FIRESIDE

Jacques Pépin

A French Chef Cooks at Home

A Fireside Book
Published by Simon and Schuster
New York

First Fireside Edition, 1980
Published by Simon and Schuster
A Division of Gulf & Western Corporation
Simon & Schuster Building
Rockefeller Center
1230 Avenue of the Americas
New York, New York 10020
Designed by Edith Fowler
Manufactured in the United States of America

3 4 5 6 7 8 9 10
1 2 3 4 5 6 7 8 9 10 Pbk.

Library of Congress Cataloging in Publication Data

Pépin, Jacques.
    A French chef cooks at home.

    (A Fireside book)
    Includes index.
    1. Cookery, French.   I. Title.
TX719.P46   1980   641.5'944   79-22583

ISBN 0-671-21946-4
ISBN 0-671-25397-2 Pbk.

To Gloria
for caring and loving so much

Contents

Introduction

To most of us, nowadays, the old adage of Harpagon in Molière's *L'Avare*—"One should eat to live and not live to eat" —is not necessarily true. Only the people who do not know how to eat properly would still subscribe to such a saying. As a matter of fact, neither should one believe that too many cooks spoil the broth, because if they are professionals, regardless of how many they are, they will enhance the broth considerably.

When one talks about food, one longs, probably more than in any other field, for the old bygone days. One looks with envy to the brilliant period of the first half of the nineteenth century praised by Brillat-Savarin and Grimod de la Reynière, to the *belle époque* at the turn of the century illustrated by Maxim's, and to the Escoffier reign which followed. However, Carême, one of the great chefs of the time who had studied the cooking of the Romans, does not hesitate to label the cuisine of Apicius ". . . intrinsically bad and atrociously heavy." Likewise, although I would not go as far as to characterize the cooking of the old practitioners of French cooking as "atrociously bad," I would certainly find it too heavy and too copious according to our modern standards.

Since we spend several hours every day preparing and consuming food, and this for the rest of our life, it seems to me that the matter is worth some recognition. As with any other subject,

11

the more you know about food the better you are able to enjoy, appreciate and recognize good cooking, and to avoid bad food and bad habits which are detrimental to your health. Cooking is just as alive today as it has ever been before. However, it has put on a different look. New equipment, new methods of packing, handling, storing and freezing food, more refined and more varied products as well as a tendency toward a lighter and a more balanced diet have changed the face of cooking somewhat. Chefs should investigate new trends. As in any other discipline, cooking will be kept alive only if its practitioners move forward with their times. Unfortunately, chefs frequently hide behind the shield of Carême or Escoffier by contending that the old masters never used such methods or apparatus. Well, they never used the blender because there were no such appliances, and if they cooked the gelatin longer, this was to get rid of some of its harsh smell and taste, a process which is not necessary nowadays because of a more refined product. Brillat-Savarin, in his *Physiology of Taste,* tried to rationalize and understand the cooking of his predecessors. We should, in the same manner, try to comprehend the cuisine of our elders. They established rules for pragmatic reasons which may not be relevant today. One should not follow precepts simply because they happen to be old and respectable. There is nothing sacrosanct about French cooking, and it is an insult to the genius of the old masters as well as to the intelligence of modern chefs to cloister cooking in a stagnant torpidity. One should demystify where there are no reasons for mysticism. As La Reynière once said: "Thirteen at a table is to be feared only if there is enough to go around for twelve."

One should not automatically criticize or discard new equipment or methods any more than one should uncritically accept them. For example, do not believe that everything freezes well. Cured pork, among other things, has a tendency to get rancid when frozen too long; egg yolk will still grow bacteria in conventional freezers but egg whites, on the contrary, will freeze quite well. Unless you have a professional freezer going down as low as ten below zero, nothing should be kept frozen too long. Wrapping is extremely important to avoid dehydration and to prevent the food from picking up odors. Defrosting should never go directly, except for stock, soup, and the like, from the freezer to the kitchen counter. Food should be defrosted under refrigeration or at least packed in a plastic bag and plunged into cold water. If you place a roast of beef unproperly wrapped in an overcrowded freezer, then defrost it in hot water and end up with a perfectly insipid and dry piece of meat, this has nothing to do with the freezer or the meat; it is your own fault. If the food is too "squeezed," it will not freeze fast enough and may start to spoil before it is completely frozen. If not properly wrapped, it will get freezer burned, and if defrosted too fast it will "run," lose moisture, and be dry.

Similarly, if you try to make whipped cream with a blender you will end up with butter. However, you can make hollandaise sauce with a blender, although it will not be as good as conventional hollandaise. You can make delicious fresh bread crumbs in seconds, providing that you cube the bread and add the pieces while the blade is turning. You may also puree fish for mousse or quenelles, but only a few small pieces at a time. Do not think either that because the fish has been pureed in the blender you do not have to push it through a sieve—it has to be strained. As for the microwave oven, it can be totally disastrous if you try to perform miracles with it. In short, one must know the limitations of one's own equipment and fully understand what one is doing.

One of the greatest principles of Escoffier: *Faites simple* (keep it simple) still holds true today. However, the standard of what is simple and what is elaborate has changed considerably in the last fifty years. By this sententious expression, Escoffier warned against excesses in cooking. It is often the case that to please a special guest one overdoes the "goodies." Too much butter, cream, cognac, reduction of sauces, will end in a dish hopelessly ruined. Remember the key word is "balance."

Of course, the seasonings will be slightly varied with different palates. I, personally, like cooking well seasoned and certain people might have to adjust my recipes to their own taste.

We are far from the cuisine of Gouffé or Fulbert-Dumonteil, a nineteenth-century gastronome, who said: "For a true gourmand there are no blue eyes, rose lips, white teeth, which can take the place of a black truffle." Quite a statement, but today the food critic would have difficulty basing his standards on the quality of truffles because they are rarely available fresh, especially in the United States, and their price is so exorbitant as to preclude anyone's purchasing and using them on a regular basis. This is not to say that one should discard truffles or goose liver pâté completely, but one should not give them the importance they used to have in earlier cooking. Many people understand classic or grande cuisine to be extremely expensive and complicated. This is partially true. An example would be a *poularde à la reine* (a chicken in cream sauce stuffed with truffles), or a galantine of duck. However, the percentage of these kinds of dishes is low in the professional life of a French chef. Consider the temples of high gastronomy in France. There are fewer than twenty restaurants worthy of the distinction, and even though they may have a few lengthy, elaborate dishes, they are known for specialties which are most of the time quite simple yet still worth a trip. It is an error to think that to earn the label of "haute cuisine," a dish should be complicated and take forever to prepare. The greatest concoctions are often the simplest, in which none of the few ingredients overpower the others but combine into one dish sublimely elegant in its simplicity. "Good cooking is when the food has the taste of what it is," said Curnonsky. This is not necessarily true unless one understands it to mean the same thing as the *"faites simple"* of Escoffier. Often a preparation becomes an entity, a taste in itself by the blending of different ingredients. Such creations as coulibiac of salmon, a pâté, a lobster americaine and even a soufflé, transcend the original ingredients to become a new taste sensation. The *cuisine soignée*, that is, thoroughly and carefully prepared food, does not involve as much boiling down of sauce as you may think. The *fond brun* (brown gravy) is used very parsimoniously in three-star restaurants. Most dishes have an existence of their own and produce their proper sauce and juices. In fact, I believe that most inferior restaurants are characterized by the standard brown sauce. Poured liberally on top of most meat, it is used as a thick blanket under which the restaurateur hides his lack of imagination and professionalism.

Although most restaurants are owned by former hotel managers or head waiters, the best restaurants in France are owned by chefs. This should emphasize that the most important factor in the life of a restaurant is the quality of the food. This seems to be a mere truism; however, you would be surprised if you knew how many restaurants are built in which the owner concentrates on the façade (that is, the dining room and the bar) and makes last-minute arrangements to have some sort of cooking area built with a minimum of expense. It certainly requires training to serve food properly, but this cannot compare to the long years of apprenticeship the chef has to endure if he wants to learn his trade correctly. However, a waiter with one or two years' experience usually makes more money than anyone in the kitchen besides the executive chef. This has caused many chefs to switch from the kitchen to the dining room where they believe they can achieve prestige and greater financial reward faster and with less effort.

This book is primarily for home cooking. This is not to say that the food will taste different from what is served in a good French restaurant, but the proportions are much smaller and the whole preparation is dissimilar. The chef works in another manner at home than he would in a restaurant where all basic sauces and varied concoctions are at his disposal. To make a coulibiac of salmon is quite an involved undertaking at home. It is an easy operation in a restaurant. The pastry chef has brioche dough and will make the crêpes (supposing you are using crêpes in your recipe), sliced mushrooms or mushroom puree is ready, the fish chef will poach the salmon and let it cool. Finally, the *garde manger* (the preparation department) will put all the ingredients together into a brioche loaf at the request of the executive chef, and the coulibiac will be cooked. It is part of the daily routine of a restaurant and it does not involve any hardship. A *cordon bleu* (a good cook) can make a great dinner for eight persons but it is quite a different matter to serve one hundred persons à la carte. The work of the chef requires a fantastic amount of speed and memory, which is not a prerequisite for the creator of a small dinner party. To improve, one has to get deeply involved with the whole mechanism of the kitchen. Basic skills are second nature to a professional. His performance relies heavily on how well he has learned the fundamentals. Cutting, chopping, slicing, poaching, peeling and cooking vegetables are the techniques which should be learned first. However, unfortunately, many people would rather learn how to make one glorious, showy dish than to labor on these tedious basic techniques.

A talented painter can only express his ideas if he possesses thorough knowledge and complete control of the techniques of his trade. By the same token, a great chef starts where the craftsman leaves off. His presentation should be as beautiful as his food is good. On the other hand, even if a ham is beautifully decorated it can be perfect only if it is first properly cooked, and if the aspic coating is crystal clear. Some chefs are better at preparation (*mise en place*), some are better working at the stove during the rush hours (*le service*); these are two different kinds of work altogether. Many chefs are solely concerned with the cooking of food when they should consider their work within a larger context which includes the serving, wines, dinnerware, flowers, decoration, etc., in brief, the whole esthetic experience that goes with the preparing and the serving of food. These chefs have the know-how, the experience and the integrity which make good chefs. However, they lack the imagination and creativity added to the experience, which make great chefs. Even though a chef expects to have all the ingredients he needs when making a dish, he should be able to perform under pressure and improvise for lack of components and still come out with a good, nicely presented dish. However, he cannot make miracles happen. Although this is not possible today, when I worked at the Plaza-Athénée in Paris, we were forty-five chefs and we never served more than two hundred and fifty persons. Likewise at the Hotel Meurice, where the limit was forty-five customers for a staff of fifteen chefs. Nowadays, in most restaurants where only a couple of professionals with a few helpers are expected (and do) serve between one hundred and fifty and two hundred dinners in a single evening, the variety and the presentation cannot be the same, regardless of the quality of the chefs. Beware of the very extensive menu. It makes more sense to limit the offerings to a few freshly and carefully prepared specialties.

The chef should have a spirit and a palate open to new taste. This is not always the case in France where the people are usually subjective and chauvinistic about what they eat, and what food should taste like. French looks for French wherever he goes, a custom already criticized in 1580 by Montaigne in the third book of his *Essays*. Despite that chauvinistic attitude, the best connoisseur and the best critics of French cooking are the French, from Alexandre Dumas the Elder to Alexandre Dumaine, known as the Great Alexandre. The best critics are often not practitioners themselves. As Grimod de la Reynière put it succinctly in his *Almanach des Gourmands:* "Its duty (the *Almanach*) is to try to stimulate the appetite of its readers, but it is the artists of the kitchen who bear the duty of satisfying it."

When one knows why and how ingredients work together, a substitution is always possible. But unless one has the necessary experience one should act with caution. It is good to be imaginative but stay within the realm of common sense; do not be extravagant. Broiled slices of pineapple are an unusual and delicious garnish for a saddle of venison sauce *grand veneur*, but I have also been served broiled sardines with hot honey poured on top and I would rather not comment on that extravagance. When the reason is health, vegetable fat can always be substituted for animal fat, oil or margarine for butter, or a mixture of butter and fat if the reason is economic. By using common sense one achieves good results. A seafood-quiche dough made with margarine instead of butter will be quite satisfactory. There are two reasons: the quiche is served hot, and the filling has a strong distinctive taste of its own. If the same dough is used for a cold raspberry tart, the difference will be noticeable; a small price to pay if your health is involved.

It is always the simplest things which are the easiest, and paradoxically the hardest to make. For example, French bread which is made from flour, water, salt and yeast. Seasoning is an area which requires a lot of training. I have had the occasion of tasting dishes which were absolutely faultless outside of a definite lack of salt or pepper. The creator of the dish knew that something was "missing" but could not recognize what it was. This might seem childishly simple to some people, but it is only with a lot of practice that one is able to put his finger on exactly what is missing in a preparation.

Recipes are made to be handled differently by different persons. The chef reads it to get an idea, and create a dish of his own from that point of departure. A beginner cook should read the recipe entirely and follow it exactly and carefully the first time he tries it. The second time, supposing that the recipe works the first time, he is likely to read it fast, checking the ingredients and the proportions as he goes along. The third time, he should be comfortable enough to improve the recipe by making it more personal and more suited to his own taste. The length of a recipe depends entirely on who is going to use it. An extended recipe of eight or ten pages is still much too short for the absolute beginner. He will still struggle with words like "poach," "braise," "mince" versus "chop" or "dice," etc. At the other extreme is the *Répertoire de la Cuisine*, a tiny French cookbook listing over seven thousand recipes, which average one and one-half to two lines each. Of course, it is a book used by professionals as a memorandum. Recipes are meant to help people; they do not perform miracles. Practice does. There are no "tricks" or "secret recipes," only practice and experience. If you keep cooking, your techniques and your presentation will improve in the same proportion that your difficulties will diminish. Cooking will become easy and fun. The cookbook you like the best *is* the best—for you. Some like recipes where the proportions and the methods are barely suggested, leaving enough freedom to their own imagination. Others want recipes to be spelled out in the most minute details. Whether your approach is poetic or scientific, you must realize that the cookbook next to you is only a mere helper, and it is still up to you to use common sense.

I have had no intention of covering the whole range of French cooking or following a pattern which could be related to specific parts of France. My choice is totally subjective; I am simply giving the recipes my wife and I enjoy cooking for our guests. Occasionally I emphasize an important point, give special advice, or suggest a technique; these are in italic type within a particular recipe. I have also tried to explain some of the reasons behind the different techniques. If I am partial and subjective, I do not profess to be right in all my assertions. I have changed my point of view several times on different issues. However, I have tried to understand honestly the problems of home cooking and have tested my recipes carefully.

I have entitled this book *Jacques Pépin: A French Chef Cooks at Home* because this is not really the kind of cooking I have seen done in restaurants, but rather the way I cook at home. "Cuisine" is an ambiguous word in French. It means "cooking," but also signifies the location, the kitchen itself. (This led my five-year-old daughter, who is completely bilingual, to ask her mother if she could help by doing the kitchen in the kitchen.)

I love to cook with my family or with friends. Remember that you almost always cook for others and very rarely for yourself. Cooking for friends is an act of love which should be accomplished willingly and joyfully to be completely successful.

Menus

Using the same dishes, you may vary the following menus according to your own taste, almost ad infinitum. I do not list salads, cheeses or wines, which could and should be served with most of these menus. The salad should be served after the vegetable, followed by the cheeses as a separate course. Wine is most enjoyable with cheeses, but does not go well with salad when the latter is seasoned with a vinegar dressing; I therefore do not recommend serving salad and cheeses together.

FRENCH	ENGLISH
Feuilleté de champignons	Mushrooms in Puff Pastry
Poulet au vinaigre	Chicken in Vinegar
Endives braisées	Braised Endive
Tarte au pommes frangipane	Apple Tart with Almond Filling

•

Soupe de poisson	Fish Soup
Lapin aux pruneaux	Rabbit with Prunes
Poireaux au gratin	Gratin of Leeks
Mousse au chocolat	Chocolate Mousse
Dentelles Lily	Lily's Lace Cookies

•

FRENCH	ENGLISH
Truites grillées à la crème	Broiled Trout with Cream
Cervelles de veau provençale	Veal Brains Provence Style
Nouilles fraîches	Fresh Noodles
Dacquoise au chocolat	Chocolate and Meringue Cake

•

Soufflé au fromage	Cheese Soufflé
Poulet fine champagne	Chicken with Cognac
Concombres persillés	Parsleyed Cucumbers
Crêpes Suzette	Thin Pancakes Flavored with Orange Liqueur

•

Crème Dubarry	Cream of Cauliflower Soup
Faisan rôti sur canapés	Roast Pheasant on Canapés
Pommes dauphine	Puff Potatoes
Bananes flambées au rhum	Bananas Flambéed with Rum

•

Cervelas truffé en brioche	Truffled Sausage in Brioche
Filet de boeuf périgourdine	Fillet of Beef with Périgueux Sauce
Laitues braisées	Braised Lettuce
Croûtes aux poires	Pear Pastry

•

Champignons à la grecque	Cold Marinated Mushrooms
Saucisson de campagne	Hard Salami
Ris de veau au madère	Sweetbreads with Madeira Sauce
Beignets de pommes de terre	Potato Fritters
Crème caramel au rhum	Caramel Custard with Rum

•

FRENCH	ENGLISH
Moules rémoulade	Mussels with Rémoulade Sauce
Poulet grillé aux herbes	Charbroiled Chicken with Herbs
Pommes Savonnettes	Potatoes Savonnette
Gâteau de fromage aux myrtilles	Cheesecake with Blueberries

•

Oeufs Jeannette	Eggs Jeannette
Cassoulet	Bean and Meat Casserole
Tarte aux pommes de ma mère	Mother's Apple Tart

•

Boudin noirs aux pommes	Blood Sausage with Apples
Poulet aux topinambours	Creamed Chicken with Jerusalem Artichokes
Roulade au chocolat	Chocolate Roll

•

Saucisson de campagne	Hard Salami
Terrine de foies de volaille	Chicken Liver Terrine
Noisettes d'agneau monégasque	Lamb Chops with Eggplant and Tomato Fondue
Paris-Brest	Paris-Brest Cake

•

Potage cultivateur	Vegetable Soup
Gâteau de foies de volaille à la tomate	Chicken Liver Custard with Tomato Sauce
Quenelles de brochet lyonnaises	Pike Quenelles Lyonnaises
Pouding au caramel	Caramel Pudding

•

FRENCH	ENGLISH
Alose en croûte nivernaise	Shad in Crust
Porc braisé aux marrons	Braised Pork with Chestnuts
Bûche de noël	Christmas Yule Log

•

Billi-Bi	Mussel Soup
Selle d'agneau provençale	Saddle of Lamb Provençale
Crêpes mère Blanc	Potato Pancakes
Soufflé glacé grand marnier	Iced Soufflé Grand Marnier
Tuiles à l'orange	Orange Cookies

•

Potage cressonnière	Watercress Soup
Escalopes de veau normande	Veal Scallopini with Cream, Calvados and Apples
Nouilles fraîches	Fresh Noodles
Pêches Ninon	Ninon Peaches

•

Crevettes provençale	Shrimp with Snail Butter
Ballotine de canard braisée	Braised Duck Ballotine
Gnocchi romaine	Gnocchi Roman Style
Omelette soufflée	Soufflé Omelet

•

Soufflé aux épinards	Spinach Soufflé
Selle de chevreuil poivrade	Saddle of Venison with Red Wine Sauce
Pommes savonnettes	Potatoes Savonnettes
Cake Anglais	Fruit Cake
Truffettes du dauphiné	Small Chocolate Truffles

•

Salade de homard	Lobster Salad
Steak au poivre	Pepper Steak
Choux fleurs au gratin	Cauliflower au Gratin
Tarte à l'orange	Open Orange Tart

•

FRENCH	ENGLISH
Oeufs en cocottes bressane	Eggs in Ramekins Bressane Style
Cabillaud grenobloise	Fresh Codfish Steaks Grenoble Style
Beignets d'aubergines	Eggplant Fritters
Petits pots de crème vanille	Rich Vanilla Custard

•

Fonds d'artichauts au safran	Saffron Artichoke Bottoms
Canard Montmorency	Braised Duck with Cherries
Purée freneuse	Puree of White Turnips
Compote de pommes au calvados	Apple Compote with Calvados
Dentelles Lily	Lily's Lace Cookies

•

Ceviche	Raw Marinated Fish
Yassa de poulet	Chicken African Style
Riz pilaf	Rice Pilaf
Salade de fruits au kirsch	Fruit Salad with Kirsch

•

Gratin d'oeufs à la crème	Gratin of Eggs in Cream Sauce
Pâté de foie en brioche	Pork Liver Pâté in Brioche
Mousse aux fraises	Strawberry Mousse
Langues de chat	Cats' Tongues

•

Soufflé au fromage	Cheese Soufflé
Côtes de porc charcutière	Pork Chops with Mustard and Pickles
Petits pois paysanne	Stewed Peas
Galette au citron	Open Lemon Tart

•

FRENCH	ENGLISH
Civier bressan	Pork Cheese
Pigeon bressane	Braised Squab
Petits pois à la française	French Style Peas
Mont Blanc aux marrons	Chestnut Puree with Meringues

•

Rillettes de porc	Pork Spread
Truites farcies au vermouth	Stuffed Trout with Vermouth
Concombres à la crème	Cucumbers with Cream
Fraises aux framboises	Strawberries with Raspberry Sauce
Cake anglais	Fruit Cake

•

Tarte aux oignons	Onion Tart
Poulet sauté Boivin	Sautéed Chicken with Artichokes
Charlotte de pommes sauce abricot	Apple Charlotte with Apricot Sauce

•

Saucisson chaud pommes à l'huile	Hot Country Sausage with Potato Salad
Choux farcis	Small Stuffed Cabbages
Beignets de bananes	Banana Fritters

•

Aspic de homard à la parisienne	Lobster in Aspic
Croûte de ris de veau à l'estragon	Sweetbreads in Pastry
Timbale d'épinards	Spinach Mold
Fraises aux framboises	Strawberries with Raspberry Sauce

•

FRENCH	ENGLISH
Consommé	Consommé
Grenadins de porc normande	Pork Chops with Cream and Calvados
Pommes Biron	Biron Potatoes
Meringues chantilly	Meringue Shells with Chantilly Cream

•

Potage crème de tomates	Cream of Tomato Soup
Carbonades de boeuf flamande	Carbonade of Beef Flamande
Pommes persillées	Parsleyed Potatoes
Beignets de pommes	Apple Fritters

•

Quiche au lard	Quiche with Bacon
Homard normande	Lobster Normandy Style
Riz pilaf	Rice Pilaf
Soufflé Rothschild	Rothschild Soufflé

•

Bisque de homard	Lobster Bisque
Canard à l'orange	Roast Duck with Orange Sauce
Pommes soufflées	Puffed Potato Slices
Diplomate au kirsch	Diplomat Pudding with Kirsch

•

Soupe aux pêches	Cold Peach Soup
Lapin farci	Stuffed Rabbit
Pommes Biron	Biron Potatoes
Pouding brésilien	Bread and Butter Pudding

•

FRENCH	ENGLISH
Terrine de ris de veau	Cold Sweetbreads Terrine
Paupiettes de veau lyonnaises	Paupiettes of Veal Lyonnaise
Gratin dauphinois	Scalloped Potatoes in Garlic and Cream
Poires Bourdaloue	Pears in a Pastry Shell

•

Oeufs pochés florentine	Poached Eggs Florentine
Saucisson chaud rôti aux pommes	Roast Sausage with Potatoes
Salade de pissenlits au lard	Dandelion Salad with Bacon and Croutons
Fromage blanc à la crème	Fresh White Cheese with Cream

•

Pieds de porc rémoulade	Pig's Feet with Rémoulade Sauce
Poulet lyonnaise	Chicken Lyonnaise
Poireaux au gratin	Gratin of Leeks
Crème au chocolat	Chocolate Cream
Langues de chat	Cats' Tongues

•

Hure de porc aux pistaches	Rolled Head Cheese with Pistachios
Paupiettes de sole Dugléré	Sole Fillets with Tomatoes
Pommes persillées	Parsleyed Potatoes
Tarte à la rhubarbe	Rhubarb Pie

•

FRENCH	ENGLISH
Soufflé de homard Plaza-Athénée	Lobster Soufflé Plaza-Athénée
Canard aux pommes	Duck with Apples
Poires braisées au caramel	Braised Pears in Caramel Sauce
Biscuit à la cuillère	Ladyfingers

•

Pilaf de moules à la crème	Rice Pilaf with Mussels in Cream Sauce
Cayettes de cochon	Pork Dumplings with Spinach
Gâteau chocolat	Chocolate Cake

•

Pâte de cervelles	Veal Brains in Pastry
Côtes de veau aux morilles	Veal Chops with Morels
Gâteau de riz sauce groseille	Rice Pudding with Red Currant Sauce

•

Bar rayé en croûte à l'oseille	Striped Bass in a Crust with Sorrel
Fricadelles de veau smitane	Veal Patties with Sour Cream Sauce
Petits pois paysanne	Stewed Peas
Gâteau Saint-Honoré	Saint-Honoré Cake

•

Pâté de foie	Pork Liver Pâté
Mayonnaise de volaille	Chicken Mayonnaise
Pouding de pommes et brioche	Apple Brown Betty

•

FRENCH	ENGLISH
Escargots forestière	Snails with Mushrooms
Jambon en croûte au madère	Ham in Crust with Madeira Sauce
Salade à la crème	Salad with Cream Dressing
Vacherin aux pêches	Meringue Cake with Peaches

•

Gratinée lyonnaise au porto	Onion Soup Lyonnaise Style
Jarret de veau provençale	Braised Veal Shank
Rizotto piémontaise	Risotto with Cheese and Saffron
Poires au vin rouge	Pears Braised in Red Wine

•

Huîtres florentine sauce diable	Oysters with Deviled Sauce
Poulet grandmère	Chicken Grandma Style
Oeufs à la neige	Meringue Balls Poached in Custard

•

Moules poulette	Mussels Poulette
Bavette farcie braisée	Braised Stuffed Flank Steak
Carottes vichy	Steamed Carrots
Platée de pommes au caramel	Apple Tart with Caramel

•

Champignons à la grecque	Cold Marinated Mushrooms
Terrine de foies de volaille	Chicken Liver Terrine
Quenelles galliera	Quenelles in Fish and Mushroom Sauce
Rognonnade de veau poêlée matignon	Veal Roast Braised with Vegetables
Salade de fruits au kirsch	Fruit Salad with Kirsch

Basic Recipes

Fond Brun

Basic Brown Sauce

•

This brown sauce is the base for many other sauces. As it stands, it is neither properly seasoned nor thick enough. It should be brought to the right taste and the right consistency, usually with arrowroot, when it is used. It is slightly thickened with flour, which has the time to clarify and lose its raw taste through the long cooking process. I believe that a clear stock thickened with arrowroot only often tends to be too gelatinous or "gooey."

> *4 pounds veal bones (shin, neck, tail, etc. I have*
> *the butcher cut them into 3-inch pieces)*
> *1 pound chicken bones (neck, wings, back, etc.)*
> *1 large carrot, cubed (1 cup)*
> *1 leek, diced (1 cup)*
> *1 rib of celery, diced (¾ cup)*
> *3 cloves garlic, crushed with skin on*

There are two ways to start the brown sauce:

A. Place all the ingredients in a large shallow cooking tray or

pan (they should not overlap) and place in a preheated 425°
oven for 1 hour. Turn the bones with a spoon after half an hour.

B. Place the chicken bones in a large heavy pot and cook on
high heat until the pieces are browned and have rendered some
fat (about 6 minutes). Add the veal bones and the vegetables.
Keep cooking for about 10 minutes, stirring with a large spoon
until the bones and vegetables start to brown.

> ¾ cup all-purpose flour
> 4 tablespoons tomato paste
> 1 cup dry white wine
> 1¾ gallons water
> 1 teaspoon black peppercorns
> 3 bay leaves
> 1 teaspoon crushed thyme (fresh is preferable)
> 1 teaspoon crushed tarragon leaves (a piece of
>   fresh tarragon is preferable)
> 2 teaspoons salt
> caramel coloring

If you use method A, transfer all the ingredients to a large
kettle, pour about 1 quart of water into the cooking tray and
bring to a boil on the stove to melt all the solidified juices.
Meanwhile, add the flour and tomato paste to the ingredients in
the large kettle and mix well. Add the water boiling in the pan,
the remaining ingredients, and bring to a boil, stirring to dilute
the flour. Simmer the sauce slowly, uncovered, for about 3 hours.
Skim the foam which comes up to the top every 15 or 20 minutes. Add 1 teaspoon of commercial caramel coloring or 1 tablespoon of homemade coloring. Strain the sauce through a fine
sieve. *Yield:* About 2 to 2½ quarts. The sauce may be kept
covered in the refrigerator up to 10 days, or it may be divided
into small plastic containers and frozen.

Note: Commercial caramel coloring is difficult to buy outside
of a wholesale restaurant supply house. The homemade caramel

coloring is not as concentrated as the commercial one and needs to be added in greater quantity:

> 2 *cups sugar*
> 1 *cup water*

Mix the sugar and the water in a heavy saucepan and cook on medium heat until it turns into caramel. Reduce the heat and keep the caramel cooking. The mixture will soon turn black, smoke, and finally decompose and become solid. Remove from the heat and add (slowly because it splashes and you may burn yourself) about 1½ cups of water. Place back on the heat, bring to a boil, simmer 2 to 3 minutes and strain the liquid into a bowl. Cool and pour into a bottle. If the syrup is too thick (it should have the consistency of a light maple syrup), add some cold water. Keep in refrigerator for months.

Glace de Viande
Meat Glaze

•

It takes time to make *glace de viande*, but it is easy to make. Choose a day and make time-consuming items such as puff paste (the classic recipe), brown sauce, *glace de viande*, pâté, etc. *Glace de viande* is often a savior and always a big helper to enhance meat or fish sauces and even vegetables (e.g., *pommes parisienne*). It will keep practically forever in a covered jar in the refrigerator and it is an excellent, dependable base. In addition to the ingredients required by this recipe, pieces or scraps of meat, chicken, bones, etc., may be added to the stock.

10 *pounds veal and beef bones cut into 3-inch
    pieces*
1 *onion, coarsely sliced (about 1 cup). It does
    not have to be peeled.*
1 *large carrot, washed and coarsely sliced
    (about 1 cup)*
2 *cloves garlic, crushed with skin on*
½ *teaspoon crushed thyme*

Put the bones, vegetables, garlic and thyme in a large oven tray and place in a preheated 425° oven for 1 hour, turning the bones after 30 minutes. Lift the ingredients with a skimmer and transfer to the largest kettle you have. Discard the fat accumulated in the bottom of the tray. Pour 2 or 3 cups of water in the tray and bring to a boil to melt all the solidified juices. Add to the kettle. Fill the kettle with water and bring to a boil over high heat. Cook simmering overnight or on a high heat for at least 6 hours. *You may have to add water if the liquid reduces too much, but it should cook at least 6 hours to get all the flavor from the bones.* Skim the top of the liquid every 2 hours to remove as much foam and fat as you can. Strain the liquid into a smaller kettle (you should have about 1 gallon of liquid left). Boil the stock on medium heat for about 2 hours, skimming the top to remove all the fat. *The reduction will not work properly unless all the fat is removed.* Strain the liquid into another smaller heavy saucepan. You should have about 4 to 5 cups of liquid left. Keep cooking on medium heat until you have about 1½ cups left. It should be brown and slightly thick and gelatinous. *Reduce to low heat because the liquid being thicker now has a tendency to burn.* Keep reducing another 1 or 2 hours. The *glace* is ready when no steam is escaping from the liquid. It should be dark brown and as thick as jam. Big blisters should form during cooking at this point and the mixture should be very shiny. You should have approximately ¾ to 1 cup of *glace de viande,* dark, sticky, and resembling a brown caramel. Pour into a bowl and let the *glace* cool and set for about 1 hour.

Unmold (it will be set into a solid block) and cut into 1-inch cubes. Place in a jar in the refrigerator. If the *glace* is reduced enough it will not spoil and will keep indefinitely. Use whenever required by a recipe.

Mayonnaise

•

One of the best of all sauces and perhaps the most useful in the world, mayonnaise is a smooth emulsion of raw egg yolks and oil that lends itself to an infinite number of variations. Actually the forerunner of hollandaise, which is made by thickening egg yolks with hot butter, mayonnaise is served with cold foods—eggs; cooked vegetables, such as asparagus, broccoli and artichokes; fresh tomatoes; vegetable salads; poached fish; shellfish; cold chicken. When other ingredients are combined with mayonnaise they take its name. Thus: Mayonnaise de Volaille (chicken), Mayonnaise de Homard (lobster), Mayonnaise de Poissons (fish). Although the classic recipe does not call for mustard, today it is used more often than not—and I think the sauce is easier to prepare.

Basic Mayonnaise

2 egg yolks
1 teaspoon Dijon mustard
1 tablespoon tarragon or wine vinegar
salt
freshly ground white pepper
1½ cups oil (imported peanut oil, vegetable oil,
    olive oil, or half vegetable and half olive oil)

Place the yolks and mustard, half the vinegar, and salt and pepper to taste in a generous bowl. Beat for 1 minute with a wire whisk. Then add the oil slowly, almost drop by drop, whipping vigorously and constantly until all the oil is incorporated. If the finished mayonnaise seems too thick, beat in the remainder of the vinegar. *Yield:* Approximately 2 cups.

To Salvage Curdled Mayonnaise

Put 1 tablespoon of the mayonnaise into a warm, dry bowl with 1 teaspoon prepared French or domestic mustard. Whip with a wire whisk until creamy. Add the remaining mayonnaise by tablespoons, beating vigorously after each addition until creamy.

A Second Way

Add 1 tablespoon of boiling water in place of the mustard and follow the same directions.

Note: Even if homemade mayonnaise turns out perfectly, if it is stored in the refrigerator for too long a time it will eventually break down. This is essentially the same thing as curdling. However, if brought to room temperature before it is stirred it will not break down. Before storing, seal the surface with plastic wrap, otherwise it will turn dark yellow.

Mayonnaise Variations

Here are some variations, all classic. However, you may use your own imagination and combine almost anything you like with mayonnaise. For example, Mayonnaise aux Câpres (with capers); à l'Estragon (finely chopped tarragon); aux Crevettes (with shrimp); aux Anchois (with anchovies).

Sauce Verte (Green Sauce)

Pick the leaves from 10 sprigs of watercress, 4 sprigs of tarragon, 4 of parsley, and 4 of chervil. Drop into a pot of boiling water. Add 10 fine spinach leaves and blanch for 1 minute. Drain. Refresh in cold water. Drain again and squeeze dry. Chop into a fine puree. Stir into 2 cups of thick mayonnaise along with 1 tablespoon of chopped chives. Serve with poached fish, such as salmon or trout. Sauce Verte is sometimes referred to as Sauce Vincent.

Note: If all the greens are not available, omit those that are not and increase the others in proportion.

Sauce Andalouse

Combine ½ cup of very thick tomato sauce with 2 cups of thick mayonnaise. Fold in half of a sweet red pepper, seeded and chopped fine, along with 1 teaspoon or so of chopped fresh tarragon or chives, or a mixture of the two. Serve with cold chicken or hard-cooked eggs.

Sauce Gribiche

To 2 cups mayonnaise, add 1 hard-cooked egg, chopped; 1 tablespoon chopped gherkins or small French sour pickles; 1 tablespoon chopped, drained capers; 1 tablespoon chopped shallots or green onion bulbs; about 3 sprigs of minced parsley; 4 or 5 fresh tarragon leaves, chopped; and ⅓ tablespoon chopped chives. Taste for seasoning. It may need salt and pepper. Especially good with fried fish or mixed with cold mussels when served as a first course.

Sauce Suédoise

To 1 cup thick mayonnaise, add 1 cup thick applesauce and 1 tablespoon freshly grated horseradish. Serve with cold pork or a handsome golden goose.

Sauce Rémoulade

To 1½ cups mayonnaise, add 1 generous teaspoon Dijon mustard; 2 tablespoons each chopped gherkins, capers, parsley, fresh tarragon or chervil; and a "whisper" of anchovy paste. Allow to mellow for a couple of hours. Serve with sliced hard-cooked eggs, shellfish, or cold meats such as tongue or chicken.

Gloucester Sauce

To 2 cups thick mayonnaise, add about 1 cup commercial sour cream, the strained juice of 1 lemon, 1 teaspoon chopped fresh fennel leaves, and 1 teaspoon Worcestershire Sauce. Serve with all cold meats.

Chantilly or Mousseline

Fold ½ cup of heavy cream, whipped, into 1 cup of thick mayonnaise. Serve with cold fish, green salads, or cold cooked eggs.

Sauce Mousquetaire

Cook 2 tablespoons of chopped shallots in ½ cup of dry white wine until all the liquid has been absorbed. Mix into 2½ cups of mayonnaise with 1 tablespoon of Meat Glaze (see page 33) and a pinch of cayenne. Serve with cold poached eggs or cold beef or chicken.

Mayonnaise Collée

To 2 cups of mayonnaise, add ½ cup lukewarm meat or fish aspic, depending on how it is to be used. Thinner than a regular mayonnaise, it is used to coat whole fish or whole chickens for a cold buffet. Since it is prepared with aspic, it will be shiny and firm when set.

Sauce Aïoli

A combination of egg yolks, garlic, oil, and the pulp of a baked potato, Aïoli is known in Provence as *la pommade*—or the butter of Provence. It is served with boiled fish, snails, hard-cooked eggs, and certain vegetables, such as·boiled potatoes and green beans.

> 1 *baked or boiled Idaho potato*
> 3 *egg yolks*
> 4 *garlic cloves, crushed and chopped into a*
> > *puree*
> *salt*
> *good pinch of freshly ground white pepper*
> *juice of ½ lemon, strained*
> 1½ *cups olive oil*

Scrape the pulp from the baked potato or peel, if boiled, and put through a ricer or food mill. Beat with an electric beater or mixer until very smooth. Then beat in the egg yolks 1 at a time; add the garlic, salt and pepper to taste, and the lemon juice, beating hard and constantly until the mixture is thoroughly combined and smooth. Then begin to add the oil very slowly, drop by drop, beating constantly with a wooden spatula. When all the oil has been added the sauce should have the consistency of a firm mayonnaise. *However, you should watch carefully as you add the oil because if the sauce becomes too thick it may separate. You can avoid this by adding a little lukewarm milk or water as you go along.* Keep the finished sauce over warm water because Sauce Aïoli is always served tepid with fish, and especially saltwater fish, such as codfish. Yield: Approximately 3 to 4 cups.

Note: The use of the potato pulp in the sauce is a variation; Sauce Aïoli is often made with just garlic and oil.

Hollandaise

•

An aristocrat among sauces, golden hollandaise adorns everything from vegetables to fish to meat to poultry. This is the counterpart of mayonnaise, a cold emulsified sauce made with raw yolks and oil. Familiar to both Spanish and French provincial cooks by the eighteenth century, it was a natural gastronomic progression to thicken egg yolks with hot clarified butter. Hence, the smooth emulsion we know as hollandaise.

Classic Hollandaise

4 *egg yolks*
2 *tablespoons water*
1½ *cups clarified butter**
salt
freshly ground white pepper
cayenne
½ *tablespoon lemon juice (optional)*

Combine the egg yolks and water in the top of a double boiler. With a wire whip, beat for 1 minute. Then place over simmering water (the bottom of the pan should not touch the water). Whipping vigorously with the whip, beat for 8 to 10 minutes or until the mixture is thick and creamy. Take care not to curdle the eggs and note that the temperature of the mixture should never be so hot you cannot dip your finger into it. When

* To clarify the butter: Cut 1½ cups (3 sticks) of sweet butter into pieces and place in a saucepan over moderate heat. When it has melted and foamed, take off the heat and let it rest so the clear liquid can rise to the top. Then pour off slowly and carefully into another small pan, discarding the milky residue in the bottom.

*it is perfectly combined you can see the bottom of the pan
between strokes and the sauce will be slow to cover the lines
made by the whip.*

Now, take the pan off the heat and place on a damp cloth
to keep it from sliding around. Add the hot butter very slowly,
in dribbles, whipping constantly. Season to taste with salt,
pepper, and cayenne. *Be careful—the hollandaise does not require much salt.* Last of all, stir in the lemon juice. If not served
immediately, keep warm in a pan of tepid water—not hot, or the
hollandaise will curdle. Hollandaise is always served lukewarm.
Yield: About 2 cups of sauce.

If the Sauce Hollandaise is too thick, with a wire whip, beat
in 1 or 2 tablespoons of hot water to bring it to the right consistency.

To Salvage Curdled Hollandaise

To salvage hollandaise that has not thickened or has curdled,
heat it slowly to make it almost hot. Allow to rest without
moving at least 30 minutes. The clarified butter will separate
from the solids. With a spoon or ladle, scoop up as much liquid
butter as you can and set aside. You now have your hollandaise
in 2 parts—thick or solid part, and liquid part. Place 1 tablespoon of hot water in a bowl that may be placed on the stove
(be sure the bowl you use is not aluminum), and set on a very,
very low flame or on the top of a double boiler. Add 1 tablespoon of the thick mixture to the water and beat with a wire
whisk until it is homogeneous (this will take only a few seconds). Continue adding the thick sauce (you may add a greater
amount at the time the sauce binds together and thickens).
Now add the liquid or butter part of the sauce you have set
aside, as if you were making the hollandaise for the first time.

Hollandaise Variations

Although specific dishes are suggested for serving with these various sauces, you will find that, on the whole, most of them can be used interchangeably.

Sauce Béarnaise

In a small saucepan, combine 2 tablespoons of dry white wine, 2 tablespoons of tarragon vinegar, ⅓ cup peeled, chopped shallots, and 1 tablespoon finely chopped parsley. Place over medium heat until all but about a tablespoon of the liquid has evaporated. Stir into the hollandaise along with 1 tablespoon of finely chopped fresh tarragon (lacking fresh, 1 teaspoon of dried, crumbled). Serve with broiled steaks or chicken and with either broiled or fried fish.

Sauce Choron (Tomato-flavored Béarnaise)

Peel and seed 1 large ripe tomato, then chop coarsely. Melt 2 or 3 tablespoons of butter in a small skillet. Add the tomato and sauté for 5 minutes over moderate heat. Stir in 1 tablespoon of tomato paste and bring to a boil. Mix into Sauce Béarnaise. Serve with steaks, fish, chicken, or poached eggs.

Sauce Valois or Foyot

Add 2 tablespoons of Glace de Viande (Meat Glaze, see page 33) to Sauce Béarnaise. Serve with broiled or deep-fried fish, or charcoal-broiled or breaded chicken breasts.

Sauce Maltaise

Stir the grated rind and strained juice of 1 large navel orange into the basic hollandaise. This variation is especially good with asparagus or broccoli.

Sauce Noisette

Cook the clarified butter long enough so that it turns a rich hazelnut (*noisette*) color. Make the hollandaise with this butter, following the classic recipe. Serve with salmon, trout, all poached fish, as well as asparagus and cauliflower.

Beurre d'Escargots
Snail Butter

•

1 pound soft sweet butter
¼ cup freshly chopped parsley
1 tablespoon fresh, finely chopped shallots, or
  2 tablespoons finely chopped chives
7 cloves garlic, peeled, crushed, and chopped
  very fine (1½ tablespoons)
1 tablespoon Pernod or Ricard or other anise
  apéritif
1½ teaspoons salt
1 small teaspoon freshly ground white pepper
1 slice white bread, trimmed, cubed, and
  blended (½ cup breadcrumbs)
2 tablespoons dry white wine

Combine all ingredients except the bread and wine and mix carefully. Then add the bread and wine and mix just enough to add it to the butter. *It is good to add some liquid like white wine to the butter because it blends with the butter during cooking and cuts the fattiness of the dish. However, bread is added to absorb the wine, which could not be incorporated into the butter when cold.* Yield: Enough butter for about 5 dozen snails. This is a very versatile mixture and may be used with snails, butterfly shrimp, tomatoes, and sautéed potatoes, to name just a few. The butter will keep up to 2 weeks covered in the refrigerator.

Variations

Escargots (Snails)

Snails are purchased in cans and the shells are packaged separately. Push ½ teaspoon of the snail butter into the shell and place the snail on top. Add another full teaspoon of the butter to the top of the snail. Place on a tray and place in a preheated 375° oven for 10 to 12 minutes or until the butter bubbles and clarifies.

Crevettes Provençales (Shrimp)

Place shrimp in a gratin dish, sprinkle with lemon juice and cover with snail butter. Place in the oven and cook as you would the snails.

Tomates Provençales (Tomatoes)

Split tomatoes in half and fry in a pan in very hot oil, seasoned with salt and pepper, about 3 to 4 minutes on each side. Place fried tomatoes on a tray, flat side up, and add some snail butter to each half. Place in a very hot oven for 5 minutes.

Toss a little butter on sautéed potatoes—a new taste experience. You may also want to try adding a little "nut" of the snail butter to each bowl before you pour in a vegetable soup. One thing must be remembered: *Be careful not to burn the butter because the garlic will taste bitter and the entire dish will be ruined.*

Pâte Brisée
Pie Dough

Same as Gourmet de France except for use of 1/4 t salt + no use of sugar

(Enough for a 9-inch pie shell)

•

This is one of the most useful doughs. Easily and rapidly done, it is the base of countless open tarts, pies, quiches, etc. The dough is always better if made a few hours in advance (it may be made and kept in the refrigerator or freezer). However, you may also make the dough and use it right away. It will not be elastic and will roll perfectly well if you follow the recipe. *Notice that the fat and the flour are worked together and the water added at the end and incorporated rapidly. This is the reason why the dough is usable right away. If the water is worked and kneaded with the flour for a period of time the dough becomes rubbery and must rest before being used.*

> 1¼ cups all-purpose flour (about 5 ounces)
> 6 tablespoons sweet butter, cut into bits (¾ of
>   a stick)
> 2 tablespoons lard or white shortening
> ⅛ teaspoon salt
> ¼ teaspoon sugar
> 3 tablespoons cold water

Place all ingredients, except the water, in a large bowl. With both hands start mashing the mixture until it has the same color and is lumpy. Add the water and mix rapidly with your fingers— just enough to assemble all ingredients into a solid, smooth mass. Wrap in plastic wrap or use immediately.

How to Line a Flan Ring

On a lightly floured pastry board (*flour the rolling pin, too*), roll out the pastry about ⅛ inch thick and at least 2 inches larger all around than the ring. Place the ring on a baking sheet. Roll up the pastry on the rolling pin, place over the ring and unroll. Ease the pastry down inside the ring, taking care not to break it, pressing it along the sides and bottom. Now press the overlapping pastry inside the sides of the ring to make them slightly thicker than the bottom of the shell. With a sharp knife, cut off the dough, following the contour of the ring all around. To make a decorative edge, press the rim of the pastry with the dull edge of a table knife, the tines of a fork, or a special crimper.

Pâte Brisée Fine

(*Enough for about two 9-inch shells*)

•

This *pâte brisée,* made only with butter, is not as short and tender as the one on page 45 but it is a flakier and finer dough, closer to puff paste than the standard *pâte brisée* recipe. Both recipes are interchangeable.

> ½ *pound pastry or all-purpose flour (about 2 cups)*
> 6 *ounces (1½ sticks) cold sweet butter, cut into*
> ¼-*inch bits*
> ¼ *teaspoon salt*
> ½ *teaspoon granulated sugar*
> 3 *ounces (about ⅓ cup plus 1 tablespoon) cold*
> *water*

Mix the flour, butter, salt and sugar in a bowl for a few seconds with your fingers (the pieces of butter should still show). Add the water, gather the mixture into a ball and knead the dough for about 1 minute. It should be kneaded enough so that the dough has body, but not so much that it becomes too elastic and dry (the pieces of butter should still show in a few places). If the dough is too elastic to be used right away, let it rest in the refrigerator for 30 minutes before rolling. This dough can be frozen if carefully wrapped.

Pâte Fine Sucrée
Sweet Pie Dough

(Enough for a 9-inch pie shell)

•

This dough is primarily used for delicate and fancy fruit pies where the shell is precooked. It is made only with butter, sweetened with sugar, and the egg yolk is added for extra richness and to make a drier and crunchier crust.

> 1¼ *cups all-purpose flour*
> ⅛ *teaspoon salt*
> 2 *tablespoons sugar*
> 1 *stick sweet butter, cut into bits (4 ounces)*
> 1 *egg yolk*
> 3 *tablespoons water*

Mix the yolk with the water until it is well blended. Set aside. Place the remaining ingredients into a large bowl and work the dough with your hands, mashing it through your fingers to have all the ingredients blend together. It will form into lumps after

1 or 2 minutes. *Pour the yolk mixture in the bowl and mix rapidly with your fingers until all ingredients are assembled together into a ball.* Knead the dough on a flat surface for 1 minute. Wrap the dough in a towel and set in the refrigerator until you are ready to use it. It should rest for at least 1 hour before it is used; however, it may be done a few days in advance.

Pâte à Brioche de Ménage
Ordinary Brioche Dough

•

This recipe will make enough dough for a 1½-pound sausage in crust or a 1-pound *roulade* of goose liver. The dough is very soft and cannot be rolled like conventional brioche dough. It rises only once, and it is used right away and therefore convenient for last-minute menu planning. Whereas a conventional dough has a tendency to separate from the item wrapped inside during cooking, this dough will adhere to it and no space will develop between the dough and the sausage or liver pâté.

> 1½ *cups all-purpose flour*
> ½ *teaspoon salt*
> ½ *ounce fresh yeast*
> 2 *tablespoons lukewarm milk*
> 3 *large eggs*
> 1¼ *sticks sweet butter (5 ounces), room*
>   *temperature*

Crumble the yeast in a bowl, add the milk and mix well. Add all remaining ingredients and work with your hands for a few minutes until everything is well blended together. Do not overwork. *The dough will have the consistency of a cake batter.*

Butter a cake mold, big enough to accommodate the sausage or the goose liver, and pour the dough into it. (It should be half full.) Place, covered with a towel, in a draft-free, lukewarm place (on top of a double boiler or in a 160° oven) for about 1½ to 2 hours, until it has doubled in volume. Push the pâté or sausage into the dough, just enough so that it is immersed or barely covered with the dough. *It should be closer to the top than to the bottom of the mold because it will sink slightly during cooking.* Place on a cookie sheet in a preheated 400° oven for about 25 minutes. Allow the brioche to rest for about 5 minutes before unmolding. Run a knife around the edge, unmold on a tray, and bring to the table. Will serve 6 as a first course.

Pâte à Brioche
Brioche Dough

(Enough for 18 to 20 small brioches)

•

1 *ounce fresh yeast (fresh yeast is available at any bakery)*
1 *tablespoon sugar*
1 *teaspoon salt*
1 *pound fresh sweet butter (4 sticks)*
7 *large eggs*
1 *pound all-purpose flour (about 3½ loose cups)*

I will explain how to make the dough using a mixer because it is easier and the result is just as good as the handmade dough. However, it is likely that your home-model mixer will not accommodate the entire above recipe. Make half the recipe at a time using 4 small or 3 extra-large eggs. Place the fresh yeast, sugar, and salt in the bowl of the mixer. Mix on medium speed, adding the butter in pieces and the eggs one by one. Use the flat beater, if you have this attachment. When everything is mixed together (it will not be smooth and the butter will still be in pieces), add the flour. Beat on medium speed for at least 8 minutes, scraping the sides and the bottom of the bowl twice during the process so that all the ingredients are well blended together. *The dough should be velvety, elastic, and should separate easily from the beater.* Place the dough in a bowl, cover with a towel and let rise in a lukewarm and draft-free place (a 160° oven is good) until it has doubled in bulk. It should take 1½ to 2 hours. Push the dough down with your fingers (flour your hands to be able to handle the dough). Wrap in foil or in a towel and place in a cold refrigerator (the meat compartment is the coolest and best area for storing the dough so it won't "develop" too much). Make the dough the day before you plan to use it and it will be more malleable after it has rested overnight. This dough may be frozen (well-wrapped) but not much longer than 1 month in a conventional freezer because the yeast is affected by the extreme cold. If you freeze it, *defrost under refrigeration* before using it.

For little brioches, cut pieces of dough (about 2½ to 3 ounces per brioche) and roll into little balls. Place the dough into buttered brioche molds. Brush with a wash (1 beaten egg) and let rise in a warm, draft-free place for about 1¼ to 1½ hours. Cook in a 400° oven for about 25 minutes.

If you make the dough by hand, knead the dough until all the ingredients are well blended. Then, work the dough on a marble or stainless-steel table by lifting part of it in the air and throwing it back on itself. It will take at least 15 minutes of working until blisters appear on the dough. Follow above procedure.

If you have no fresh yeast replace 1 ounce with 2 packages of dry yeast. Place the yeast with ½ cup of lukewarm water into a bowl and add the sugar. Let the mixture soften and bubble. Use

½ cup of additional flour to absorb the water necessary to melt the yeast. Follow above procedure.

Pâte à Pâté
Pâté or Ham Dough

(Enough for 1 large ham or pâté in crust)

•

Pâté dough must be strong, not elastic, otherwise it will "work" during the cooking and the dough will lose its shape. We use less fat than in a regular pie dough in order to make it stronger and the egg yolks so that the dough takes on a nice color and does not contract during cooking.

> 1 *pound all-purpose flour*
> 1 *stick sweet butter (4 ounces)*
> 4 *ounces lard (pork fat) (if you cannot obtain*
>   *lard replace with butter)*
> ½ *teaspoon salt*
> ½ *teaspoon sugar*
> 4 to 5 *egg yolks, depending on the size*
> *approximately ½ cup cold water*

The butter and the lard should be at room temperature. Place the flour, butter, lard, salt, and sugar in a large bowl. Start working the fat and flour with both hands "squishing" the mixture together until it becomes lumpy (about 1 or 2 minutes). Reach into the bowl with both hands, take up some of the mixture and rub both hands together so that the mixture crumbles and falls back into the bowl. Continue this operation until you have all of the mixture the same color and looking very much like cornmeal or sand as it runs through your fingers. Mix the yolks and the water together with a fork until they are well blended. Make a large hole in the middle of the flour mixture and pour the yolks and water into it. With your fingers, mix well and rapidly until all the ingredients assemble into a large solid mass. Knead the dough on a flat surface for 1 minute to have all of the ingredients well blended. Wrap in a towel and allow to rest in the refrigerator for at least 1 hour before using. This dough may also be made a day, or even a few days, in advance.

Pâte Feuilletée
Puff Paste

(Enough to make 1 fish in crust, page 155, and 1 mille-feuille)

•

Feuilletage or puff paste is probably one of the most difficult doughs to make and even for professionals it has its pitfalls. The puff pastry must be perfect to make *bouchées* or a *vol-au-vent*. However, for a pie shell, quiche, *bandes des fruits* (fruit strips), *fleurons*, a *demi-feuilletage* (half puff paste) is often used. The *demi-feuilletage* is the trimming of regular puff paste gathered into a ball and kept in the refrigerator or freezer. There are several ways to make puff paste. We will give one very classic recipe and one fast version, easier to make and quite satisfactory. The puff paste is always made with flour and butter in equal proportions, and a liquid, usually water, to bind the elements. The butter is never incorporated into the flour as in the *pâte brisée, sucrée*, etc. The flour and water agglomerate into an elastic dough. Then the butter is placed on the dough. By folding, rolling, and folding again, a multi-layered effect is achieved composed of layers of elastic dough covered with butter. During cooking the butter heats and develops steam which tries to escape by "pushing up" the layers. Thus, the "thousand leaf" effect. If you understand the principle of puff paste you will know that *the butter and the basic dough have to be at the same temperature to roll uniformly.* A soft butter will be "squished" and will run between layers and vice versa if the dough is too soft. *The flour used to roll out the dough must be dusted from the surface before folding. Dry flour imprisoned between layers will make a dry and tough pastry.* The rolling must be light and uniform. If you push the rolling pin down and forward too hard the butter will mash into the layers of dough and be smeared with the flour, then the layers will be broken and the butter will bleed during cooking. Beware of hot and humid summer days, the ingredients are limp and have a tendency to blend together. When cutting a strip, circle, or any shape from the dough, use a sharp cutter or knife to have a neat cut. If the knife is dull the layers will again be squished together and will not rise properly. For the same reason, when brushing the top of the pastry with egg wash, avoid brushing the cut so that the layers do not stick together. The best puff paste of all is the one made with heavy cream instead of water. It is extremely light, tender, and flaky and it develops beautifully. The dough is also more malleable and rolls easier. The 1½ cups of cream used in this recipe may be replaced with 1 cup of water for a more conventional dough.

> 1 *pound (about 3½ cups loose flour), plus ¾
>   of a cup to roll out the dough (pastry flour
>   makes the dough less elastic, although all-
>   purpose flour can be used)*
> 1½ *cups heavy cream*
> 1 *teaspoon salt*
> 1 *pound sweet butter (4 sticks)*

Place the 1 pound of flour, salt, and cream in the bowl of an electric mixer. Mix on the second speed, using the flat beater, for 1 to 2 minutes. The dough should be velvety and elastic. It may be done by hand just as well working the mixture for a few minutes. Set the basic dough in the refrigerator and allow to "rest" a few minutes. Meanwhile, place the butter in the bowl of the mixer and work with the flat beater for 1 or 2 minutes until you have a homogeneous paste, not too soft. Now you want to roll the dough and the butter together. However, the butter cannot be rolled or it will stick to the pin. It must be enclosed in the dough first and the whole mixture rolled together. Spread the basic dough with your hands or a rolling pin. Place the butter in a block in the middle and fold the sides of the dough so that it joins and seals up the butter in the middle. Squeeze the joints together so that it adheres and does not split open during the rolling. *Allow the mixture to rest in the refrigerator for 15 minutes. This will allow time for the dough and the butter to reach the same temperature and consistency, insuring proper rolling.* Sprinkle the board with some of the reserved flour. Using a rolling pin, start rolling the dough without pushing too hard. Check to see that you have enough flour underneath the dough so that it can slide and expand during rolling. *Proceed slowly. The first 2 turns are the most delicate. If some patches of butter appear, sprinkle with flour.* You should make a rectangle 16 to 18 inches long by 6 to 8 inches wide. With a soft brush or a towel, dust off any excess flour from the surface of the dough. Fold the dough so the narrow ends meet in the center. Make it as equal as possible. Again, brush excess flour from the surface and fold the 2 halves together, which will give you a 4-layer package. This is known as a double turn. (The single turn has only 3 layers). By this time the dough will probably be limp or too elastic to handle. Place it on a tray, dust with flour, and place in the refrigerator for 15 to 20 minutes so that it may again set to a proper temperature. Next, place the dough on the floured board with the narrow side of the dough facing you. Roll into a 20- by 8-inch wide rectangle. Dust off the surface and make a double turn again. Repeat the operation 3 more times (a total of 5 double turns), making sure to dust off the flour between the folds. You may try to make 2 double turns in a row if the dough is still workable—otherwise place in the refrigerator once more. When finished, cover with plastic wrap. It may be kept in the refrigerator for a few days or in the freezer for a couple of months. (If kept in the refrigerator too long, the dough has a tendency to become rubbery and difficult to roll out.) If you freeze it, be sure to defrost it under refrigeration before using. The finished dough usually resembles a rectangle. When using only a piece, cut it "widthwise." Keep the trimmings for a *demi-feuilletage*.

Feuilletage Rapide
Fast Puff Paste

(Same amount as classic recipe, page 52)

•

This dough is made with granulated instant flour. It rolls very easily. It will not take more than 30 minutes for the dough to be completed. However, it is satisfactory, although not quite as tender and flaky as the classic recipe.

1 *pound instant flour (4 cups), plus ½ cup for*
   the rolling
1 *pound cold sweet butter (4 sticks), cut into*
   1-inch pieces
1 *teaspoon baking powder*
½ *teaspoon salt*
1 *cup very cold water*

Place all of the ingredients, except the ½ cup of flour used for rolling, into a large bowl and mix together with your hands for a few seconds, just enough to gather all ingredients into a ball. The butter should still be in pieces.

Sprinkle the board with some of the reserved flour and roll the dough into a rectangle about 18 inches long by 8 inches wide. You will be surprised to see how malleable this dough is. Be sure to have enough flour on the board so that the dough can slide and expand during the rolling. Sprinkle generously with flour to coat all the pieces of butter. This is why the butter should be very cold. Brush excess flour from the surface of the dough and give a double turn (see classic recipe, page 52). If the dough is still workable give another double turn. Allow to rest refrigerated for 15 minutes and then give 2 more double turns (a total of 4 double turns) in a row if possible. Allow the dough to rest refrigerated a few minutes before using. Follow the same storing and using procedures as for classic puff paste.

Génoise
Basic Cake

•

The *génoise* is the base for many desserts from a mocha cake to a Croûte aux Fruits (page 310), also petits fours, *glacés*, or a wedding cake. After being cooled the *génoise* can be kept covered with plastic wrap in the refrigerator for at least 1 week. The *génoise* is easier to make with an electric mixer, however, it may also be made by hand. *The most delicate step in making a* génoise *is folding (see page 296) the flour into the mixture. This is best done with your hand or with a rubber spatula. If the flour is not folded in enough you will have lumps, however, you must not overwork the mixture. This will result in a greenish, heavy and dry cake.* Enough air should be absorbed by the eggs during the beating to give the cake its airy quality. If the eggs are cool and over-beaten the cake will lack texture, will run over during cooking, go up and down like a soufflé, and result in a flat and crumbly cake.

> *butter and flour to prepare the cake pans*
> 6 *large eggs*
> ¾ *cup sugar*
> ½ *teaspoon vanilla extract*
> *grated rind of* ½ *lemon*
> 1 *cup sifted pastry or all-purpose flour* (*it is*
> *imperative you sift the flour*)
> 1 *tablespoon melted butter*

The batter may be cooked in a large flat tray or in square molds, depending upon what it is to be used for.

Generously butter two 9-inch cake pans. Add 1 tablespoon of flour to one pan, tipping the pan back and forth so that the flour coats the bottom and sides of the pan. Pour the excess flour into the second pan by tapping the bottom of the prepared pan to remove all excess flour. Coat the second pan in the same manner, discarding the excess flour. Set the prepared pans in the refrigerator.

Place the eggs, sugar, vanilla, and lemon rind in the bowl of an electric mixer, or if you are making it by hand, use a stainless-steel, copper, or porcelain bowl. Stir with a whisk over boiling water for ½ minute, or until the mixture feels warm to your touch. Place the bowl on the machine and beat on high speed for about 6 to 8 minutes, or until the mixture is very pale yellow and as thick as a light mayonnaise. Remove the whip and sprinkle the flour on top, folding it in with your hand or a rubber spatula as you go along. Fold in the melted butter. *Do not over-mix.* Pour the batter into the cake pans and place on a cookie sheet in a 350° oven for 25 to 30 minutes. When cooked the cake should spring back when touched, or when inserting the

blade of a small knife into the middle it should come out clean.
Cool on a rack at room temperature.

Cakes, pies, and soufflés should not be placed directly on oven
wire racks because the transfer of heat is not proper. They
should be placed on a solid sheet of metal first (cookie sheet or
jelly-roll pan) to insure proper cooking.

If you find it difficult to make the cake as explained above
you may separate the eggs and beat the sugar and egg yolks
together for 2 minutes with a whisk. Add the vanilla, lemon,
and flour and mix with a whisk until smooth. Beat the egg
whites until stiff, add about ⅓ of it to the yolk mixture and mix
with the whisk. Fold in (see page 296) the remaining egg whites
and butter and cook as explained above. This is closer to a
biscuit de Savoie, gives good results, and is easy to make.

Soufflés

•

A soufflé—from the French verb *souffler*, to breathe, inflate,
puff up—is nothing more than a thick sauce base into which
beaten egg whites are incorporated. The air "trapped" in the
egg white in the form of little bubbles expands as the soufflé
cooks, and pushes it into its magnificent puff. The flavoring
element can be varied from chocolate to orange, spinach, or
cheese. The cheese soufflé—using Gruyère or Emmenthal—is
one of the easiest soufflés to make because the cheese melts and
holds the ingredients together. The chocolate, on the other
hand, is heavy and difficult to make perfectly. Do not make a
chocolate soufflé on your first try.

A few points are important: A soufflé should not be too
cooked in the center, but still soft. It should rise only about

2 or 3 inches above the edge of the mold, and it should not break and spill over or "fall" right away. It should have a "bite" to it and hold its shape for several minutes before starting to deflate. If the soufflé goes very high, breaks and spills over the rim, the base sauce is too light; you have too many egg whites and the soufflé is only air. The soufflés holding the longest are the ones cooked in a double boiler at low temperature (between 325° to 350°). But even cooked the conventional way, a soufflé should hold if the mixture is the right consistency. Place a baking sheet under the soufflé in the oven to insure a proper distribution of heat. Be careful when separating the egg whites not to get any yolks mixed with the whites, because yolks, being fat, will prevent the whites from expanding. Be sure the vessel into which you beat the egg whites is clean and not made of aluminum. The most delicate part of the soufflé is adding the whites to the sauce. It is delicate because as soon as you stop beating the whites to mix some into the sauce, the remaining whites start to become granular and break down. If it is possible, the ideal situation is to have two people working, one incorporating the egg whites into the sauce and the other still beating the whites. If you are alone, be sure to go as fast as possible during this step. It is hard to incorporate the stiff whites with a spatula. Therefore approximately ⅓ of the whites are beaten into the base with a whisk to lighten the base. Then the remaining whites are "folded" into the mixture. The objective is to retain the air in the whites.

Be sure to butter and coat the mold (either with sugar, flour, or cheese) and refrigerate the prepared mold before pouring in the mixture. This detail will help the soufflé to rise straight up. After the mold is filled with the mixture (it should be filled up to the edge), you can keep the soufflé in the refrigerator for at least 3 to 4 hours. When you are ready to cook it, transfer it from the refrigerator straight to the oven.

Champignons
Mushrooms

•

How to Cook Fresh Mushrooms in Advance

In French cooking we use mushrooms in a fantastic number of ways: with meat, fish, and chicken, as a vegetable, in omelets, as a garnish, or an hors d'oeuvre. For many dishes the mushrooms can be cooked ahead and refrigerated in their broth in a covered bowl. They will keep for 1 or even 2 weeks. In cooking mushrooms, lemon juice is essential and you must cook them as fast as possible. When done this way, they will remain white.

Wipe the mushroom caps with a clean, damp cloth. Do not soak them in water. Using a sturdy French knife, slice the caps and stems separately if the mushrooms are large, or through the whole mushroom if they are small.

Pour the strained juice of 1 lemon into a medium-sized saucepan. Do not use an aluminum pan as it will discolor the mushrooms.

Add ¼ cup of water, 1 tablespoon sweet butter, and ½ teaspoon salt. Place the pan over a high heat and bring to a boil. Add 2 cups of sliced mushrooms—stems and caps—(about ½ pound) all at once. Bring to a boil again and boil hard for 4 to 5 minutes, stirring a few times. Pour immediately into an earthenware bowl and cover tightly with foil or plastic wrap.

First Courses

Billi-Bi
Mussel Soup

(Serves 8 to 10)

•

5 *pounds mussels, washed and cleaned (see
  page 131)*
1 *clove garlic, crushed with skin on*
1 *medium onion, coarsely chopped (about ½
  cup)*
8 to 10 *shallots, coarsely chopped (about ½
  cup)*
1 *tablespoon sweet butter*
2 *cups dry white wine*
½ *teaspoon thyme, crushed (fresh is better)*
1 *crushed bay leaf*
5 to 6 *sprigs of parsley*
2 *teaspoons salt*

Place all ingredients in a large casserole (do not use aluminum, as it will discolor) and bring to a rolling boil, shaking the
pan to move the mussels and have them open. Boil 1 minute.

> 2 *cups heavy cream*
> 1 *tablespoon arrowroot diluted with ½ cup cold*
>   *water*

Mix the arrowroot mixture with the cream and pour on the mussels. Let come to a high boil and keep boiling for 1 minute, mixing the mussels with a long wooden spoon. Strain the mixture. Dish the mussels onto a large tray. Try to leave all the juices in the casserole.

> 2 *egg yolks*
> ¼ *cup heavy cream*

Mix the cream and yolks carefully so that the mixture is homogeneous. Add about 1 cup of mussels and cream juices from the casserole to the above mixture, mixing carefully to prevent the egg yolk from curdling. Pour the whole mixture into the casserole and heat, stirring constantly to avoid "scrambling" the eggs, until the mixture coats the spoon. *Temperature should be about 180°, which means that the mixture should not boil, but come close to a simmer.* Immediately, strain the Billi-Bi through a very fine sieve or a cheesecloth. Chill before serving, as this soup is usually served cold. *Yield:* 2 quarts. This soup is very rich and creamy and a 6-ounce serving is enough.

Note: Shell the mussels (you will have approximately 2 full cups of mussels), mix with about ¾ cup of Rémoulade (see page 109) and serve cold as an hors d'oeuvre.

Gazpacho
Cold Raw Vegetable Soup

(Serves 6 to 8)

•

1 *cup peeled, diced onions (about 2 medium-to-small onions)*
2 *large-sized cucumbers (or 3 medium), peeled and seeded*
4 *medium-sized, well-ripened tomatoes (seeds removed)*
1 *large green pepper (seeds removed)*
1 *piece of celery rib, cleaned and cut into cubes (about ⅓ cup)*
2 *cloves garlic, peeled and crushed*
2 *eggs, separated*
¾ *cup water*
1 *tablespoon white wine vinegar*
2 *tablespoons olive oil*
1 *teaspoon salt*
dash tabasco or cayenne pepper
1½ *cups croutons (make with 3 slices of bread and sauté in a mixture of oil and butter)*

Dice separately ½ cup onions, ⅓ of 1 cucumber, 1 tomato, ⅓ of the green pepper. Place in individual bowls and refrigerate. This will be used as a garnish for the soup. Place, a little at a time, the remaining onions, cucumbers, tomatoes, green pepper and celery in the blender and blend. Add the garlic and egg yolks. Use the water to help the ingredients to puree properly. They should be reduced to a liquid. When all of the ingredients have been blended, add the vinegar, oil, salt, and tabasco. Taste for seasoning and add salt and pepper if needed. Next, push the soup through a food mill or metal sieve and refrigerate overnight before serving. Serve with the diced vegetables and the croutons.

Note: You do not have to put the soup through a food mill. However, this will eliminate stringy pieces which have not blended properly and will give the *gazpacho* a creamier and smoother texture.

Germiny
Cold Sorrel Soup

(*Serves 6 to 8*)

•

1 *bunch* (*about 3 ounces*) *fresh sorrel. Remove
the biggest part of the stem. Slice thin
(about 2 cups)*
1 *tablespoon sweet butter*

Melt the butter in a pan and then add the shredded sorrel. Cook 4 to 5 minutes and set aside.

6 *egg yolks*
4 *cups chicken stock*
1 *cup heavy cream*
1 *tablespoon fresh chopped chervil*
salt and pepper to taste (*depending on the
saltiness of the chicken stock*)

Place egg yolks and ½ cup cold chicken stock in a saucepan and cook on very low heat, beating constantly with a wire whisk for about 6 to 7 minutes. *The mixture should have the con-*

sistency of a light mayonnaise and should never get so hot that you cannot hold your finger in the mixture. When the sabayon is cooked, you should be able to see the bottom of the saucepan between the strokes of the whisk. Bring the remaining stock to a boil in a separate pan. Mix the cream (cold) with the sabayon and add to the hot stock. Place back on the stove on medium heat and cook just enough for the mixture to coat a spoon, about 170° to 180° on a thermometer. Strain through a fine sieve or a towel, add the sorrel mixture and cool in refrigerator until very cold. Serve sprinkled with the fresh chervil.

Soupe aux Pêches
Cold Peach Soup

(Serves 6 to 8)

•

This is really a fantasy adapted from an old French recipe. You may also serve it as a dessert poured directly over slices of pound cake and decorated with whipped cream. As a soup, it will surprise and delight your guests if they like the unusual.

1½ cups water
4 cloves
¾ cup sugar
1 stick cinnamon, broken into small pieces
2 tablespoons cornstarch, diluted with ¼ cup
    cold water
1½ cups dry white wine
3½ pounds ripe peaches (about 12 peaches)
1 cup heavy cream
1 cup fresh blueberries

Place the water, cloves, sugar, and cinnamon in a small kettle and bring to a boil. Let simmer for 10 minutes and add the cornstarch diluted in water, stirring with a wire whisk to blend the starch with the syrup. Bring the syrup to a boil again and set aside. Let cool. When cold, add the wine to the syrup and refrigerate. Clean the peaches (remove the skin with a knife or dip the peaches in boiling water for 30 seconds before peeling by hand). You may also make the soup without peeling the peaches. Split them lengthwise and remove the pits. Slice 2 cups of the nicest peaches (these will be served as a garnish in the soup) and set aside. Place the remaining peaches in the blender, puree them, and add to the syrup with the reserved slices. Refrigerate overnight or for a few hours before serving. Whip the cream and set aside. At serving time, fill individual bowls, sprinkle the blueberries on the soup, and top with a generous tablespoon of whipped cream.

Consommé

(Serves 8)

•

Consommé is the beef or chicken concoction that, when perfectly made, is a beautifully clear and sparkling soup or base for other soups. It has all of the proteins of meat and none of the fat. Clarification is the process that gives the consommé its crystal-clear appearance. Be sure to use a fat-free stock and immaculate equipment.

1 pound very lean ground beef
⅓ cup coarsely chopped celery

½ cup coarsely chopped parsley
1 cup coarsely chopped leek tops (the green
     part)
¾ cup coarsely chopped carrots
1 tablespoon black peppercorns
2 bay leaves
½ teaspoon crushed thyme
4 egg whites
¼ teaspoon caramel coloring (see page 32)
8 cups beef or chicken (or a mixture of both)
     stock (not concentrated)
1 cup water
dash of salt, depending on the saltiness of the
     stock

Combine all the ingredients except the caramel coloring and
the stock in a large heavy casserole. Mix by hand until homogeneous. Add the stock and mix with a spatula. Bring to a boil
over *high heat*, stirring constantly to avoid scorching. *Do not
worry if the stock becomes very cloudy and a white foam forms.
The albumin in the egg whites and the meat is solidifying and
this is the process that will clarify the stock.* When the mixture
comes to a boil, a rolling boil, stop stirring *immediately*. Reduce
the heat to a simmer. As the mixture simmers, you will notice
that the ingredients form a crust on the surface of the liquid
with one or two holes, through which the liquid slightly boils.
Allow the consommé to simmer very gently for 1 hour without
disturbing the little "geysers" in any way. After 1 hour add the
caramel coloring to the consommé through one of the openings
—just enough to turn it to a light gold color. Do not add any
coloring if the consommé is already dark enough, which depends
on the stock. Strain the consommé through a sieve lined with
several layers of cheesecloth wrung out in cold water, taking care
not to disturb the crust. Use a ladle to dish the liquid out. After
the consommé has "rested" 1 hour, check to see if there is any

fat on the surface. If so, remove it by blotting the top with paper towels. The crust is usually discarded. However, with the addition of whole eggs, breadcrumbs, and seasonings (providing you remove the peppercorns), it can be turned into a satisfying meatloaf. *Yield:* About 7 measuring cups, enough for 8 persons. *If the consommé is too reduced and too strong dilute it with some plain water.* This is a plain consommé and it can be served as such or with a garnish like Célestine (shredded crêpes), Royal (cubed custard), etc. Consommé is also the base used to make aspic.

Gratinée Lyonnaise au Porto
Onion Soup Lyonnaise Style

(*Serves 6 to 8*)

•

2 *tablespoons sweet butter*
1 *large onion, peeled and sliced thin*
3 *cups beef or chicken broth*
salt, depending on seasoning of broth
freshly ground pepper, depending on seasoning
 of broth
15 to 20 *thin slices French or Italian bread,*
 *toasted**
¾ *cup grated Gruyère cheese*
2 *egg yolks*
½ *cup sweet port wine*

---

* The loaf of bread should be about 3 inches in diameter, and the slices ¼ inch thick. Toast them by placing the bread flat on a cookie sheet and cook in a hot oven until browned.

Melt the butter in a saucepan. Add the onion and sauté for 10 to 15 minutes or until nicely browned. Add the broth, salt and pepper to taste, and bring to a boil. Cook for 20 minutes. Strain, pushing on the onions with a spoon to extrude as much as you can. Place ⅓ of the bread in the bottom of an ovenproof soup tureen or large casserole. Sprinkle with some cheese, add more bread, then more cheese, saving enough to sprinkle over the top of the soup. Fill the tureen with the hot soup, sprinkle the remaining cheese on top, and place in a 400° oven for approximately 35 minutes.

At serving time, bring the *gratinée* to the table. Combine the yolks with the wine in a deep soup plate and whip with a fork. With a ladle, make a "hole" in the top of the *gratinée*, pour in the wine mixture and fold into the soup with the ladle.

Note: This recipe from the Lyon region is for a soup that is much thicker than the usual onion soup. For a "lighter" soup, use about half the amount of bread.

Potage Cressonnière
Watercress Soup

(*Serves 6 to 8*)

•

This soup is usually served hot but may also be served cold. When making a watercress salad, the leaves are used and the stems discarded. However, with Potage Cressonnière you may use all of the watercress or save the leaves for salad and use only the stems.

½ stick fresh sweet butter
1 medium onion, coarsely sliced
1 large leek (white and light green parts only),
    washed and sliced
2 bunches watercress
4 to 5 medium potatoes, peeled and sliced
1 quart chicken stock
approximately 1 teaspoon salt (depending on
    the seasoning of the chicken stock)
¼ teaspoon freshly ground white pepper
1 pinch thyme leaves
1½ cups milk
1 cup heavy cream

Melt half of the butter in a large pot, add the onion, leek, and watercress. Cook, stirring often, until all the ingredients become soft (about 5 minutes). Add the potatoes, chicken stock, salt and pepper, and thyme. Bring to a rolling boil. Reduce heat, cover, and let it simmer for 1 hour. Allow soup to cool off a bit so that you may handle it. Blend 2 cups at a time in the blender. When the soup is blended, strain through a metal sieve to remove stringy pieces of watercress. Return soup to a large pot and add the milk and cream. Bring to a boil, slowly stirring with a wooden spatula. Taste for seasoning. Stir in the remaining butter, bit by bit, just before serving. Stir after each addition until the butter is well incorporated into the soup. *Do not boil the soup after the addition of the butter.* If the soup is too thick for your taste add a little milk or water.

This soup is a perfect start for an elegant dinner.

Potage Cultivateur
Vegetable Soup

(Serves 6 to 8)

•

3 tablespoons sweet butter
1 leek, thoroughly washed, thinly sliced (white
    and light green parts only)
1 medium onion, peeled and thinly sliced (¾
    cup)
1 small turnip, peeled and thinly sliced (¾ cup)
2 medium carrots, peeled and thinly sliced
    (about 1¼ cups)
10 parsley sprigs, coarsely chopped (about ⅓
    cup)
2 quarts water
1 celery rib, thinly sliced (about ½ cup)
3 medium potatoes, peeled and thinly sliced
    (about 2½ cups)
1½ teaspoons salt
minced parsley

Melt the butter in a large enameled casserole. Add all the
ingredients except the potatoes, water, salt, and the minced
parsley. Steam over moderate heat, stirring occasionally, for 3
to 4 minutes. Do not allow the mixture to brown. Add the
potatoes, water and salt. Bring to a boil, then cook uncovered
over a moderate heat for 1 hour and 15 minutes. *Yield:* About
2½ quarts. If the soup reduces too much during cooking, add
water to get the proper yield. Serve in heated cups with a garnish
of minced parsley.

Crème Dubarry
Cream of Cauliflower Soup

•

½ cup flour
4 cups water
4 cups chicken broth
2 medium onions, peeled and sliced (about 1½
      cups)
1 leek, peeled, washed, and sliced (use only the
      white part)
1 medium cauliflower, washed and cut into
      chunks with leaves discarded (about
      1 pound)
1 cup heavy cream
salt
freshly ground white pepper
4 tablespoons chopped fresh chervil (if unavail-
      able, replace with parsley)

Mix the flour with 1 cup of water until smooth. In a large kettle place the mixed flour, remaining water, chicken broth, sliced onions, sliced leek, and cauliflower. Bring to a boil and simmer slowly for 1¼ hours. Put through a food mill or puree, a small amount at a time, in the electric blender. Add the cream and taste for seasoning. Add the chopped chervil and bring to a boil. This soup can be served hot or cold. Yield: About 2 quarts. If the liquid reduces too much during cooking, add water to bring up to the correct yield.

Note: When the soup is served cold, be sure to "overseason" it as salt has a tendency to lose strength in cold dishes.

Potage Crème de Tomates
Cream of Tomato Soup

(Serves 6 to 8)

•

4 *tablespoons* (½ *stick*) *sweet butter*
1 *tablespoon olive oil*
1 *yellow onion, peeled and sliced thin* (*about*
    1¼ cups)
3 *ripe tomatoes, chopped coarsely*
3 *tablespoons tomato paste*
4 *tablespoons all-purpose flour*
2½ *cups or 2 cans* (10½-*ounce size*) *chicken*
    broth
½ *teaspoon sugar*
dash salt (*depending on saltiness of chicken*
    broth)
dash freshly ground white pepper
1 *cup heavy cream*

Heat 2 tablespoons of the butter with the oil in a saucepan. Add the onion and sauté for about 5 minutes. Stir in the tomatoes and tomato paste and cook for 2 to 3 minutes. Sprinkle with the flour and mix well with a wooden spatula. Add the broth, sugar, salt, and pepper. Simmer 15 minutes.

Pour into the container of the electric blender and blend at high speed for a couple of seconds. Strain through a fine sieve. Pour into a saucepan and add the cream. Bring to a boil. Reduce heat and simmer 2 to 3 minutes.

At serving time, stir in the remaining butter, bit by bit. Serve with or without croutons.

Soupe de Poisson
Fish Soup

(*Serves 6 to 8*)

•

This is one of those wonderful hearty soups everybody loves
and are so delicious on a cold night. The fish couldn't be less
expensive, but what gives the soup its marvelous flavor is the
combination of the fish with the vegetables and aromatic herbs
all cooked together.

> 1 *big onion, diced (1¼ cups loose)*
> 1 *leek, diced (1 cup)*
> 1 *rib celery, diced (½ cup)*
> ½ *cup parsley, minced*
> ½ *cup fennel bulb, cleaned and diced*
> 2 *carrots, peeled and diced (1¼ cups)*
> 3 *tablespoons olive oil*

Heat the olive oil in a heavy 8½-quart kettle. When hot, add
the vegetables and herbs and cook together for 5 minutes.

> 6 *cloves garlic, crushed with skin on*
> 2 *very ripe tomatoes, cut into chunks (2 cups)*
> 3 *bay leaves*
> 3 *pounds fish and fishbones (1 head of striped*
>   *bass, gills removed and cleaned; the heads*
>   *and bones of 2 flounders, gills removed and*
>   *cleaned; 3 blowfish; 1 whiting)*
> 1 *pinch dried thyme (or 2 sprigs fresh thyme)*
> *large pinch real saffron pistils*
> 1 *teaspoon freshly ground black pepper*

Mix together in the kettle with a wooden spoon and cook 3 minutes longer.

> ½ cup tomato puree
> 2 cups dry white wine
> 3 quarts water

Add these ingredients and bring to a boil in the kettle. Boil for 25 to 30 minutes. Put through a food mill. *Yield:* Approximately 2 quarts of soup.

Cook 4 large Idaho potatoes in boiling, salted water until they seem tender when pierced with the point of a sharp paring knife. Drain. When cool enough to handle, peel and cut into large, thick slices. Set aside for the moment.

> 12 slices French bread, cut about ¼ inch thick
> ½ cup vegetable oil
> 2 large cloves garlic, peeled

To make croutons with the bread, brush both sides with vegetable oil and cut each slice into 4 squares. Place in a baking pan in a preheated 375° oven until brown. Cool. When cold, rub each square with the garlic cloves.

To serve the soup, place slices of the cooked potatoes and croutons in large soup bowls, then fill the bowls with boiling hot fish soup. Serve at once.

Bisque de Homard
Lobster Bisque

(Serves 6 to 8)

•

One of the richest among the French soups, *bisque de homard* is served for elegant dinners. Crab or crayfish can replace the lobster.

> 1 *live fresh lobster, 3½ pounds*
> 3 *tablespoons dry white wine*
> ¾ *cup flour*
> 3 *tablespoons sweet butter*

Cut the lobster with a cleaver or a large knife. Cut the legs, claws, and tail into 3 or 4 chunks and separate the front in half lengthwise. Place the coral (red part in the breast), the tomalley (brownish-green part in the breast, if any), and the liquid, which congeals fast, into a bowl. Add the wine (*you will notice that the mixture will turn whitish if the lobster is very fresh and the wine will stop the mixture from congealing*). Add the flour and butter and work with a spatula to make a paste. This will be the thickening agent for the soup.

> 2 *tablespoons olive oil*
> ¼ *cup cognac*
> 1 *medium onion, coarsely chopped (¾ cup)*
> 1 *carrot, coarsely chopped (¾ cup)*
> 1 *leek, coarsely chopped (the white part only,*
>   *about ½ cup)*
> 2 *tomatoes, coarsely chopped (about 2 cups)*
> 2 *tablespoons tomato paste*

½ teaspoon crushed thyme (fresh is better)
1 tablespoon chopped fresh tarragon (or 1
    teaspoon dry tarragon)
1¾ cups dry white wine
2 cups water
2 teaspoons salt
1 teaspoon freshly ground black pepper
2 cups chicken stock

In a very large, wide skillet or sauté pan, place the oil, and when very hot, add the pieces of lobster. Cook for 4 to 5 minutes stirring the pieces, which should turn bright red. Add cognac and ignite. Add the remaining ingredients, cover, and simmer for 18 to 20 minutes. With a skimmer, remove the lobster pieces to a tray. When cool enough to handle, remove the meat from the shells and set aside. Discard the shells which have no meat attached to them; keep the small legs, pieces of breast, and any hollow pieces of shell with meat in them. Chop these coarsely with a cleaver and add back to the pan. Cook for 12 to 15 minutes. Strain through a metal sieve, pushing with a spoon or ladle to extract as much liquid as possible.

2 cups heavy cream
1 cup milk
1 tablespoon good cognac
salt and pepper as needed

Add the cream and milk to the pot and bring to a boil, add salt and pepper if needed. A bisque *should be peppery*. Stir in cognac at the last minute. Serve hot in small cups, about 6 ounces per person.

Note: The lobster meat can be diced and served as a garnish for the soup, but I believe the pieces get rubbery in the soup. Just as good a use for it is to make a lobster salad. Dice the meat and add ¾ cup of Gribiche Sauce (see page 37); serve with sliced avocado as a first course.

Ceviche
Raw Marinated Fish

(*Serves 6 to 8*)

•

1 *pound scallops (bay scallops if possible) cut*
    into ½-inch cubes
1 *bluefish, approximately 2½ to 3 pounds as*
    purchased. It will give approximately 1½
    pounds of flesh after it has been boned and
    skinned. Cube in the same manner as the
    scallops. If bluefish is not available, use any
    plump, meaty fish.
juice of 4 limes (¾ cup)
juice of 1 lemon (¼ cup)
3 *tomatoes, peeled, seeded, and diced into ¼-*
    inch cubes (about 1¾ cups)
2 *onions (red onions if possible), peeled and*
    chopped (about 1 cup)
1 *sweet green pepper, seeded and diced (about*
    1 cup)
2 to 3 *hot chili peppers, seeded and chopped*
    very fine (⅓ cup)
2 *stalks celery, peeled and diced (about ⅔ cup)*
4 *shallots, minced fine (about ¼ cup)*
3 *cloves garlic, peeled and chopped (about 1*
    tablespoon)
½ *cup olive oil*
1 *bunch parsley (about ⅓ cup), chopped*
1 *bunch fresh coriander, chopped (also called*
    Chinese parsley or cilantro) (about ⅓ cup)
1 *small avocado, peeled and diced (about 1 cup)*
1 *teaspoon coriander seeds, crushed*
1 *tablespoon salt*
½ *teaspoon freshly ground black pepper*

Mix all ingredients together in a tureen and cover with a piece of plastic wrap. Place in a refrigerator overnight. The mixture has to macerate at least 6 to 7 hours. Serve cold as an appetizer. *This dish may be kept for several days under refrigeration, and it even improves with time.*

Escargots Forestière
Snails with Mushrooms

(Serves 8)

•

48 *heads white cultivated mushrooms about*
   1½ inches in diameter (Break the stems
   off at the base of the caps and use for
   Champignons à la Grecque, see page 80;
   puree of mushrooms; or soup.)
½ *teaspoon salt*
3 *tablespoons vegetable oil*

Place the caps, hollow side up, flat on a cookie sheet and sprinkle with the salt and oil. Place in a preheated 400° oven for about 8 minutes. *There will be some liquid accumulated in the caps. Turn the caps upside down and let cool.*

4 *dozen big snails, canned (Fresh snails are very*
   rarely available.) Choose the largest size.
1½ *tablespoons sweet butter*
½ *teaspoon salt (Snails are usually unsalted in*
   cans. If yours are salted, omit the salt in
   this recipe.)
¼ *teaspoon freshly ground white pepper*

Drain the can of snails in a colander and rinse thoroughly under cold water. Melt the butter in a frying pan, add the salt, pepper, snails, and toss gently for a few seconds. Set aside. *This step is only to get rid of the canned taste that the snails may have acquired. If you do not think it is necessary, you may omit this step.*

Snail Butter (*see page 43*)

Place ½ teaspoon of snail butter in the hollow part of each cold mushroom cap. Push 1 snail in each buttered cap and top with 1 teaspoon of the butter, enough to cover the snail. When all prepared, the snails and mushrooms can be refrigerated. Place 6 filled mushroom caps per dish in small au gratin dishes. Place on a cookie sheet in a preheated 400° oven for 12 minutes. Serve immediately.

Champignons à la Grecque
Cold Marinated Mushrooms

(*Serves 8*)

•

This dish will keep several weeks in a jar in the refrigerator. In fact, the flavor will improve after a few days.

> 2½ pounds fresh mushrooms
> 3 medium-to-large onions, peeled and quartered,
>   with the layers separated
> 3 bay leaves
> ½ teaspoon crushed thyme (fresh is better)
> 2 teaspoons whole black peppercorns
> 2 teaspoons salt

½ teaspoon coriander seeds, crushed
⅓ cup olive oil
1 cup dry white wine
juice of 1½ lemons

Wash the mushrooms in cold water. Quarter the large ones and split the medium mushrooms into halves. Place in a heavy saucepan with all remaining ingredients. Bring to a boil on high heat and boil on high heat for 6 to 8 minutes, covered. Transfer to an earthenware container and let cool to room temperature. Cover with plastic wrap and refrigerate until serving time.

Fonds d'Artichauts au Safran
Saffron Artichoke Bottoms

(Serves 6)

•

Trim the artichokes to make Artichoke Bottoms (see page 258).

6 raw, medium-sized artichoke bottoms, cut
    into eighths (Remove the choke with a
    paring knife.)
1 cup water
½ cup dry white wine
½ lemon (the juice only)
¾ cup thinly sliced onion (about 1 onion)
2 tablespoons olive oil
1 teaspoon salt
¼ teaspoon freshly ground black pepper
1 bay leaf
¼ teaspoon of real saffron, crushed

Place all of the ingredients into a large pot and bring to a boil. Simmer gently for 20 minutes. Transfer to a nice earthen vessel and cool, covered with plastic wrap. Serve cold as a first course or appetizer. This dish will keep in the refrigerator for at least 10 days.

Oeufs en Cocottes Bressane
Eggs in Ramekins Bressane Style
(Serves 6)

•

6 *large eggs*
2 *tablespoons sweet butter*
3 *tablespoons heavy cream*
salt
freshly ground white pepper

This will be a new way to cook eggs for many Americans because this method is not well known in the United States.

Butter 6 small porcelain ramekins (*ramequins* in French) or soufflé molds, then sprinkle lightly with salt and pepper. Break an egg into each *cocotte* or ramekin. Set the ramekins in a shallow pan with enough water, cold or warm, it does not matter, to reach about ⅔ of the depth of the ramekins. Cover the eggs, bring the water to a boil and cook for 1 minute. Add ½ tablespoon of cream on top of each egg, cover and cook another minute. Place the ramekins on a plate and serve immediately with thin buttered toast.

The eggs should be soft in the middle like poached eggs. If you use metal rather than porcelain containers the eggs will cook faster. If you like your eggs more done, increase the cooking time.

Gratin d'Oeufs à la Crème
Gratin of Eggs in Cream Sauce

(Serves 6 to 8)

•

6 *hard-cooked eggs, sliced (¼ inch thick)*
5 *tablespoons sweet butter*
2 *tablespoons chopped onion*
3 *tablespoons water*
6 *tablespoons all-purpose flour*
1 *cup condensed chicken broth*
1 *cup milk*
1 *cup heavy cream*
salt (depending on saltiness of chicken broth)
freshly ground pepper to taste
2 *ounces Swiss cheese, grated (about ½ cup)*

Melt the butter in a saucepan, add the onion, 3 tablespoons water, and cook over moderate heat for about 2 minutes until all the water is evaporated. Do not allow the onion to brown. Stir in the flour. Cook on a low heat, whipping constantly with a wire whisk for 1 to 2 minutes. Add the chicken broth and bring to a boil, whipping constantly. Next, add the milk, still stirring, and bring to a boil again. Reduce the heat and simmer 5 minutes. Stir in the cream and once more bring the sauce to a boil. Season with salt and pepper to taste.

Butter a shallow baking dish that can go on the table. Arrange the sliced eggs on the bottom, cover with the sauce. Sprinkle with the cheese and slide under a preheated broiler for 8 to 10 minutes, or until nicely browned.

Oeufs Jeannette
Eggs Jeannette

(*Serves 6 to 8*)

•

6 *hard-cooked eggs**
¼ *cup minced parsley*
4 *cloves garlic, peeled, crushed, and chopped*
  fine
¼ *cup heavy cream*
½ *teaspoon salt*
¼ *teaspoon freshly ground white pepper*

Cut the eggs in half and place the yolks in a bowl. Using a fork, mash the yolks until smooth. Mix in the parsley, garlic, cream, and salt and pepper to make a smooth paste. Fill each egg half with the paste, level with the top. Set aside.

Sauce

1 *tablespoon wine vinegar*
1 *teaspoon Dijon mustard*
½ *cup vegetable oil*

Add the vinegar and mustard to any mixture remaining in the bowl and beat well with a wire whisk. Now add the oil slowly, almost drop by drop, beating constantly until you have the consistency of a light mayonnaise. Set aside.

* Be careful when making hard-cooked eggs not to cook them too long or the yolks will turn slightly black around the outside. They should be placed in boiling water, boiled 10 minutes, and cooled under cold water.

2 *tablespoons sweet butter*

Heat the butter in a large heavy skillet. When sizzling, add the stuffed eggs, flat side down, and sauté on medium heat until lightly brown (about 2 to 3 minutes); turn on the other side and brown for another 2 to 3 minutes. Arrange on a heated platter and coat with the sauce. Serve immediately.

Oeufs Pochés Florentine
Poached Eggs Florentine

(*Serves* 8)

•

8 *eggs*
½ *cup white vinegar*
3 to 4 *cups water*

Take a wide shallow pan (about 8 inches wide, 3 inches deep). Add the water and white vinegar (this helps to "firm" the whites) and bring to a boil. Break the eggs, 1 at a time, into a saucer or plate and slip each egg into the boiling water. Do not cook any more than 4 eggs at one time. Turn the heat down, allowing the water to barely simmer or "shiver" (*frémir*), as we say in France. As the eggs cook, drag the bottom of a large metal spoon or skimmer across the surface of the water to move the eggs and to prevent them from sticking to the bottom of the pan. Cook for 2½ to 3 minutes. At this point, the whites should be set and the yolks soft to the touch. Lift from the hot water with a slotted spoon and place in a bowl of ice water. This washes off the vinegar and stops the cooking. When cool enough to handle, trim the eggs. Cover your left hand with a clean dry cloth, lift the egg with the slotted spoon into the palm of this hand and trim with a sharp knife or a pair of scissors.

2 pounds fresh (about 2 cups cooked) spinach
2 teaspoons salt
½ teaspoon freshly ground pepper
¼ teaspoon freshly ground nutmeg
3 tablespoons sweet butter

To prepare the spinach, remove the stems and use the leaves only. Drop into a large kettle of boiling salted water (do not use an aluminum or iron pan because the spinach picks up a metallic taste). Boil uncovered for about 6 minutes, or until the spinach tastes tender. Drain through a colander. Refresh immediately under cold running water to stop the cooking and keep the color. Drain again, pressing the spinach to extract as much water as possible. Place on a chopping board and chop coarsely. Sprinkle with salt, pepper, and nutmeg.

Place the butter in a frying pan over high heat. When the butter turns black, add the spinach and mix well with a fork. Sauté for 3 minutes. Arrange the spinach on the bottom of an ovenproof dish large enough to accommodate 8 poached eggs. Place the cold poached eggs on top with a little space between.

Sauce Mornay

2 tablespoons butter
2 tablespoons flour
1 cup milk
½ teaspoon salt
¼ teaspoon freshly ground white pepper
1 egg yolk
3 tablespoons grated Swiss cheese or 1½
tablespoons grated Parmesan

Heat the butter in a heavy saucepan. Stir in the flour until smooth and cook, stirring constantly, until the mixture froths (about 2 minutes) without browning. Add the milk, whipping constantly with a wire whisk. Cook until it boils, whipping constantly. Stir in the seasonings, and continue cooking on low heat for 2 to 3 minutes, stirring constantly with the whisk. Cool slightly, for 6 to 8 minutes, then add the egg yolk, beating very fast and hard. Fold in the cheese with a rubber spatula. Do not use a whip, or the cheese will "string."

1½ tablespoons freshly grated Parmesan cheese

Coat the eggs with the sauce and sprinkle with the cheese. Place under a broiler for 3 to 4 minutes until nicely browned. Serve immediately.

Omelette Savoyarde

(Serves 4)

•

¼ pound (about 5 or 6 lean slices) lean bacon
3 tablespoons sweet butter
1 medium potato, peeled and finely diced
1 leek (white part only), washed and sliced into
*   thin rounds*
8 eggs
salt
freshly ground pepper
½ cup finely diced Gruyère or Swiss cheese
*   (2 ounces)*
3 or 4 sprigs parsley, minced

Blanch the bacon in salted water. Drain, dry with paper towels and fry until brown in one tablespoon melted butter. Remove the bacon to paper towels to drain. Fry the potato in the remaining hot fat. Cook the sliced leeks in a little of the remaining butter.

Break the eggs into a bowl, season with salt and pepper and beat well. Add the potatoes, leek, bacon, cheese and parsley.

Melt the remaining butter in a large skillet. When the butter is sizzling, pour in the egg mixture and stir gently as the omelette cooks. Take care not to overcook.

The egg should be slightly runny.

You do not fold this omelette, but slide it, like a big pancake, onto a heated round serving plate.

Terrine de Foies de Volaille
Chicken Liver Terrine

(*Serves 8 to 10*)

•

This terrine is easy and fast to make compared with other kinds of terrines. It is quite delicious and similar in texture to a goose liver pâté. You may add chopped truffles to the mixture if you can afford it.

> 1 *pound fresh chicken liver* (*trimmed of nerves*)
> 1 *medium onion, sliced thin* (*½ cup*)
> 1 *cup chicken stock*
> *½ teaspoon salt, depending on the saltiness of
> the stock*

Place all ingredients in a saucepan (do not use aluminum, or the stock will discolor). The liver should be barely covered with the liquid. Bring to a boil, lower the heat, cover, and simmer for 10 minutes, not allowing the water to boil. Remove from the heat, leave the liver in the poaching liquid for 10 minutes, then strain through a colander. Reserve the liquid.

The Cooked Liver

> 3 *sticks soft sweet butter*
> 1¼ *teaspoons salt*
> ¾ *teaspoon freshly ground white pepper*
> ¾ *teaspoon good cognac*
> ½ *cup heavy cream*

Place some of the liver-and-onion mixture in an electric blender. Add 1 stick of very soft sweet butter, some of the salt, pepper, and cognac and blend until you have a very smooth, homogenized mixture. Transfer to a clear bowl and repeat until all the butter, liver, salt, pepper, and cognac have been used. Place the mixture in the refrigerator for 15 minutes. Mix well with a wooden spatula and place again in the refrigerator for 15 minutes. Mix again. Meanwhile, whip the cream until stiff and gently fold into the pâté mixture. Pour the mixture into a nice earthenware terrine, cover with plastic wrap and refrigerate.

Aspic

> *the poaching liquid from Step I, strained*
> *through cheesecloth or paper towel (about*
> *1 cup)*
> 1 *envelope unflavored gelatin*
> 1 *egg white*

Mix the gelatin with the broth. Beat the egg white with a fork for a few seconds and add to the liquid. Place on medium heat and cook until it comes to a boil, stirring constantly with a spoon to avoid scorching. As soon as the liquid boils (there will be a heavy crust forming on top of the liquid), strain through a double layer of cheesecloth or through a sieve lined with a paper towel. You should have about ¾ cup of very clear liquid. Let the liquid cool.

Decorate the top of your pâté with little pieces of truffle or red tomatoes and the green of a leek, blanched, or any vegetable cut-outs that will make the terrine attractive. When the aspic is cool enough and has the consistency of a heavy syrup, pour a layer on top of the pâté. Let cool at least 4 to 5 hours before serving. Serve using a spoon, with thin toast.

Pâté de Foie
Pork Liver Pâté

(*Serves 6 to 8*)

•

A very Gallic dish, pâté of meat or liver is served and appreciated all over France. Eat it with crusty bread and robust country red wine. This is a good first course for an evening meal or main course for a light lunch. It is customarily served cold with French mustard and small *cornichons* (small gherkins in vinegar).

> 1¼ *pounds diced pork liver* (*nerves and sinews removed*)
> 1 *pound ground fresh pork fatback*
> ½ *pound ground fresh pork meat*
> ¾ *cup dry white wine*
> 2½ *teaspoons salt*

⅓ *teaspoon freshly ground white pepper*
¼ *teaspoon ground thyme leaves*
1 *small clove garlic, crushed and chopped very*
   fine
¼ *teaspoon saltpeter**
½ *pound caul fat or thin lard leaves*
2 *bay leaves*

Preheat oven to 350°. Place the liver in the blender and emulsify for 35 to 50 seconds or until smooth, using about ¼ the quantity at a time. Repeat until all the liver is blended. Set aside. Blend together the pork fat and the ground pork in the same way, blending a small amount at a time, using the wine as you go to help the blending. After all of the pork fat and ground pork have been blended, combine together in a large bowl with the blended liver and mix well with a spatula or wire whisk. Add the salt, pepper, thyme, garlic, and saltpeter. Mix carefully.

Line a small terrine or pâté mold with the caul fat or lard leaves (see Bardes, page 95). The mold should be about 8 to 10 inches long, 4 to 5 inches wide, and 4 to 6 inches deep. Allow the caul fat to hang over the sides so that you will be able to cover the top of the mixture with it after the dish has been filled.

Fill the terrine with the mixture and cover with the caul fat. Place the bay leaves on top. Cover the terrine with aluminum foil. Place the terrine in a saucepan and pour lukewarm water into the saucepan—enough water to come at least ¾ of the way up the sides of the terrine. Cook for 2½ hours in a preheated 325° to 350° oven. Remove from the oven and water and allow to reach room temperature (2 to 3 hours). Refrigerate overnight

* Saltpeter, sometimes called Prague powder, is available for a small cost at drugstores. This ingredient will give the pâté a nice pink color that is found in ham, frankfurters and sausages.

before serving. This pâté will keep 1¼ to 2 weeks under refrigeration.

Slice in thin ¼-inch slices and serve with salad, fresh country bread, pickles and mustard.

Rillettes de Porc
Pork Spread

(*Serves 12 as an appetizer*)

•

Although *rillettes* can be made out of goose or rabbit, pork is always added to give it its texture and smoothness. *Rillettes* is served very cold, packed in small crocks. It is excellent as an hors d'oeuvre with Dijon mustard, crusty French bread, and dry cold white wine. Like many other dishes it is good because of its extreme simplicity. I have made *rillettes* using wine, stock, or different seasonings and it never was as good as this simple recipe.

> 3 *pounds fresh pork from the chuck or the neck*
> (*you should have about ⅓ lean meat to ⅔ fat*)
> 1 *tablespoon salt*
> ½ *teaspoon freshly ground black pepper*
> *water*

Cut the meat into 2- to 3-inch cubes and place in a large heavy saucepan with the salt, pepper, and enough water to reach 1 inch above the surface of the meat. Bring to a boil and cover. Simmer very slowly for 5½ to 6 hours. Skim the foam of the liquid every 20 minutes during the first 3 hours of cooking. *The meat should poach gently in the liquid. You may have to add water during the cooking process because the fat melts, and if the water reduces completely the fat gets hot and the meat fries instead of poaching.* After 5½ or 6 hours of cooking practically all water should have evaporated from the mixture. You will know when this has happened as the liquid starts to sizzle when all the water has gone. Let the mixture cool overnight. The next day, crush the pieces of meat between your thumbs and fingers to separate the fibers from the meat. This separation is better done by hand. To grind it or to beat it with a machine to emulsify it is no good. When you mash the pieces of meat by hand the mixture does not look homogeneous but it will be melted again and everything will blend together. Melt the mixture and taste for seasonings. It will probably need pepper and maybe salt. *Remember that it should be slightly over-seasoned. Seasonings tend to lose their strength in going from a hot to a cold dish.* Scoop about ¾ of a cup of pure fat from the kettle and set aside. Place the rest of the mixture over ice and work it with a wooden spatula stirring every 5 or 10 minutes until it turns into a thick, homogeneous mass. When the whole mixture has set, work it with the wooden spatula for 1 or 2 minutes to whiten it and make it more fluffy. Remember, it should not be too fluffy. Therefore, do not *overwork* it. Place in small crocks and smooth out the top with a spatula. Pour a thin layer of the reserved fat on top to seal it. When cold, cover with plastic wrap. Well sealed, the small crocks will keep a few weeks in the refrigerator.

Terrine de Ris de Veau
Cold Sweetbreads Terrine

(Serves 10)

•

1¼ *pounds ground pork (it should be half lean
    and half fat, the shoulder or butt is good)*
8 *strips lean pork meat, about ¾ inch wide by
    8 inches long (about 6 ounces)*
6 *strips fresh backfat, about ¾ inch wide by 8
    inches long (about 3 ounces)*
½ *cup dry white wine*
¼ *cup good cognac*
2½ *teaspoons salt*
1½ *teaspoons freshly ground white pepper*
½ *teaspoon thyme, chopped fine (fresh thyme
    is better)*
1 *bay leaf broken into pieces and chopped with
    a knife into powder (¼ teaspoon)*
⅛ *teaspoon saltpeter (see footnote, page 91)*
¼ *cup shelled and peeled pistachio nuts
    (Plunge the shelled pistachios into boiling
    water for 2 minutes, the skin will then slide
    off.)*
1 *egg yolk*
2 *truffles (if one can afford), diced in small
    pieces (about ¼ cup)*

Mix all ingredients together carefully. Place in a vessel, cover
with plastic wrap, and macerate for 48 hours in the refrigerator.

When buying sweetbreads, insist on getting the big roundish
chunks. This is the larger and juicier gland of the veal. Soak in
cold water for 2 to 3 hours to whiten the meat. Cover with cold
water, bring to a boil, and let boil for 1 minute. Place under cold

running water until cold. Pull out the sinews, *i.e.*, the rubber-like pieces adhering to the meat. Place a towel on a flat tray, put the sweetbreads on top, and cover with another towel. Then, place a flat tray or a platter on top and press down by putting weight on the tray. A 3- or 4-pound weight should suffice (canned foods or a pot of water may be used as a weight). *Pressing the sweetbread extrudes the undesirable pinkish liquid and provides a white and compact sweetbread. Keep pressed for a few hours.*

> 1¼ *pounds sweetbreads, blanched, sinews*
> *removed and pressed*
> 2 *tablespoons sweet butter*
> 1 *teaspoon salt*
> ½ *teaspoon freshly ground pepper*
> 1 *small carrot, diced* (¼ *cup*)
> 1 *small tomato, diced* (½ *cup*)
> 1 *medium onion, diced* (½ *cup*)
> 3 *sprigs parsley, coarsely chopped*
> 2 *tablespoons dry sherry*
> ¼ *cup Brown Sauce or 1 tablespoon Glace de*
> *Viande* (*see pages 31 and 33*)

Melt butter in a heavy saucepan and roll the sweetbreads in it. Add salt, pepper, carrot, tomato, onion, parsley, cover with a piece of waxed paper and place in a preheated 400° oven for 20 minutes. Remove the paper and add the sherry and the gravy. Cook uncovered for 10 more minutes. Remove the sweetbreads to a plate and strain the juices, pressing with a spoon to extrude all the juices. Reduce the juices to ⅓ of a cup. Add the reduced juices to the meat mixture and mix well.

Bardes

Use ¾ of a pound of fresh pork fatback, sliced with a machine parallel to the rind into ⅛-inch thick, 3-inch wide by 8-inch long slices. These "leaves" of fat are used to line the mold before placing the mixture in it. It serves to protect and enrich the terrine during cooking. Line an earthenware or Pyrex terrine (about 8 inches long by 4½ inches wide and 3 inches deep) with the *bardes*. Let the fat hang over the sides so that it can be folded back over the mixture to cover it completely.

If you have large pieces of sweetbreads, cut into halves lengthwise. Place enough of the meat mixture in the bottom of the terrine to cover 1 inch. Layer sweetbreads, pork strips and fatback strips alternately with more meat mixture until all ingredients are used. Fold the *bardes* over the terrine. Place in a deep tray and add water so the level comes to about ⅔ of the height of the terrine. Cook in a 325° oven for 2½ hours. The internal temperature should reach about 155° to 160°. Remove the terrine from the water and cool at room temperature. Cover with plastic wrap and refrigerate. Let rest in the refrigerator at least 1 day before slicing. Serve slices with diced Aspic (see page 89) and small sour pickles. Keeps for 1½ weeks in the refrigerator.

Civier Bressan
Pork Cheese

(*Yield: About 20 slices*)

•

This is a kind of head cheese made around Lyon and served sliced plain or with the slices covered with thinly sliced onions and an oil and vinegar dressing. The pig's knuckles may be replaced with the pig's head and tongue and done in the same manner.

3 *pounds pig's knuckles* (*about 2 or 3, depending on size*)

3 *pounds pig's feet* (*about 4 to 5, depending on
  size*)
½ *gallon water*

Put all ingredients in a large kettle, bring to a boil, and
simmer very slowly for 2½ hours, skimming every 20 to 30
minutes. Let cool enough to handle, pick the meat off the bones,
and place in a clean kettle. Strain the juices on top of the meat.

½ *teaspoon thyme, crushed* (*fresh is better*)
3 *carrots, peeled and sliced* (*about 1⅓ cups*)
2½ *cups dry white wine*
½ *teaspoon freshly ground white pepper*
1 *bay leaf*

Add the above ingredients to the meat and bring to a boil and
simmer gently for 45 minutes.

3 *tablespoons French mustard* (*strong Dijon
  style*)
¼ *teaspoon freshly ground black pepper*
⅓ *cup tiny French sour gherkins* (cornichons),
  sliced thin

Stir the above ingredients into the mixture. *Yield:* 9 cups of
mixture. Pour into a meat-loaf container or terrine. Cool and let
set overnight before using. Cover with plastic wrap to cool so
that the top doesn't harden. *If the seasonings are added too
early in the recipe, they lose most of their flavor through the long
hours of cooking.*

Hure de Porc aux Pistaches
Rolled Head Cheese with Pistachios

(*Serves about 10*)

•

The *hure* is different from the Pork Cheese (see page 96) because it is not set into a jellied broth but rolled into a sort of galantine.

> 1 *pig's head (about 13 pounds) Ask the butcher to bone it out. Boned out it will yield approximately 6 pounds of meat with the tongue (ask for the tongue). Try to have the skin in 1 or 2 pieces because you will need it as an envelope or wrapper for the meat.*
> 2 *carrots, peeled*
> 3 *cloves garlic, crushed with skin on*
> ½ *cup parsley stalks (reserve the top or curly part of parsley and chop)*
> 2 *leeks (use the green only—chop the white and set aside)*
> 3 *bay leaves*
> ½ *teaspoon thyme*
> 1 *teaspoon whole black peppercorns*
> 6 *cups chicken stock*

Place the meat in a large pot. Place all of the other ingredients except the chicken stock into a cheesecloth and tie. Add to the pot. Add the chicken stock and bring to a boil. Cover tightly and simmer very slowly for 1½ hours.

> ½ *tablespoon freshly ground white pepper*
> ½ *tablespoon salt*

16 to 18 *shallots, peeled and chopped (1 cup)*
2 *cups dry white wine*
the reserved chopped parsley
the reserved chopped leek

Add all of the above ingredients to the meat and simmer for an additional hour. Discard the cheesecloth package. Remove the meat to a tray and cool off enough to handle. Be careful not to break the large piece of skin. Spread the largest pieces of skin on a towel. Arrange the meat, ears, snout, tongue in the middle. With a slotted spoon, dish out the shallots, leek and chopped parsley and sprinkle on the meat. Taste the meat for salt and pepper. It should be over-seasoned, otherwise when the meat is cold it will be bland. Add salt and pepper if needed. Roll the skin with the towel into a tight loaf. Tie both ends and the middle of the roll with string. Place the roll back into the broth and bring to a boil. Simmer slowly for 20 minutes. Allow the roll to cool in the broth. When cold, unwrap the roll. Skim the fat from the broth, bring to a boil and reduce to about 1½ cups. Cool the broth. It should be jellied. Serve with the cold sliced *hure.*

Saucisson de Campagne
Hard Salami

(Yield: 6 to 8 salami, depending on casing)

•

Making salami is a simple operation. However, as with basic food such as bread or wine, all the factors involved in the production must be one hundred percent correct. The seasoning is important, but most of all, the drying is vital to the finished product. This simple operation consists of hanging the salami and allowing them to dry. However, if the temperature or the humidity is not just right, the salami will spoil. They may be dried in a cellar or a garage but the place must be dry, airy, and preferably dark. Summer is too humid and hot and winter too cold for making salami. The salami may be cured in a liquid brine for 1 or 2 days or by the addition of regular salt. Prague powder, also called saltpeter or potassium nitrate, helps the salami to achieve a nice color. Use it sparingly though, because it tends to toughen the meat. Natural casing may come from beef ("beef middle" is about 3 inches in diameter), or from pork (1½ to 2 inches in diameter). Lamb casing (about 1 inch in diameter) is used for link sausages. Casing can be ordered from your butcher and comes in bundles preserved in salt. It keeps for years in the refrigerator, packed in salt in a jar. Pull whatever length you need and wash it under lukewarm water. Fit the end of the casing to the opening of the faucet and allow the water to run through the inside. Wash the casing again and allow to soak in cold water for about 10 minutes. It is now ready to use. If you have any left over, repack in salt and keep refrigerated.

> 5½ pounds fresh pork butt or shoulder. It
>   should be ground through a large screen
>   with about ¼- to ⁵⁄₁₆-inch holes. The meat
>   should be about ⅓ fat to ⅔ lean.
> 2¾ ounces salt (5½ tablespoons) This large
>   amount of salt is necessary.
> ½ teaspoon saltpeter
> 2 teaspoons freshly ground white pepper
> 1½ teaspoons whole black peppercorns
> 2 small cloves garlic peeled, crushed, and
>   chopped into a puree (1 teaspoon)
> ¼ cup dry and robust red wine

Combine all ingredients together carefully. Insert the end of a funnel (you need a funnel with a large opening—at least ¾ of an inch) in the opening of the casing. Slip some of the casing around the tapered part of the funnel so that you have a good grip. Push the meat through the funnel and into the casing with your fingers, squeezing along the length of the casing to push the meat forward. (The casing may also be filled using a pastry bag and a plain tube.) Tie one end of the casing with a string. The correct way to tie the salami is to make a simple flat knot first, then fold the casing back on top of the knot and tie it again. With one hand, push the meat to the tied end of the casing, pricking the sausage with a skewer as you go along to let the air escape. Tie the sausage at the other end at the desired length. Be sure that there is no air trapped in the meat, or the salami will be black inside. If the drying area is not ventilated enough, use a fan to create some air. The first 2 weeks are the most critical. The salami should be dry after 1 week. *If the outside of the salami becomes white, it is a good sign; the meat is curing properly.* Salami can be consumed after 6 weeks, when they are semi-firm. However, they will keep for months after they have completely dried.

Note: For a differently flavored salami, omit the garlic and replace the red wine with white wine.

Andouillettes de Troyes
Chitterling Sausage

(Serves 8)

•

The *andouillette* is one of the greats of French *charcuterie*. They are often made with the lacy membrane (chitterlings) of the calf mixed with the pork chitterlings. Since only the pork chitterlings are available in the United States, our recipe might be slightly different from the *andouillettes* you may have enjoyed in France. The *andouillettes* are normally poached slowly for a few hours to cook them. However, the pork casings available nowadays are very fragile and burst easily during cooking. Therefore, we have precooked the chitterlings before stuffing the casing to lower the cooking time and avoid too much bursting.

> 10 *pounds cleaned raw pork chitterlings, fresh*
>   *if possible*

Place the cleaned chitterlings in a large kettle, cover with cold water, bring to a boil and simmer gently for 1½ hours. Drain the chitterlings in a colander. *You will notice that they shrink considerably.* When cold enough to handle, cut into 2-inch pieces.

> *hog casing prepared for stuffing (see page 99,*
>   *Saucisson de Campagne)*
> 2 *tablespoons sweet butter*
> 12 *shallots, peeled and chopped fine (¾ cup)*
> 1 *onion, peeled and chopped fine (½ cup)*
> ¼ *pound fresh, firm mushrooms, cleaned and*
>   *chopped fine (about ¾ cup)*
> 2¼ *tablespoons salt*
> 1⅓ *tablespoons (4 teaspoons) good French*
>   *mustard*
> 1½ *teaspoons freshly ground black pepper*
> 1 *tablespoon freshly chopped parsley*
> 1 *cup dry white wine*

Melt the butter, add the shallots and onion and cook for 4 to 5 minutes on low heat without allowing the mixture to brown. Add the mushrooms and cook for a few minutes until the liquid rendered by the mushrooms has all evaporated. Mix all the other ingredients except the casing with the pieces of chitterlings. Stuff the casing using a funnel with a broad opening. Tie the casing every 4 to 5 inches. You should have approximately 18 to 20 pieces.

>*dry white wine*
>*chicken stock*

Place the pieces flat in an oven roasting pan. Add the dry white wine and chicken stock in equal proportions, just enough to cover the *andouillettes*. Bring to 180° and continue poaching in an oven or on top of the stove at the same temperature for 1 hour. *Be extra careful not to let the mixture boil or the* andouillettes *will burst. Let cool in the liquid overnight. If some links have burst, you may restuff the pieces into casing and poach for 5 or 10 minutes to cook the casing.* When cold, remove from the liquid (you can keep the liquid to use as stock or clarify it to make an aspic) and dry the *andouillettes* with a paper towel. Keep refrigerated until ready to use.

Use 2 *andouillettes* per person as a main dish or 1 as a first course. Melt about 1 teaspoon sweet butter per *andouillette* and brown in a small au gratin dish or skillet on very low fire until slightly browned. Deglaze with about ¼ cup dry white wine and place in a 425° oven for 6 to 8 minutes until piping hot. Serve immediately. The casings often break during the last step of cooking. This doesn't change the taste of the dish, merely its appearance.

Saucisson à Cuire
Large Country Sausage

(*Yield: 3 or 4 sausages, depending on casing*)

•

2½ pounds fresh pork butt or shoulder, cut
    coarsely by hand or ground through the
    machine using a large screen hole (about
    ¼ inch)
1½ tablespoons salt
¾ teaspoon freshly ground white pepper
¼ teaspoon saltpeter (see footnote, page 91)
½ cup dry white wine
1 small clove garlic, peeled and chopped into a
    puree (optional)

Mix all the ingredients together carefully and stuff the casing as explained on page 100. Keep the sausages at least 2 days in the refrigerator before using.

Note: This rough and flavorful country sausage can be poached, roasted, and eaten either hot or cold. To make a more delicate and fancier sausage (what is called *cervelas* in French), the meat has to be chopped finer—about ⅛ inch thick. Omit the garlic and add 1 large black truffle, chopped (about 2 tablespoons), and ¼ cup of shelled pistachio. The *cervelas* is usually cooked in Brioche (see page 48), or served hot with a Potato Salad (see page 106).

Saucisson Chaud Rôti aux Pommes
Roast Sausage with Potatoes

(Serves 3 to 4)

•

1 *sausage (about 1 pound, see page 104)*
15 *small new potatoes or 5 regular potatoes,*
    peeled and quartered (about 1½ pounds)
1 *medium onion, split into halves*
2 *tablespoons sweet butter*
¼ *teaspoon salt*
¼ *teaspoon freshly ground white pepper*

Melt the butter in a large casserole with a cover. Prick the sausage all around with a fork. Brown in butter on low heat (about 5 to 6 minutes). Add the onion and potatoes, cover and cook on low heat for 30 minutes. Turn the sausages and the potatoes after 15 minutes so that they brown all around. *If you brown or cook the sausage on high heat it will burst.* Remove the sausage to a warm platter and sprinkle the potatoes with the salt and pepper. Transfer the potatoes and onion to the serving platter, arrange the sliced sausage next to it and serve immediately.

Saucisson Chaud Pommes à l'Huile
Hot Country Sausage with Potato Salad

(*Serves 4 to 6*)

•

1 *pound sausage (1 or 2 sausages, depending on the casing; see page 104).It may be a regular sausage or a* cervelas *sausage.*
5 to 6 *potatoes, depending on size (about 2 pounds), washed*
½ *cup oil (It may be vegetable oil or a mixture of olive and vegetable oil depending on your taste.)*
2 *tablespoons good wine vinegar*
2 *tablespoons dry white wine*
⅓ *cup chopped onions (1 small onion)*
1 *teaspoon salt*
½ *teaspoon freshly ground white pepper*
½ *cup chopped fresh herbs—parsley, tarragon, chervil and chives. (Do not substitute dry herbs. It is better to omit the herb you do not have.)*

Place the potatoes in a large casserole, cover with cold water and bring to a boil on high heat. Lower the heat and simmer for 35 to 40 minutes, depending on the size of the potatoes, or until tender when pierced with a knife. Drain the water off the potatoes right away or lift them out of the water and let cool uncovered. Peel the potatoes when they are still warm and slice into ½-inch slices. Add all the remaining ingredients, except the sausage, mix lightly and let the mixture macerate at room temperature for 1 or 2 hours.

Prick the sausages on all sides with a fork or a skewer. Place the sausage or sausages in a saucepan and add just enough cold water to cover the sausages. Add ½ teaspoon of salt. Bring to a boil on medium heat. As soon as it simmers, turn the heat down and poach slowly for 12 to 20 minutes, depending on the size of the sausage. Remove from the heat and let the sausages cool slightly in the cooking stock. Add ¼ cup of the cooking liquid to the potato salad. *The salad should be lukewarm.* Arrange the potatoes on a platter, slice the sausage and place next to or on top of the potatoes. Serve immediately.

Cervelas Truffé en Brioche
Truffled Sausage in Brioche

(Serves 6)

•

1 cervelas (*about 1 to 1½ pounds, see page 104*)
1 *egg, beaten* (*to use as egg wash*)

Prick the sausage all around with a fork. Place in a small casserole and cover with cold water. Add ¼ teaspoon of salt. Bring the sausage to a boil on medium heat. As soon as it boils, remove the sausage from the heat and set aside. When cold enough to handle, remove sausage from the liquid and take the skin off. If you use the Pâte à Brioche de Ménage, follow the instructions on page 48. If you use the regular Brioche Dough, see page 49, you will need about ⅓ of the dough recipe. Push the dough with your hands on a very lightly floured board. It is better to spread the dough with your hands because you do not want any flour inside the dough. It should be about ¼ inch thick in the middle. Place the skinned sausage on top of the dough. The sausage should still be warm to assure that the dough will not separate from it during cooking. Gather the sides of the dough so that it joins on top. Squeeze the ends together so that the seams do not release during cooking. Brush a cookie sheet with butter and place the sausage on it upside down so that the seams are underneath. *After it is wrapped and turned upside down, there is more dough on the sides and under the sausage. However, the sausage will sink down during cooking and should end up in the middle of the dough.* Brush the sausage with the egg wash and let rise in a lukewarm and draft-free place for 35 minutes. By that time the dough will not have developed completely, but it should not rise too much. Place in a preheated 375° to 400° oven and cook for 25 to 30 minutes. Let the dough rest for 5 minutes before slicing the *cervelas*. It is usually served as is, but it can also be served with fresh or melted butter.

Pieds de Porc Rémoulade
Pig's Feet with Rémoulade Sauce

(*Serves 6*)

•

6 *pig's feet, split lengthwise* (*about 4½ pounds*)
2 *bay leaves*
½ *teaspoon thyme*
1 *leek, cooked*
1 *peeled carrot*
4 to 5 *sprigs parsley*
½ *teaspoon black pepper*
5 *cups beef or chicken stock*
salt, if necessary—depending on the stock

Place all ingredients in a large casserole. Bring to a boil, cover tightly and simmer very gently for 4½ hours. Set aside.

Rémoulade

> ½ tablespoon French mustard
> 1 egg yolk
> ½ teaspoon salt
> ⅛ teaspoon freshly ground pepper
> 1½ tablespoons wine vinegar
> ¾ cup vegetable oil, or half olive and half
>   vegetable oil

With a whisk, work the mustard, yolk, salt, pepper, and vinegar in a bowl for 1 minute. Add the oil slowly, mixing with the whisk to have all ingredients blend together. It should have the consistency of a very light mayonnaise.

> ½ cup chopped onion
> 3 tablespoons herbs—parsley, chives, chervil,
>   tarragon (Use only fresh herbs, even if you
>   just have parsley.)

The feet should be served lukewarm. Lift from the broth with a slotted spoon. Drain on a towel. Arrange on a serving platter removing the biggest bone. Sprinkle the chopped onion over the meat, pour the sauce over and sprinkle the herbs on top. It is better if allowed to macerate for 1 hour before serving.

Tarte aux Oignons
Onion Tart

(*Serves 8*)

•

1 *recipe of Pâte Brisée* (*see page 45*)

Roll out on a floured board, then line a 9-inch pie pan. Flute the edge of the pastry. Refrigerate while making the filling.

Filling

2 *slices bacon*
1½ *cups thinly sliced onions* (*about 2 medium onions*)
¼ *cup chopped parsley*
¼ *cup chopped chives*
dash dried thyme
2 *tablespoons all-purpose flour*
2 *cups milk*
½ *cup heavy cream*
3 *eggs*
salt to taste (*depending on the saltiness of the bacon*)
¼ *teaspoon freshly ground pepper*
⅛ *teaspoon freshly ground nutmeg*

Cut the bacon into chunks and fry in a large, heavy skillet until brown and crisp. Add the onions directly to the bacon bits and fat and sauté until they have taken on a little color (about 3 to 4 minutes). Stir in the parsley, chives and thyme thoroughly. Sprinkle the flour over the mixture and stir in well. Add the milk and bring to a boil, stirring constantly with a spatula or spoon. Allow the mixture to simmer for 3 to 4 minutes after it has thickened. Remove from heat and let cool for 10 minutes. Beat the cream and eggs together lightly, then stir into the mixture along with the salt, pepper, and nutmeg. Pour into the pastry shell, place the filled shell on a cookie sheet, and bake in a preheated 400° oven for 45 to 50 minutes, or until the crust is golden and the custard is firm. Let rest 5 to 8 minutes before serving.

Pissaladière
Provence Pizza

(*Serves 8*)

•

Although this dish can be made with regular Pâte Brisée (see page 45) it is better and customarily made with a bread dough.

> 1 *pound all-purpose flour* (3½ *to 4 cups*)
> 1 *cup lukewarm water*
> 1 *ounce fresh yeast* (*or 2 packages dry yeast*)
> ⅓ *cup olive oil*
> 1 *teaspoon salt*
> ½ *teaspoon sugar*

If you have a heavy-duty mixer, use it with the flat beater. If not, make the dough by hand. Mix the water and yeast together until the yeast is dissolved. Mix all ingredients together and work with the mixer for about 2 minutes on medium speed, or about 5 minutes by hand, kneading the dough until it is satiny and smooth. Place in a bowl, cover with a towel, and set in a warm place (such as an oven with the pilot on) and let rise until it doubles in volume (about 60 minutes). *At this point, if you push the dough with your finger it should not spring back and the indentation should remain.* Break the dough down and divide into halves. Spread each half on a cookie sheet (use your hands, you do not need a rolling pin or flour to spread the dough). Spread it to obtain two wheels, each at least 12 inches in diameter. The dough will be thicker on the edges.

Filling

> 2½ pounds onions (about 10 to 12 onions,
>   depending on size), peeled and sliced very
>   thin (about 8 cups)
> ⅓ cup olive oil
> 1 cup water
> 1 teaspoon salt
> ½ teaspoon freshly ground black pepper
> ¹⁄₁₆ teaspoon (small dash) ground cloves
> 4 to 6 cloves garlic, peeled, crushed, and
>   chopped fine (2 teaspoons)

While the dough is rising, make the filling. Place all ingredients except garlic into a large kettle and bring to a boil. Let boil on high heat until all the water has evaporated (about 12 to 14 minutes). By this time the onions are cooked. Keep cooking on medium heat to brown the onions slightly (about 8 minutes), mixing once in a while. Add the garlic, mix, and set aside.

> 2 dozen anchovy fillets in oil*
> 1 cup of small dry black olives (found in Greek
>   or Italian markets)

Spread the onion mixture evenly on both wheels. Arrange the anchovy fillets on top in a crisscross pattern and scatter the olives over the surface. Cook in a preheated 425° oven for 20 to 30 minutes, or until the dough is nicely browned.

* If the anchovies are too salted, place in cool water for a couple of hours to unsalt. Drain on paper towels before using.

Quiche au Lard
Quiche with Bacon

(*Serves 6 to 8*)

•

Pastry

> 1½ *cups flour*
> ¼ *teaspoon salt*
> 6 *tablespoons* (¾ *stick*) *sweet butter*
> 1 *tablespoon vegetable shortening*
> ¼ *cup cold water*

Work the flour, salt, butter, and shortening together until you have a coarse yellow mixture. Sprinkle on the water and gather together into a ball.

Line a 10½-inch flan ring and refrigerate for at least 1 hour.

Filling

> ¼ *pound bacon, all in 1 piece* (*you may*
>   *substitute sliced bacon*)
> 4 *eggs*
> 1½ *cups milk*
> ½ *cup heavy cream*
> 1 *teaspoon salt*
> ¼ *teaspoon freshly ground white pepper*
> 5 *ounces Gruyère or Emmenthal cheese, diced*

Cut the bacon into small strips (*lardons*—see page 237) and blanch in boiling water for about 3 minutes.

Beat the eggs only until well mixed. Then stir in the milk, cream, salt, and pepper. Scatter the bacon and cheese over the bottom of the pie, add the egg mixture and bake in a preheated 400° oven for 1 hour. Remove from the oven and let cool for a few minutes before removing the ring. Slide onto a serving platter. The quiche is best after it has rested for at least 15 to 20 minutes. Serve lukewarm.

Feuilleté de Champignons
Mushrooms in Puff Pastry

(Serves 6 to 8)

•

½ recipe for Puff Paste (see page 52)
1 egg, beaten

Mushroom Filling

> *¾ pound firm, fresh mushrooms, washed and*
> *   sliced*
> *3½ tablespoons all-purpose flour*
> *2 tablespoons sweet butter*
> *¾ cup milk*
> *¾ cup heavy cream*
> *1 teaspoon salt*
> *½ teaspoon freshly ground pepper*

Place the mushrooms in a heavy skillet over moderate heat and cook until all their liquid has extruded and boiled away.

Melt the butter in a saucepan, whip in the flour and cook for a couple of minutes. Add the milk and cream and bring to a boil, whipping constantly. Whip in the salt and pepper. Then add the mushrooms and bring to a boil. Pour into a bowl, cover with foil and refrigerate until cold.

To complete the *feuilleté*, roll the pastry on a lightly floured board into a strip 16 inches long and 10 to 12 inches wide. Cut into halves lengthwise. Spoon the cold mushroom mixture down the center of one strip—the full length of the pastry, leaving an edge all around. Dampen the edge of the pastry around the mushrooms with water. Place the second strip on top, then press the edges together tightly. With a sharp knife, trim the edge all around. Brush the pastry with the beaten egg. Then score the top, making a design, and make 3 small holes, equidistant, to allow steam to escape. Place in the refrigerator and allow to rest for 30 minutes.

Bake in a preheated 375° oven for 20 minutes. Reduce heat to 350° and bake another 20 minutes. Allow the *feuilleté* to rest a few minutes before serving.

Soufflé au Fromage
Cheese Soufflé

(*Serves 4 to 6*)

•

(See Soufflés, page 58)

Butter a 1½-quart soufflé mold, making sure you coat the curve at the bottom. Add a couple of tablespoons of flour. Holding the mold in your hands, roll it around and around so that the sides and bottom are evenly but lightly coated. Turn upside down and give it a good bang to get rid of any excess flour. Refrigerate the mold. *It is important to have the mold well coated and cold because it will help the soufflé to rise straight up. Cook the soufflé in a 350° oven in a double boiler* setting the soufflé mold in a pan of hot water, (bain-marie) *for 1 hour without allowing the water to boil. This gives an excellent result.*

> 3 tablespoons sweet butter
> 3 tablespoons flour
> 1 cup milk
> ½ teaspoon salt
> dash freshly ground pepper
> dash freshly grated nutmeg
> 4 whole eggs, separated

Melt the 3 tablespoons of butter in a heavy saucepan over low heat. Stir in the flour and cook slowly, stirring constantly, until the butter and flour froth (about 3 minutes) without browning. Take off the heat and add the milk, salt, pepper and nutmeg, whipping constantly with a wire whisk. Bring to a boil, still whipping. Take off the heat and cool for 5 minutes. Add the egg yolks, 1 at a time, whipping vigorously after each addition.

> 3 *extra egg whites (plus 4 from step II)*
> ¾ *cup freshly grated Gruyère or Emmenthal cheese (good imported Swiss cheese)*

With a rotary or electric beater, whip the 7 egg whites until they hold firm, shiny peaks when the beater is held straight up. Using the whip, beat about ⅓ of the whites into the yolk mixture. Add the grated cheese and fold in (see page 296) the remaining whites.

> 1 *slice Swiss cheese cut into diamonds*

Pour the batter into the prepared mold, smooth the top with a metal spatula, and arrange the diamonds of cheese on top. Bake in a preheated 400° oven for 20 to 25 minutes, or in a *bain-marie* double boiler as explained above. For a firm rather than a creamy center, bake an additional 5 minutes.

Fish

Truites Grillées à la Crème
Broiled Trout with Cream

(Serves 6)

•

This is an excellent dish when made with fresh trout, but quite tasteless when made with frozen trout. It is much better when real charcoal or wood is used for the barbecue. Charcoal briquets do not give the same flavor.

> 6 *fresh trout, about 8 to 10 ounces each, or*
> *several smaller trout (cleaned and washed)*
> 1¼ *teaspoons salt*
> 1 *teaspoon freshly ground white pepper*
> 1 *tablespoon oil*
> 1 *cup heavy cream*

Dry the trout thoroughly with a towel. Sprinkle inside and out with 1 teaspoon salt and the pepper. Place the trout on a tray and sprinkle with oil. Place the trout on a clean and very hot charcoal grill shelf. If the grill is not ultra clean the trout will stick. (*Be sure that the flames have completely died out and*

117

you only have a bed of hot ashes. Otherwise the flames and smoke will burn and give a bad flavor to the fish.) Cook about 3 to 5 minutes on each side, depending on the size of the fish. They should be nicely browned on each side. When they are browned, place the trout in a nice row in a gratin dish. Pour the cream on top, add salt, cover and place on medium heat and bring to a boil. Let simmer 2 to 3 minutes. Serve immediately; 1 trout and a tablespoon of cream for each person.

Truites Farcies au Vermouth
Stuffed Trout with Vermouth

(*Serves 8*)

•

8 8-ounce trout, fresh and not cleaned (See How to Bone Trout, page 120.)

Mousse

1 pound fillets of sole, cut into small pieces
1 egg white
1 cup heavy cream
½ teaspoon salt
dash freshly ground white pepper

Place ⅓ of the sole in an electric blender and puree. Repeat until all the sole is pureed. Push through a metal sieve with a spoon or your fingers. Add the egg white and beat it with a wooden spatula. Refrigerate. When cold, place on a bed of ice cubes and add the cream, a spoonful at a time, beating carefully after each addition to keep the mixture homogeneous and to prevent it from breaking down. Add the salt and pepper at the end; this should help to tighten the mixture.

Puree of Mushrooms

1 tablespoon sweet butter
3 shallots, chopped (2 tablespoons)
¼ pound mushrooms, washed and chopped
    (2 cups whole mushrooms when purchased;
    ¾ cup after pureed)
⅓ cup heavy cream
½ teaspoon salt
¼ teaspoon freshly ground white pepper
½ teaspoon arrowroot diluted with 1 tablespoon
    water

Melt the butter in a saucepan, add the shallots and sauté for 1 minute. Add the mushrooms and cook for a few minutes, until the water from the mushrooms has evaporated. Add the cream, salt, pepper and bring to a boil. Add the diluted arrowroot, stirring as you pour, bring to a boil, remove from the heat, cover and cool in the refrigerator. When cold, mix with the mousse. Place the mixture in a pastry bag, stuff the fish and cover the backs with buttered pieces of waxed paper.

4 tablespoons sweet butter
12 shallots, chopped very fine (¾ cup)
1 teaspoon salt
½ teaspoon freshly ground white pepper
½ cup red sweet vermouth
1 cup dry white vermouth
1½ cups heavy cream
2 tablespoons flour

Butter a large ovenproof dish with half of the butter. Sprinkle with the shallots, the salt and the pepper. Place the trout so that they touch one another. Add the two different vermouths, cover with a piece of buttered waxed paper, bring to a boil on top of the stove and then place in a 400° oven for 20 minutes. Pour the juices into a saucepan (not aluminum), bring to a rolling boil and let reduce for 5 minutes. Add the cream and let boil another 2 minutes. Meanwhile, mix the remaining butter with the flour. Add the flour mixture to the sauce with a whisk, mixing rapidly to prevent the mixture from becoming lumpy. Simmer 5 more minutes, then add salt and pepper to taste. Remove the waxed paper from the fish. Pour the sauce over the trout and serve immediately.

How to Bone Trout

It is difficult to find fresh fish that has not been cleaned and you may have to order it at your fish store a few days before the date of your dinner party. If the fish has been cleaned, the belly will be split open. Since you are boning the fish through the back the result would be two separate fillets. To avoid cutting the belly, the fish may also be cleaned through the gills.

With a scissors or shears cut the fins off the fish and wash under cold running water. Place the trout on its side and make an incision with a sharp knife just above the backbone following its line from the head to the tail. Keep cutting, following the backbone, until one side of the bone is completely uncovered. Be careful to follow the shape of the rib bones with your knife and not to cut through them.

Repeat the same operation with the other side of the fish, cutting as close as you can to the backbone.

Sever the bone at the tail and at the head and pull it out of the fish. Clean the inside of the fish with cold running water.

With a pastry bag, fill up the cavity with a mousse or your favorite stuffing. You may also use a spoon instead of the pastry bag. Butter rectangles of waxed paper and cover the back of the fish to hold the stuffing in during cooking. Place the fish one against the other and cook them following your own recipe or the one given on page 118.

Bar Rayé à la Russe
Cold Striped Bass with Russian Salad

(Serves 8 to 10)

•

Fish

> 4 *skinless and boneless striped bass fillets (about 2½ to 3 pounds total weight)*
> 1 *teaspoon salt*
> 1 *teaspoon freshly ground pepper*
> 2 *tablespoons sweet butter*
> 1 *cup thinly sliced onion*
> ½ *cup coarsely chopped carrot*
> ⅓ *cup finely chopped parsley*
> 3 *sprigs fresh thyme or ½ teaspoon dried*
> 2 *bay leaves*
> 1¼ *cups dry white wine*

Sprinkle the fillets with salt and pepper. Butter the bottom of a baking dish. Scatter the sliced onion, carrot, parsley, thyme, and bay leaves over the dish. Arrange the fish fillets on top and sprinkle with the wine. Cover with a piece of buttered waxed paper cut to fit the dish. Place the dish on the stove and bring to a boil. Then place on a baking tray and bake for 12 minutes in a preheated 400° oven. Remove. Let the fish cool in the cooking liquid.

Mayonnaise

> 4 egg yolks
> 1½ teaspoons salt
> ¼ teaspoon freshly ground pepper
> 2 tablespoons prepared mustard, preferably
>   imported, such as Dijon or Dusseldorf
> 2 tablespoons vinegar
> 3 cups oil (either peanut, vegetable, corn, or
>   olive oil)

Place the yolks in a mixing bowl and add salt, pepper, mustard and vinegar. Gradually add the oil, beating with a wire whisk or an electric beater. When thickened, set aside.

Salade Russe

> 1¼ pounds unpeeled potatoes
> ¾ pound string beans, trimmed and cut into
>   ½-inch or smaller lengths (about 2 cups)
> ½ pound green peas (about 2 cups shelled)
> ½ pound carrots, peeled (3 to 5 carrots)
> 3 small white turnips, peeled
> ¾ cup finely chopped onion
> ¼ cup finely chopped parsley
> 2 tablespoons finely chopped basil (optional)

Boil the potatoes in salted water until tender. Drain and let cool. Cook the string beans in boiling salted water about 10 minutes. Drain and put under cold running water. Drain again and set aside. Cook the peas about 5 minutes (if frozen peas are used, cook according to package directions) and drain. Put under cold water, drain and set aside. Cook the carrots and turnips in separate saucepans of salted water until crisp and tender (12 to 15 minutes). Drain, rinse under cold water and drain again. Set aside. Peel the potatoes and cut them into ½-inch cubes. There should be about 3 cups. Cut the carrots and turnips into ½-inch cubes. There should be about 1½ cups of each.

In a large bowl, combine the vegetables with the chopped onion, parsley, and basil. Add half the mayonnaise and salt and pepper to taste. Blend well.

Take 2 of the fillets and place each on a serving dish. Spoon ¼ of the *salade russe* on top of each fillet. Smooth it over just to the edges of each fillet. Cover each with another fillet. Add a few tablespoons of mayonnaise on top of each fish. Smooth it over adding enough mayonnaise to coat the fillets nicely. Chill well.

Aspic

> *cooking liquid from Step I*
> 1 *egg white*
> 1 *envelope gelatin*
> 3 *tablespoons coarsely chopped parsley*
> ¼ *cup dry white wine*

Strain the cooking liquid into a saucepan; there should be about 1¼ cups. Put the egg white into a small mixing bowl and add the gelatin. Blend well. Add the gelatin mixture and the parsley to the cooking liquid and bring it to a boil, stirring constantly. Line a sieve with a paper towel and strain the aspic through it. Add the wine and stir. Let cool on ice. When the aspic is cool, becoming oily and gelatinous, but not set, spoon it over the fish, coating as evenly as possible.

Bar Rayé aux Aromates
Stuffed Striped Bass with Herbs

(Serves 6 to 8)

•

Prepare the stuffing first, then the other ingredients you will use in cooking the bass.

Stuffing

> 1 *tablespoon sweet butter*
> 3 *tablespoons minced shallots (about 5), or*
> *green onion bulbs*
> ½ *cup mushroom stems, minced*
> ½ *small rib celery, minced (⅓ cup)*
> 1 *clove garlic, peeled, crushed, and minced*
> 1 *hard-cooked egg, chopped*
> 4 to 5 *sprigs parsley, minced*
> 1½ *cups fine breadcrumbs*
> ½ *teaspoon salt*
> ½ *teaspoon freshly ground black pepper*

Melt the butter in a skillet. When sizzling, add the shallots and sauté for about 2 minutes. Add minced mushroom stems, celery, and garlic. Sauté 3 more minutes. Combine in a mixing bowl with all remaining ingredients. Take care not to overmix.

Bass

> 1 *4-pound striped bass, cleaned*
> ½ *cup (1 stick) sweet butter*
> ½ *cup (about 10) shallots, peeled and minced*
> 2 *teaspoons salt*
> 1 *teaspoon freshly ground white pepper*

⅓ cup (about 15 sprigs) parsley, minced
⅓ teaspoon thyme
2 cups (about ½ pound) thinly sliced
    mushroom caps
2 bay leaves
1½ cups dry white wine
2 cups heavy cream
4 tablespoons flour

Stuff the bass and sew up the opening. Set aside. Butter a large roasting pan, sprinkle with the shallots, salt, pepper, parsley and thyme. Place the stuffed bass on top and sprinkle with the sliced mushrooms. Add the bay leaves and pour the wine over all. Cover the fish with foil. Bring to a boil on top of the stove, then place in a preheated 375° oven for 25 to 30 minutes. When cooked, using 2 wide spatulas, lift from the pan onto a large heated serving platter. Peel off the skin, remove the string, and keep warm in a 180° oven.

Pour the liquid from the pan into a saucepan. Add the cream and bring to a boil. Work the flour into 3 tablespoons of butter to make a *beurre manié*. Add to the hot sauce, bit by bit, stirring constantly with a wire whisk. Bring to a boil and let simmer slowly for 5 minutes. Coat the fish with some sauce and serve the remainder in a heated sauceboat.

Bar Rayé en Croûte à l'Oseille
Striped Bass in a Crust with Sorrel

(*Serves 6 to 8*)

•

1 4-pound whole striped bass, boned, skinned
    and filleted

Fish Fumet

the fishbones, cut into pieces
2 tablespoons butter
1 small rib celery, diced
1 small yellow onion, peeled and diced
1 leek, well washed and diced
1 teaspoon dried thyme
1½ cups dry white wine
2 cups water
1 teaspoon salt
¼ teaspoon white peppercorns, crushed

Melt the butter in a large, heavy saucepan. Add the fishbones and steam for 3 to 4 minutes. Then add the celery, onion, leek, and thyme. Cook 1 minute. Add the wine, water, salt and peppercorns. Bring to a boil and let boil for 15 minutes. Strain through a fine sieve and set aside.

Pâte à Choux (Cream Puff Pastry)

1½ cups water
6 tablespoons (¾ stick) sweet butter
pinch salt
1½ cups all-purpose flour
6 eggs

Combine water, butter, and salt in a heavy saucepan and bring to a boil. Take off the heat and add the flour all at once, mixing hard and fast with a wooden spatula. Place back over very low heat and work vigorously with the spatula until the dough leaves the sides of the pan and forms a ball. Take off the heat and transfer to a clean bowl and cool for about 25 minutes, covered. Then add the eggs, 1 at a time, beating briskly after each addition until the dough is smooth. (*If you add the eggs when the mixture is still too hot, you will make scrambled eggs.*)

Mousse

½ cup (4 ounces) of the fish cut into small
    pieces (trim the bass fillets)
1 egg white (reserve the yolk)
¼ cup (2 ounces) heavy cream
2 tablespoons sorrel, chopped
2 tablespoons pâte à choux
salt
freshly ground white pepper

Combine the fish and egg white in an electric blender. Blend until you have a smooth puree. Add the cream and blend 5 seconds longer. Strain through a metal sieve using a metal spoon or your fingers to push the mixture through. Pour into a bowl and stir in the sorrel and *pâte à choux* with salt and pepper to taste.

To finish the dish, take a large ovenproof tray and butter well. Then coat with flour, knocking off any excess. Cover the bottom of the tray with *pâte à choux* in an area as large as the fish, using a pastry bag with a plain tube. Place 1 of the fish fillets on top, season with salt and pepper, then coat completely with the mousse. Place the other fillet on top and cover with the remaining *pâte à choux*, again pushed through a pastry bag. Smooth with a metal spatula wet with water. Mark with the back of a spoon or with a fork to imitate the scales of a fish. Take the reserved egg yolk beaten with 1 teaspoon of water and brush the entire surface of the *pâte à choux*. Bake in a preheated 375° oven for 45 minutes. *During cooking the dough may break or open on the top. If this happens, after you remove the tray from the oven, push the dough back together. Even though the dough is crisp when it comes out of the oven, it will soften and have a consistency between a pancake and a pie dough.*

Sauce

> 4 *tablespoons* (*½ stick*) *sweet butter*
> 6 *shallots, peeled and chopped* (*about ½ cup*)
> 1 *cup sorrel, chopped*
> *fish fumet*
> *½ cup heavy cream*

Heat 2 tablespoons of the butter in a saucepan. Add the shallots and sauté for 1 minute. Add the sorrel and cook over medium heat for 3 to 4 minutes. Add the fish fumet. Bring to a boil and allow to boil rapidly until it has reduced by about half. Stir in the cream and boil another 10 minutes. You should have about 1½ cups of sauce. Take off the stove and taste for seasoning; it may need salt and pepper. To finish the sauce, just before serving add the remaining butter, bit by bit, shaking the pan as you add the butter so that it blends with the sauce. Serve at once with the fish.

Huîtres Florentine Sauce Diable
Oysters with Deviled Sauce

(*Serves 6*)

•

> 1 *pound fresh spinach* (*Remove the longest
> stems and yellow leaves, wash under cold
> water.*)

Place the spinach in a lot of salted boiling water and cook *uncovered* for 5 to 6 minutes. Place the kettle directly under cold running water until the spinach is cold. Drain and press the spinach into a ball. *If the spinach is not cooked in a lot of salted water, and not cooled off rapidly, the leaves will not be as green and flavorful as they should. This rule can be applied to practically all green vegetables.*

8 *slices bacon, each slice cut into 5 or 6 pieces*
4 *tablespoons sweet butter*
1 *clove garlic, peeled, crushed, and chopped fine*
½ *teaspoon salt*
¼ *teaspoon freshly ground black pepper*
⅛ *teaspoon freshly ground nutmeg*

Place the bacon in a skillet and cook for 2 to 3 minutes until it is brown and slightly crisp. *It should not be cooked too much.* Drain the bacon on a paper towel and set aside. Melt the butter in a skillet and let it cook until it turns black and smokes. (Make sure that it is a real black, burned butter.) Meanwhile, coarsely chop the drained and pressed spinach and sprinkle with salt, pepper and nutmeg. Add to the black butter and mix with a fork for 1 or 2 minutes. Add the garlic and cook until the spinach is hot.

2 *dozen oysters (bluepoint or malpeque,*
medium size) (separate the oysters from
the shell, strain the juice and set aside)

Place a little bit of the spinach in the bottom of each shell. Place 1 oyster in each shell and top with 2 pieces of bacon. *The bacon should cover most of the oyster to protect it from drying up during baking in the oven.* Place the oysters in a 425° oven for about 10 minutes until they are hot, but not dry or chewy.

Sauce Diable

> 2 teaspoons chopped shallots
> ½ teaspoon crushed black peppercorns (called
>   mignonnette in French) Use a large knife
>   or pound with the bottom of a skillet.
> ⅓ cup dry white wine
> juice or liquor of oysters
> ¾ cup Basic Brown Sauce (see page 31)
> 2 tablespoons sweet butter

Place all ingredients except the brown gravy and butter in a heavy saucepan. Bring to a boil and let cook on high heat until it is reduced by half. Add the brown gravy and bring to a boil, let reduce for 2 minutes. Remove from heat and strain the sauce. Add the butter, bit by bit, whipping with a whisk to incorporate it into the sauce. Add salt if necessary.

After the oysters have been removed from the oven, add about 1 teaspoon of sauce on top of each oyster. Serve immediately.

Moules Poulette
Mussels Poulette

(Serves 8)

•

10 pounds mussels
2 medium-sized yellow onions, peeled and diced
1 garlic clove, peeled and chopped
large handful parsley sprigs, chopped
dash dried thyme
1 bay leaf
freshly ground white pepper

2 *cups dry white wine*
½ *cup (1 stick) sweet butter*
3 *tablespoons all-purpose flour*
1 *cup heavy cream*
3 *egg yolks*

Cleaning Method

With a small, sharp knife, first scrape off any encrustations that are on the shell, then cut off the "beard," which looks very much like old dried grass. After scraping the shells and removing the "beard," wash the mussels under cold running water, rubbing the mussels against each other to clean the shells further. *Press each mussel separately, on the bias, to determine if it is full of mud or sand. If so, the shells will slide open and, obviously, these are to be discarded.* Place the mussels in salted cold water (a handful of salt per gallon of water) for a couple of hours so that any sand that's left will be rinsed off. Following that, rinse them all again, 2 or 3 times, in fresh cold water. Lift the mussels from the water and place in a heavy kettle. (Do not drain through a colander first, as any sand remaining will then go back onto the mussels and into the cooking pot.)

Combine the cleaned mussels with the onions, garlic, 3 tablespoons of the parsley, the thyme, bay leaf, pepper to taste, the wine, and 5 tablespoons of the butter. Cover tightly. Place over a high heat for 5 to 10 minutes or until the mussels have opened. Discard any that do not open. While they cook, shake the kettle occasionally to move the mussels from one level to another.

Lift the mussels from the broth. Break the mussels apart, keeping only those shells containing mussels. Place in a deep earthenware casserole or tureen. Set aside and keep warm on side of stove or in a low oven.

Strain the broth into a clean pan (not aluminum), leaving a small amount in the bottom of the first pan just in case some of the sand eluded you in cleaning. Work the remaining butter into the flour to make a *beurre manié*. Add to the broth, bit by bit, whipping constantly with a wire whisk until smooth. Bring to a boil, reduce heat, and cook for 8 to 10 minutes. Slowly stir in ½ cup of the cream. Bring to a boil again, then take off the heat.

Meanwhile, beat the remaining cream and egg yolks together. Gradually whip into the broth. Bring up to a boil, but *do not actually boil or the mixture will curdle.* Finally, pour the mixture over the warm mussels and then sprinkle with the remaining chopped parsley. Serve immediately.

Moules Marseillaise
Mussels Marseillaise

(Serves 6)

•

6 *pounds mussels, cleaned (for method see page 131)*
2 *tablespoons butter*
2 *tablespoons olive oil*
2 *small onions, chopped (¾ cup)*
1 *small green pepper, seeded and finely chopped (½ cup)*
2 to 3 *cloves garlic, chopped (2 teaspoons)*
3 *tomatoes, skinned, seeded and chopped (1½ cups)*
1 *teaspoon freshly ground pepper*
1 *cup dry white wine*

In a large kettle (that has a cover) heat the butter and oil and add the onion and sauté for 1 minute. Add the green pepper and garlic and sauté for 1 more minute. Add the tomato and ground pepper and sauté for 2 more minutes. Add the wine and mussels, cover, and allow to boil for 2 to 3 minutes or until the shells are open. While they cook, shake the kettle occasionally to move the mussels from one level to another. Lift the mussels from the broth with a slotted spoon. Break the mussels apart, keeping only those shells containing mussels. Place in a deep earthenware casserole or tureen. Cover and set aside to keep warm. A good place would be on the side of the stove or in a very low oven.

> ½ teaspoon saffron (use the stigmas, not the
>   powder) broken into pieces or crumbled
> ½ stick sweet butter (2 ounces)
> salt and pepper if necessary
> ¼ cup chopped parsley

Add the saffron to the broth and allow to reduce by half (you should have about 2 to 2½ cups left). Add salt and pepper if necessary. Thicken the sauce with the butter (called *monter au beurre* in French). Over medium heat, add the butter bit by bit to the hot broth, shaking the pan vigorously back and forth so that the bits of butter emulsify into the broth and thereby thicken it. *If the pan is not shaken properly the butter will not combine with the broth and will come up to the surface.*

Pour over the mussels, bring to a boil and sprinkle with the chopped parsley. Serve immediately.

Pilaf de Moules à la Crème
Rice Pilaf with Mussels in Cream Sauce
(Serves 6 to 8)

•

Mussels

> 5 pounds mussels (about 5 dozen), cleaned
>   (see page 131)
> 1 medium onion, peeled and chopped
> 1 small clove garlic, peeled, crushed, and minced
> 10 to 12 sprigs parsley, coarsely chopped
> ½ tablespoon chopped fresh tarragon
> dash dried thyme
> ½ bay leaf
> salt
> freshly ground white pepper
> 1 cup dry white wine
> 4 tablespoons (½ stick) butter
> 3 tablespoons flour
> ½ cup heavy cream
> 1 tablespoon chopped parsley

Place the cleaned mussels in a big kettle (not aluminum) with the onion, garlic, coarsely chopped parsley, tarragon, thyme, bay leaf, salt and pepper to taste, wine, and 2 tablespoons of the butter. Cover tightly and cook over a high heat for 10 to 12 minutes or until all the mussels have opened.

Since this is actually steaming, shake the kettle in an up-and-down motion occasionally to move the mussels from one level to another. Lift the mussels from the broth. Remove and discard the shells and place the mussels in an earthenware casserole. Set aside and keep warm. Strain the broth into a clean saucepan (not aluminum) leaving a small amount in the bottom of the kettle in case some of the sand was missed in cleaning.

Make a *beurre manié* by mixing the remaining butter with the flour into a smooth paste. Add to the broth, bit by bit, whipping constantly until smooth. Bring to a boil, reduce heat and cook for 8 to 10 minutes. Stir in the cream and bring to a boil again. Take off the heat. Add chopped parsley.

Pilaf

> 1 *tablespoon sweet butter*
> ½ *onion, peeled and minced* (¼ *cup*)
> 1½ *cups converted rice*
> 3 *cups chicken broth, your own or canned*
> *salt*
> *freshly ground white pepper*
> *dash dried thyme*
> 1 *bay leaf*

Heat the butter in a deep saucepan. Add the onion and sauté for 2 minutes. Do not allow it to brown. Add the rice, mix well with the butter. Then add the broth and all the seasonings. Bring to a boil on top of the stove. Cover tightly and place in a 400° oven for 20 minutes.

Serving

For each individual serving, spoon about 2 tablespoons of the rice into a small bowl, add about 8 to 10 mussels with 2 tablespoons of the sauce, then cover with more rice. Press down firmly. Invert on a heated serving platter and surround with the remaining sauce.

Homard Normande
Lobster Normandy Style

(*Serves 6*)

•

Like all people living close to the sea, the Normands are very fond of shellfish, fish, and any other ocean-going delicacies. Although lobsters are very expensive in France, they are featured quite often in Normandy restaurants. As in the majority of the dishes made in that part of the country, cream, butter, and wine are used generously.

> 4 *fresh, live lobsters, about 1½ pounds each*
> ½ *cup (1 stick) sweet butter*
> 2 *teaspoons salt*
> 1 *teaspoon freshly ground white pepper*
> 6 *shallots or ½ cup finely chopped scallions*
> ½ *cup calvados*
> 3 *cups heavy cream*
> 3 *tablespoons all-purpose flour*
> *juice of ½ lemon*
> *dash cayenne pepper*
> 2 *tablespoons fresh parsley, finely chopped*

Split the lobsters lengthwise with a big knife and break the shells off the claws with a hammer or a cleaver. Pour the liquid and the tomalley into a small bowl. Discard the stomach. Melt half the butter in a large, heavy saucepan. When the butter turns to a hazelnut color, add the lobsters and sprinkle with salt and pepper. Cook on high heat for 8 to 10 minutes, turning the lobsters as you go along. They should turn an even red all over. Remove the lobsters from the saucepan. Arrange in a large roasting pan and place in a preheated 200° oven to keep them warm and to finish the cooking. Add the chopped shallots to the saucepan and sizzle 1 minute without burning. Add the calvados, ignite, and when the flame dies out, add the cream. Work together the remaining butter and the flour. When the sauce starts boiling, add the flour mixture bit by bit, stirring vigorously with a wire whisk to dissolve any lumps. Slowly bring to a boil. Then mix in the tomalley and lemon juice. Taste for seasoning and add salt and cayenne pepper if necessary. You may let the sauce reduce a bit if you like it thicker. Stir in the parsley. Pour the sauce over the lobsters and serve piping hot.

Aspic de Homard à la Parisienne
Lobster in Aspic

(Serves 6 to 8)

•

Lobster and Lobster Stock (This step is done 2 days ahead.)

> 1 *live 5-pound lobster or 2 smaller lobsters, or*
> *about 2¼ pounds fresh lobster meat. (If*
> *lobster meat is used, use 2 pounds of fish-*
> *bones to make the stock for the aspic.)*
> 4 *pints water*
> 1 *cup loose parsley*
> 2 *onions, coarsely sliced (1½ cups)*
> 2 *carrots, coarsely sliced (1½ cups)*
> 1 *rib celery, coarsely sliced (1 cup)*
> 1 *teaspoon dried thyme*
> 3 to 4 *bay leaves*
> 1 *tablespoon black peppercorns*
> 1 *tablespoon salt*

Place all ingredients except the lobster in a large kettle (do not use aluminum) and boil for 10 minutes. Add the lobster. When the liquid comes to a boil again, reduce the heat to low and simmer for 10 minutes. Cool overnight *in the broth*. This will flavor the lobster meat considerably. Remove the lobster the following day and strain the stock.

Aspic

4 cups of the strained cold broth
½ cup coarsely chopped parsley
½ cup coarsely cut celery leaves
1 carrot, coarsely chopped (¾ cup)
4 egg whites
5 envelopes unflavored gelatin

Combine all ingredients in a saucepan and bring to a boil on high heat, stirring with a spoon. As soon as the mixture comes to a boil, stop stirring. Let simmer 1 minute. Then strain through a sieve lined with a wet paper towel or a kitchen towel rinsed in water and wrung out. Cool the mixture until it gels. Whenever gelatin is used it is important to follow the directions carefully. If the gelatin is mixed to a liquid and boiled, the gelatin will lose its strength. *The more gelatin cooks, the more it weakens. If you let a stock boil with gelatin for 30 minutes you need almost double the amount of gelatin.*

Vegetable Salad

3 medium carrots, peeled
3 small white turnips, peeled
1 large Idaho potato, washed (unpeeled)
½ cup peas
¼ cup chopped onion
⅔ cup Mayonnaise (see page 35)
½ teaspoon freshly ground white pepper
½ teaspoon salt

Cook the carrots in salted boiling water until tender (about 12 to 15 minutes). Refresh under cold water and cut into ¼-inch dices. Cook the turnips in boiling salted water until tender (about 12 minutes). Refresh and cut into ¼-inch dices. Cook the potato in salted water for about 30 minutes until tender. Drain. When cold enough to handle, peel and dice into ¼-inch dices. Place the peas in boiling salted water and boil 4 to 5 minutes. Refresh under cold water and drain. Mix all remaining ingredients together with the vegetables and set aside.

Mold and Garnishes

> 1 *hard-boiled egg, sliced*
> 1 *well-ripened tomato*
> 1 or 2 *black olives*

Remove the meat from the lobster. Cut the tail into ⅜-inch slices and dice the remaining meat into ¼-inch dices. Mix the coral and tomalley with the vegetable salad. Melt the aspic. Chill a mold, a round mold or a charlotte mold is fine; it should have a 1½- to 2-quart capacity. Place a bowl of crushed ice on the table. Pour about ¾ cup of aspic in the mold and roll the mold around on the ice so that it is coated all over with a thin layer of aspic. Chill until well set. Arrange the lobster slices in the bottom of the mold. Place pieces of black olive and red diamonds of tomato skin to your own fancy to decorate the mold. *Remember that it will be unmolded upside down and the bottom will become the top.* Pour some almost-set aspic on the lobster, enough to cover it, and refrigerate until well set. Keep building, decorating the side of the mold with tomato skin, hard-boiled eggs, and olive until ⅓ of the mold is filled and the side well coated. Place the vegetable salad and the diced lobster meat in the center of the mold, filling it up to ¼ of an inch from the top. Pour some gelatin on top to glaze and seal in the vegetable salad. *Remember that the aspic should not be too liquid, otherwise it will run through the ingredients. Keep melt-*

ing the aspic and cooling it off on ice to arrive at the right consistency. It should be like a heavy pancake syrup so it will spread
evenly just before it sets. Refrigerate the mold overnight.

At serving time, unmold on a bed of Boston lettuce leaves.
Place a hot towel on the mold for 30 seconds to help the
unmolding.

Soufflé de Homard Plaza-Athénée
Lobster Soufflé Plaza-Athénée
(Serves 8)

•

Lobsters and Sauce

> 2 live lobsters, 1½ to 2 pounds each
> 5 tablespoons all-purpose flour
> ¾ cup dry white wine
> ¼ cup vegetable oil
> 6 tablespoons (¾ stick) sweet butter
> ¼ cup cognac
> 1 tomato, chopped coarsely (about 1 cup)
> 3 tablespoons tomato paste
> ¼ cup carrot, minced (about 1 small carrot)
> ½ cup minced onion (about 1 small yellow
>   onion)
> ¼ cup minced celery (about ½ rib)
> 1 clove garlic, peeled and crushed
> ½ teaspoon minced fresh tarragon (or a big
>   pinch dried)
> 2 bay leaves
> ½ teaspoon dried thyme
> salt
> freshly ground pepper
> ½ cup heavy cream

Cut the lobsters into pieces with a heavy, sharp knife. Discard the stomach (the small sac behind the eyes) and the intestinal vein which runs from the stomach to the tip of the tail. Place the coral, if any, the green liver (tomalley), and any juices in a bowl with the flour and ¼ cup of the wine. Mix thoroughly and set aside.

Combine the oil and half the butter in a large heavy enameled skillet. When very hot, add the lobster pieces and sauté 2 minutes. Add the rest of the wine and half of the cognac. Ignite. When the flames die out, add all remaining ingredients except the cream and the wine-flour mixture. Bring to a boil, then simmer 15 minutes, covered. Lift the lobster pieces to a tray and remove the meat from the shells. Cut into 1½-inch pieces. Add the wine-flour mixture to the sauce and mix with a wire whisk. Bring to a boil, then simmer 5 minutes. Strain, pushing hard with a metal spoon against the sieve to extrude all the juices. Pour ½ cup of the sauce into a second saucepan and combine with the cream. Bring to a boil. Add the remaining cognac and butter. Mix well and set aside. This sauce is served on the side.

Add the lobster to the first saucepan. Set aside.

Soufflé

> 2½ tablespoons sweet butter
> 3 tablespoons all-purpose flour
> ¾ cup milk
> salt
> freshly ground pepper
> 4 whole eggs, separated
> 1 extra egg white
> ½ cup grated Swiss cheese (about 2 ounces)

Melt the butter in a heavy saucepan. Stir in the flour until smooth and cook, stirring constantly (do not allow it to brown), over moderate heat for about 1 minute. Add the milk, salt and pepper to taste, and cook, whipping constantly with a wire whisk until the *sauce béchamel* comes to a boil. Cook for 2 minutes at a boil. Take off the heat and beat in the yolks. Beat the whites with a rotary beater or an electric beater until they hold firm, shiny peaks when the beater is held straight up. Whip about ⅓ of the whites into the yolk mixture thoroughly with a wire whisk. Fold in the remainder with a rubber spatula along with the cheese. *Go as fast as you can when adding the whites, otherwise they will be grainy.*

Bring the sauce with the lobster to a boil and pour into an au gratin dish, 2 to 3 inches deep. Spoon the soufflé on top, smoothing the surface with a metal spatula. Bake on a cookie sheet in a preheated 400° oven for 20 to 25 minutes. Meanwhile, heat the reserved sauce.

As soon as it comes out of the oven, serve the soufflé, giving each guest some of the top and some of the bottom mixture. Serve the extra sauce on the side.

Red Snapper Romulus

(Serves 8 to 10)

•

1 *red snapper, approximately 4½ pounds*
     cleaned, gills removed but with the head
     left on
½ *pound roe (the sole or flounder roe is good*
     and quite inexpensive)
2 *tablespoons olive oil*
1 *cup peeled and diced shallots*
½ *pound mushrooms, diced (about 2½ cups)*
2 *leeks (only the white parts), diced (about*
     1 cup)

1 *zucchini, washed and cut into ½-inch dices*
(about 2½ cups) Do not peel the zucchini
but cut the ends off.
¼ *cup chopped parsley*
3 *cloves garlic, peeled, crushed, and chopped (a*
good tablespoon)
1 *teaspoon salt*
½ *teaspoon freshly ground white pepper*
2 *large bay leaves split into halves lengthwise*

Place the oil in a saucepan, add the shallots and sauté for 2 minutes. Add the mushrooms, leek, zucchini, parsley, and garlic and cook for 5 minutes. Add the salt, pepper and the roe, coarsely chopped. Mix with a spoon for a few seconds. *The roe will bind all ingredients together and will turn it a whitish color. Cook it just enough until it changes color and holds together.* With a spoon, fill the cavity of the fish. Stuff also where the gills were. All the stuffing should go inside the fish. Make 4 little incisions on 1 side of the fish and insert the pieces of bay leaves so that half of each piece still shows.

1 *teaspoon salt*
1 *teaspoon freshly ground white pepper*
½ *stick sweet butter*
½ *teaspoon dried thyme (or 1 teaspoon fresh*
thyme)
½ *teaspoon dried tarragon (or 1 tablespoon*
fresh tarragon)
1 *cup dry white wine*
2 *cups homemade tomato sauce (or 1 cup*
chopped stewed tomatoes and 1 cup
tomato puree)

Rub the fish with the salt and pepper on both sides. Place in a large baking dish and add the butter (cut into bits), the thyme, tarragon, wine and tomato sauce. Place in a 400° oven for 45 minutes, basting the fish with the sauce regularly every

6 to 8 minutes. You need 2 large spatulas to lift the fish from the baking dish and arrange it on a serving platter. Coat with the sauce and serve immediately. Excellent with tiny boiled potatoes and a dry white wine.

Paupiettes de Sole Dugléré
Sole Fillets with Tomatoes

(*Serves 6*)

•

7 tablespoons sweet butter
1 teaspoon salt
½ teaspoon freshly ground white pepper
½ cup chopped shallots or green onion bulbs
12 single or 6 double fillets of sole (about 1½
  pounds)
2 large ripe tomatoes, peeled, seeded and
  chopped (2 cups)
3 tablespoons chopped parsley
1½ cups dry white wine
1 cup water
4 tablespoons flour
1 cup heavy cream
3 egg yolks
2 tablespoons cognac

Butter a heavy shallow baking pan, sprinkle with half the salt and pepper, and scatter 6 tablespoons of the shallots over the bottom. Line up the fillets, rolled, on top. *When rolling the fillet, be sure that the outside of the roll is the fleshy side of the meat, the whitest side, otherwise the fillet will unroll during cooking.* Scatter remaining shallots over the fish and sprinkle with salt and pepper. Add the tomatoes, 2 tablespoons of the parsley, and the wine mixed with the water.

Butter a piece of waxed paper large enough to cover the pan and place it, buttered side down, on top. Bring the liquid to a boil over high heat. Take the pan off the heat and place in a preheated 400° oven for 10 to 12 minutes, or until a fork pierces the flesh of the fish easily. Remove from the oven. Arrange the fillets on a buttered platter, cover again with the buttered waxed paper, and keep warm on top of the stove or in a 160° oven.

Pour the broth from the baking pan into a clean saucepan and reduce to ⅔ of the liquid. Make a *beurre manié* with 3 tablespoons of the butter and the flour. Add to the broth, bit by bit, whipping with a whisk, and cook, stirring, for 10 minutes.

Add ¾ cup of the cream and bring to a boil. Take off the heat. Beat the egg yolks and remaining cream together in a bowl, then little by little combine this mixture with the hot sauce. First add some hot sauce to the yolk mixture and mix carefully. Then pour back into the sauce. *Be careful not to boil the sauce after the addition of the yolks or it will curdle.* Add the cognac and remaining butter, whipping vigorously. Check for seasoning and add salt and pepper if needed. Pour the sauce over the fillets and sprinkle with the rest of the parsley.

Filets de Sole Claudine

(*Serves* 8)

•

2 large heads iceberg lettuce (use only the large
  green leaves and wash carefully. Save the
  hearts for salad or another use)
2¾ pounds grey sole fillets (12 fillets)
1½ teaspoons salt

½ teaspoon freshly ground white pepper
1¼ sticks sweet butter
¾ pound fresh mushrooms, washed and coarsely
    chopped
8 to 10 shallots, peeled and chopped fine
    (½ cup)
1 to 2 carrots, depending on size, cut into fine
    julienne strips (see page 170) (2 cups)
1 cup dry white wine
½ cup sweet vermouth
3 tablespoons flour
1½ cups heavy cream

You should have 12 large lettuce leaves. Plunge them into boiling water, bring to a boil again and let boil for 1 minute. Cool immediately under cold water. When leaves are cold, dry on paper towel.

Cut each fillet into halves lengthwise, discarding the strip of little bones that separates the 2 halves. Sprinkle the fillets (you now have 24) with ½ teaspoon of salt and ¼ teaspoon of pepper. Set aside.

Melt 3 tablespoons of butter in a saucepan and add the mushrooms, ½ teaspoon salt and ⅛ teaspoon pepper. Cook until all the liquid rendered by the mushrooms has evaporated. Set aside to cool slightly.

Butter a large, shallow au gratin dish with 2 tablespoons of butter and sprinkle with the shallots and the remaining salt and pepper. Drop the carrot julienne in boiling water, boil for 1 minute, drain and sprinkle on top of the shallots. Spread the lettuce leaves on the table and place 1 tablespoon of the mushrooms in the center of each leaf. Roll 2 pieces of fish and place side by side on top of the mushrooms. (Be sure that the whitest part of the flesh shows on the outside. This means that the fillets are rolled the proper way.) Fold the lettuce leaf on top of the fillets, and place on top of the carrot upside down so that the folded part is underneath. Repeat the operation until you have 12 neat little packages. They should be tight, one against the other, without overlapping. Add the wine and vermouth, cover with a piece of parchment paper and bring to a boil on top of the stove. As soon as it boils, place in a 400° preheated oven for 8 to 10 minutes.

Remove the fish from the oven, and lift the packages to a serving platter. Keep warm in a 180° oven. Place the juices and garnishes in a large saucepan and reduce by half on high heat. Mix the flour and 3 tablespoons of butter together and add to the broth, mixing fast with a whisk to avoid lumps. Bring to a boil and simmer for 12 to 15 minutes. (At this point you may pour into the sauce any liquid which accumulated in the platter around the fillets.) Add the cream, bring to a boil and simmer slowly another 5 minutes. Check for seasonings, as more salt and pepper may be needed. Add remaining butter bit by bit, shaking the saucepan as you add, so that the butter blends well with the sauce. Serve immediately. Be sure each fillet is coated with the sauce.

Cabillaud Grenobloise
Fresh Codfish Steaks Grenoble Style

(Serves 4)

•

1 *large fillet of codfish (about 1½ pounds), cut into 4 steaks*
4 *tablespoons vegetable oil*
2 *slices white bread, trimmed and cubed (about 1 cup)*
1½ *teaspoons salt*

½ teaspoon freshly ground white pepper
½ cup flour
1 stick sweet butter
1 large lemon, peeled (the white as well as the
        yellow skin) with a knife and cut into ½-
        inch cubes. Remove seeds as you cut the
        lemon. (It should yield about ⅓ cup.)
3 tablespoons capers, drained
2 tablespoons brown gravy (optional)
2 tablespoons chopped parsley

Place 2 tablespoons of oil in a skillet and add the bread. Cook turning your bread with a spoon so that it gets uniformly browned on all sides. Drain the bread in a sieve and set aside. Sprinkle the salt and pepper on both sides of the fish and dip in the flour so that all sides of the steaks are coated with the flour. Shake any excess flour. Melt ⅓ of a stick of butter in a heavy skillet, add the remaining oil. When the mixture is foaming, add the fish, each piece flat and not overlapping so that they may cook and brown properly. The side of the fillet where the skin has been removed is usually flatter and darker in color than the other side which was next to the bone. *Place the steaks with the darker side to brown first. Being flatter, this side browns uniformly and all the steaks will have the same color.* Cook on medium heat for about 8 minutes. With a wide spatula, turn on the other side and cook another 8 minutes. They should be browned and crusty on both sides. Arrange the pieces on a serving platter with the nicest side showing, sprinkle with croutons, lemon and capers on top and keep in a warm place (an oven with a pilot light is a good place). Melt the remaining butter in a skillet until it takes on a hazelnut color. Pour the brown gravy around the steaks (if you are using brown gravy) and pour the hot butter on top of the fish. Sprinkle with the parsley and serve immediately. The last part should be done at the last moment and the fish served as soon as the butter is poured on the dish. Excellent with tiny boiled potatoes and a dry white wine.

Brochet Sauce Génoise
Pike with Red Wine Sauce

(Serves 6)

•

2 *pikes* (*about 1¾ pounds each, scaled and*
    cleaned)
2 *onions, peeled and chopped fine* (*¾ cup*)
6 to 8 *shallots, peeled and chopped fine* (*½ cup*)
1 *clove garlic, crushed, peeled and chopped fine*
    (*½ teaspoon*)
2 *carrots, peeled and chopped fine* (*¾ cup*)
¼ *cup chopped parsley*
1 *bay leaf broken into pieces*
¼ *teaspoon thyme*
¼ *teaspoon whole black pepper, crushed fine*
    (*this can be done with a rolling pin*)
1½ *teaspoons salt*
1 *bottle* (*1½ pints*) *good dry red wine*
    (*Beaujolais, Macon, Corbières, etc.*)
4 *tablespoons* (*½ stick*) *sweet butter, softened*
1½ *teaspoons anchovy paste* (*or about 6 fillets*
    in oil, mashed)
1 *teaspoon cornstarch*

Place the onions, shallots, garlic, carrots, parsley, bay leaf, thyme, pepper, ½ teaspoon of the salt and the wine in a heavy saucepan (not aluminum because of discoloration). Bring to a high boil and continue to boil for about 15 minutes, until the liquid has reduced to half.

Sprinkle the fish, inside and outside, with the remaining salt and rub with 1 tablespoon of butter. Place in a baking dish, pour the wine mixture and 1 cup of water over the fish. Cover with waxed paper. Bring to a boil on top of the stove, and place in a 425° preheated oven for about 15 minutes.

Pour the juices into a saucepan, place over a high heat and reduce by about one third (about 3 to 4 minutes). Meanwhile, combine the remaining butter, the anchovy paste and the cornstarch. Add to the wine mixture and whisk well with a wire whisk. Bring to a boil; take off the heat immediately. Pour the sauce over the fish. Serve immediately. Serves 6.

Quenelles de Brochet Lyonnaise
Pike Quenelles Lyonnaises

•

This is a large recipe which will yield approximately 45 quenelles, 3 ounces each. We made it large because of the work involved and because the mixture freezes quite well. However, you may cut the recipe in half.

1 fresh pike, approximately 3 pounds

Have the fish boned and skinned if you cannot do it yourself. Cut the fillets into cubes and puree *a few at a time* in the blender. When all the fish has been pureed, push the puree through a metal sieve using a metal spoon or your fingers. The fish must be strained as you will realize when you see the fibers accumulated in the sieve. This is the hardest and most tedious part in the making of quenelles. You will have about 1½ pounds of flesh remaining. Cover and refrigerate.

Panade

    2 pounds all-purpose flour
    1 quart water
    1 stick sweet butter (4 ounces)
    1 teaspoon salt
    ¼ teaspoon freshly ground pepper

Bring the water, butter, salt and pepper to a boil in a large heavy pot. Sift the flour. When the mixture is boiling, add the flour all at once. Mix rapidly with a large wooden spatula and cook on low heat for 5 minutes, stirring with the spatula. It is hard work to mix the panade because the mixture is quite stiff. Place the panade in a tray, cover carefully with plastic wrap (to prevent a skin forming on top) and refrigerate.

    14 large eggs
    2 pounds sweet butter at room temperature
    1 ounce salt (2 tablespoons)
    ½ teaspoon freshly ground white pepper

In a restaurant where one has sophisticated equipment, such as a cutter or the Cuisinarts food processor (a large blender holding 1 gallon), the fish is blended first with the cold panade. Lacking that equipment you have to have a mixer. Place the cold panade in the bowl of the mixer, add 2 eggs and mix on medium speed until the eggs are incorporated. Repeat until you have used 10 eggs. Add the fish and mix on high speed until the mixture is very smooth. Add the remaining eggs, mix, then the butter and seasonings and mix again until smooth. The basic mixture is ready and you may divide it into containers, cover them and freeze them. *When you need the mixture defrost it for at least 1 day under refrigeration.* Use it to make quenelles, stuffed fish, turban of sole or *pain de brochet* (pike's bread).

The quenelles are poached in a large shallow pan of salted, simmering water. They may be shaped with 2 large spoons dipped into the hot water, 1 dishing the mixture out and the other pushing it down into the water. The mixture may be rolled into a cylinder 1½ inches thick, and cut on a bias into pieces shaped into the form of a lozenge or diamond-shaped form about 2½ inches long. Then, the lozenge is rolled into the flour to smooth it all around. The mixture may also be rolled into a thinner cylinder (about 1¼ inches thick) and cut into segments 3 inches long. In any case, all the quenelles should weigh about 3 ounces each. Lower about 6 to 8 quenelles into the simmering water. You will notice that as the water comes to a boil again the quenelles rise to the surface and roll over in the water. Let them poach slowly for 10 minutes, then remove them with a slotted spoon and place them in cold water. *Do not allow them to boil and do not cover them during the cooking. They should not expand during the first cooking.* When cold, remove them from the water and place them in a covered container in the refrigerator. The quenelles are now ready to be used. It is in this form that they are bought in the *charcuterie* in France.

Quenelles Galliera
Quenelles in Fish and Mushroom Sauce
(*Serves 8*)

•

16 *basic Quenelles* (*see page 150*)

Fish Fumet

> 2 *pounds fishbones* (*Flat fish, like sole, are best; avoid heads and be sure to clean the gills or the fumet will be bitter.*)
> 2 *tablespoons sweet butter*

1 *onion, sliced* (¾ *cup*)
10 *sprigs parsley*
1 *teaspoon white peppercorns*
½ *teaspoon crushed thyme* (*fresh is better*)
2 *bay leaves*
1 *teaspoon salt*
1 *cup dry white wine*
4 *cups water*

Melt the butter in a large pot (not aluminum). Add the bones and cook, stirring, on medium heat for 1 minute. Add all the other ingredients except the wine and water and mix with a spoon. Cover and cook on medium heat for 3 to 4 minutes. Add wine and water, bring to a boil and let gently boil for 20 minutes. Strain through a fine sieve. *Yield:* 4 cups of fumet. At this point you may freeze the fumet for future use.

Velouté

4 *cups fumet*
5 *tablespoons butter*
¾ *cup all-purpose flour*

Melt the butter in a heavy saucepan. Stir in the flour and cook on low heat for 1 minute, constantly stirring with a whisk. Add the 4 cups of fumet and bring to a boil, stirring to avoid scorching. Let cook slowly for 30 minutes, stirring once in a while. *Yield:* 2½ cups.

Note: The *velouté* is used as a basic white sauce. There are meat and fish *veloutés*. The first is made with a white stock using veal or poultry; the second with a fish stock or fish fumet, as with this recipe. It is the base of countless sauces with different names according to the ingredients added to the *velouté*. It should be cooked a long time so that the consistency will not change when recooked with other ingredients. The *velouté* can be kept frozen or covered in the refrigerator for up to 2 weeks.

Duxelles of Mushrooms

> 1 *pound mushrooms, chopped fine (about 3 cups)*
> 5 *shallots, peeled and chopped fine (2 tablespoons)*
> 3 *tablespoons sweet butter*
> ½ *teaspoon salt*
> ¼ *teaspoon freshly ground white pepper*

Melt the butter in a skillet, add the shallots and cook on medium heat for 1 minute. Add the chopped mushrooms, salt, and pepper and cook, mixing with a wooden spoon, for about 10 minutes. *The mushrooms will render some liquid; when the liquid is cooked down and the mixture is dry and starts sizzling, it is ready.* Transfer to a bowl, cover with waxed paper and set aside.

Galliera

> 2 *cups heavy cream*
> 1 *cup milk*
> *velouté*
> *duxelles*
> 1 *cube of Glace de Viande, if available (see page 33)*
> 1 *tablespoon good cognac*

Place the cream, milk, *velouté, duxelles,* and *glace de viande* in a large, flat saucepan with a cover. (The dish should be nice enough to be brought to the dining-room table.) Bring to a boil, stirring with a whisk. Add the 16 quenelles (they should fit without overlapping), cover and simmer for 25 minutes. It is better if the pan is placed on asbestos to prevent the sauce from sticking. *Shake the pan every 5 minutes to move the quenelles and prevent them from sticking.* The quenelles should almost double in volume. Bring the pot to the table and serve on hot plates, 2 quenelles per person with a few tablespoons of sauce.

Note: You may have to use two separate dishes for serving if the 16 quenelles do not fit into one.

Alose en Croûte Nivernaise
Shad in Crust

(Serves 8)

•

1 *shad (about 3½ pounds), boned it will yield*
1½ pounds including fillets, the roe and
liver. (Shad is a very bony fish and difficult
to bone properly. Try to buy it already
boned.)
½ recipe for Puff Paste (see page 52)

Duxelles

¾ *pound mushrooms, finely chopped (2 cups)*
2 *tablespoons sweet butter*
½ *teaspoon salt*
½ *teaspoon freshly ground pepper*

Melt the butter in a skillet, add the mushrooms, salt and pepper. Cook over medium heat, stirring with a spoon until the mushroom mixture is dry and starts to sizzle. This should take about 6 minutes. Set aside.

1 *slice bread, trimmed*
1 *tablespoon almonds*

Cut the bread into pieces and place in a blender. Add the almonds and blend a few seconds until it is all chopped. Set aside.

Green Butter

> 1 *stick soft sweet butter* (*4 ounces*)
> 4 *tablespoons chopped parsley*
> 1½ *tablespoons chopped shallots*
> 1 *teaspoon chopped garlic* (*1 clove*)
> 2 *teaspoons Pernod, Ricard or any anisette*
> ¼ *cup dry white wine*
> 1 *tablespoon fresh tarragon, chopped* (*1 tea-*
> *spoon if dry*)
> ½ *teaspoon salt*
> ½ *teaspoon freshly ground black pepper*

Mix all of the above ingredients together, including the bread-almond mixture from Step III, to have a green butter.

> 1 *egg, beaten* (*for egg wash*)

Split each fillet in half removing the center line that joins the fillets and is full of bones. You now have 4 single fillets. Butter-fly the fillets as well as you can and sprinkle with salt. To butter-fly: Place the fillet flat on a board. Slice the fish horizontally, but do not slice through completely, stopping ½ inch before the end. Once opened you will have a large flat fillet twice the original size. Using a spatula, spread half of the green butter mixture on all 4 fillets. Then close the fish fillets back to their original size.

Roll the puff paste about 18 inches long by 16 inches wide. It will be about ¼ inch thick. Place 2 of the stuffed fillets side by side on the dough (about 2 inches from the edge). Sprinkle the fish with half of the mushroom *duxelles*. Arrange the 2 last fillets on the mushrooms. Brush the edges of the dough with the egg wash. Fold the dough over the fillets pressing the edges together so that the dough does not separate during cooking. It should look like a long apple turnover. Trim the dough all around giving it the shape of a fish. Brush the "fish" with the egg wash. With the remaining dough, cut a strip about 1 inch wide and place it all around where the edges have been trimmed. Brush with the egg wash. *The extra strip of dough makes the seam thicker and it puffs up higher during cooking.* Cut little "fins" out of the dough and decorate the fish. With the back of a pastry tube or a teaspoon, press down along the dough to make half circles simulating the scales of a fish. Let the "fish" rest in the refrigerator for at least 30 minutes. Place in a preheated 425° oven for 40 minutes.

Sauce

> ¼ *cup chopped shallots* (*about 6 shallots*)
> 1 *cup dry white wine*
> ½ *teaspoon salt*
> 1 *tablespoon* (*about 2 small cubes*) *Glace de*
>   *Viande, if available* (*see page 33*)
> 3 *egg yolks*
> ½ *stick sweet butter* (*2 ounces*)
> *remainder of the Green Butter*

Place the shallots, wine, salt, and *glace de viande* in a heavy saucepan and cook on high fire until the sauce is reduced by half (about 10 minutes). Take off the heat, add the yolks and whip with a whisk on a very, very low fire for about 5 minutes. *The mixture is ready when you can see the bottom of the saucepan between the strikes of the whisk.* Be careful not to scramble the eggs. Add the butter and butter mixture bit by bit whipping with the whisk until it is all incorporated. It should be smooth, creamy and well blended. Keep in a lukewarm to hot double boiler. Serve with the sliced fish.

Vol-au-vent de Fruits de Mer
Seafood in a Puff-Paste Shell

(Serves 8)

•

Patty shells (*bouchées*) are made from simple circles of puff paste, approximately 4 to 5 inches wide by ¼ inch thick, and cooked in the oven. They are filled with a variety of garnishes and are served 1 per person. The *vol-au-vent* is an extra large patty shell served for a dinner party of 6 to 8 persons. To make it the conventional way, one needs a perfect, classic Puff Paste (see page 52). In our recipe, either puff paste may be utilized. Our method results in a more decorative *vol-au-vent* than what could be achieved with a conventional method. However, although it is called a *vol-au-vent*, it is in fact a deep decorated shell. The *vol-au-vent* is usually filled with poached fish or shellfish in a sauce, sweetbreads in brown sauce, chicken in cream sauce, pike, or veal quenelles, etc.

> 1 *egg, beaten (for egg wash)*
> ½ *recipe for Puff Paste (see page 52 or 55)*

Roll the dough out into a long rectangle approximately 10 to 12 inches wide by 26 to 30 inches long. Wrap the dough on your pin and unroll onto a wet cookie sheet about 12 by 16 inches (half of the dough will still be hanging outside the sheet). Make a ball of aluminum foil about 8 inches in diameter. *The ball should be loose and light so that it can be removed easily from the shell later on.* Place it on the tray in the middle of the dough, wet all around with water, and fold the dough over so that the aluminum ball is enclosed inside the shell. Press the dough gently all around the ball to seal the edges together.

Trim the dough all around as neatly as you can, approximately 1 inch from the base of the aluminum foil. Brush the *vol-au-vent* with the egg wash. Cut a long strip of dough from the trimmings (about ½ inch wide) and place it all around the ball to outline the lid of the shell. Pierce a small hole with the tip of a knife on top of the shell so that the steam can escape during cooking. With the knife, score a design on the lid. Cut another strip of dough (about 1 inch wide) and place it all around on the flat part of the base. You may cut out "leaves" or "flowers" from the dough and decorate according to your own taste. Brush again with the egg wash, and let the *vol-au-vent* rest for 30 minutes in the refrigerator before cooking. Place in a 400° oven and cook for 35 minutes. Cool slowly at room temperature. When cool, cut the "hat" off following the top strip of pastry that encircles the *vol-au-vent*. Insert your fingers into the shell and press the aluminum foil to make it smaller and lift it out through the hole.

> 5 *pounds of mussels* (*washed and cleaned, see*
> *page 131*)
> 1 *cup dry white wine*
> ¼ *cup sliced shallots* (*about 5 or 6*)
> 10 *sprigs parsley*
> 2 *bay leaves*
> ½ *teaspoon crushed thyme* (*fresh is better*)
> 1 *onion, sliced* (*about 1 cup*)
> 1 *teaspoon salt*
> ½ *teaspoon freshly ground white pepper*

Place all the ingredients in a large casserole with a cover and bring to a boil over high heat. Let cook for 5 minutes, stirring once or twice with a large spoon, until all the mussels are open. *Do not overcook or the mussels will be tough.* Remove the mussels from the broth with a slotted spoon and, when cool enough to handle, remove the meat from the shells and set aside. *Yield*: About 1 quart of juices.

> 1 *pound of bay scallops*
> 1 *pound of fish fillets cut into 2- to 3-inch pieces*
>   (*sole, halibut, etc.*)
> 1 *tablespoon sweet butter*
> ¼ *cup chopped shallots* (*about 5 or 6*)
> ½ *teaspoon salt*
> ½ *teaspoon freshly ground pepper*
> 8 *ounces mushrooms, washed and sliced*
> 2 *large ripe tomatoes, peeled, seeded, and*
>   *coarsely chopped* (*see page 170*)

Butter a large au gratin dish. Sprinkle the shallots, salt and pepper in the bottom and arrange the fish and scallops on top. Sprinkle with the mushrooms and tomatoes. Pour the broth from the mussels on top, discarding any sediment, and cover with a piece of buttered waxed paper. Bring to a boil on top of the stove and place in a preheated 425° oven for about 4 to 5 minutes. Do not overcook. Set aside.

> ¾ *cup flour*
> 4 *tablespoons butter* (*½ stick*)
> 1¼ *cups heavy cream*
> 2 *small cubes of Glace de Viande, if available*
>   (*see page 33*)

Melt the butter in a heavy saucepan, add the flour and cook over medium heat for 1 minute, stirring with a whisk. Pour the poaching liquid from the fish into the *roux*, stirring rapidly with the whisk. Bring to a boil, mixing with the whisk to avoid scorching. Simmer on low heat for 5 minutes. Add the cream and the *glace de viande* (if any) and bring to a boil. Add the reserved mussels to the fish, pour the sauce over, and bring the whole dish to a light simmer on top of the stove using low heat. Taste for seasoning as it may need salt and pepper. Add 1 tablespoon of good cognac if you like a highly seasoned sauce. Meanwhile, place the *vol-au-vent* in a warm oven for 1 or 2 minutes.

Transfer to a serving platter and fill with the seafood. Pour some of the sauce around the *vol-au-vent* and place the lid on top. Serve immediately, giving some seafood and some of the crust to each guest.

Meat and Poultry

Steak au Poivre
Pepper Steak

(*Serves 4*)

•

4 *shell steaks, boned and well trimmed, about*
    8 *ounces each*
1 *teaspoon salt*
3 *tablespoons crushed black peppercorns*
4 *tablespoons* (½ *stick*) *sweet butter*
3 *shallots, peeled and minced* (1½ *tablespoons*)
2 *tablespoons good cognac*
¼ *cup red wine*
1½ *cups brown beef gravy*

    Sprinkle both sides of the steaks with salt, then coat both sides with the peppercorns. This is done by spreading the crushed pepper on the table and pressing the steak on the pepper. Heat 2 tablespoons of the butter in a large, heavy skillet. When the butter is a rich hazelnut color, sauté the steaks 3 to 4 minutes on each side till medium-rare. Lift the steaks from the pan to a warm platter and keep warm in a 180° oven. Add the shallots to the pan and sauté for 1 minute. Add the cognac and ignite. When the flames die out, add the wine and bring to a boil. Reduce to about half, add the beef gravy and bring to a boil again. Boil for a few minutes to reduce the sauce and bring it to the right consistency. Add the remaining butter, strain, and taste for seasoning as it may need salt. Pour the sauce over the steaks.

Sometimes the shallots and wine are omitted and the steak is made just with cognac and brown gravy.

Or the steaks can be deglazed with cognac and 3 to 4 table-spoons of heavy cream can be added to the brown gravy before it is reduced.

Bavette Farcie Braisée
Braised Stuffed Flank Steak

(Serves 6 to 8)

•

Flank steak, usually roasted or charcoal-broiled, is served as London broil when thinly sliced. The meat is fibrous and tough if not cut against the grain. This particular recipe will serve, inexpensively, 6 to 8 persons. With any left over, you may serve it cold, sliced with lettuce and tomatoes.

1 flank steak, 2 to 2¼ pounds untrimmed (1¾
pounds trimmed), prepared for stuffing

If you should buy the steak untrimmed, pull out the "skin" and trim off the fat, which is heavy on one end. Have the butcher cut a pocket in the steak for stuffing, or cut one in yourself.

Stuffing

¼ cup vegetable oil
3 tablespoons sweet butter
3 cups small bread cubes (make with white
    bread—½-inch cubes)
1 pound lean ground beef
1 egg
1 onion, peeled and chopped (about ¾ cup)
½ stalk celery, chopped
1 tablespoon chopped parsley
2 cloves garlic, peeled and chopped fine
1½ teaspoons salt
½ teaspoon freshly ground black pepper
¼ teaspoon crushed thyme or savory

Heat the oil and butter in a skillet. Add the bread cubes and sauté over medium heat until brown on all sides. Combine the remaining ingredients in a large bowl and then add the bread cubes, mixing in lightly to avoid making it too mushy.

To make the pocket for the stuffing, place the steak on a board with your palm on the meat. Hold your knife so that the blade is flat. Cut into the meat lengthwise, parallel to the board. Be careful not to cut all the way through to the other side or come out at either end. Stuff the flank steak, then bring the lower lip of the steak back against the stuffing and then bring the top lip down over this so that you form a nice loaf. Salt and pepper the loaf all around and tie with a few strings to keep securely closed.

2 tablespoons butter
1 tablespoon oil
1 medium carrot, peeled and diced fine (about
    ¾ cup)
1 onion, chopped (about ¾ cup)
2 bay leaves
1 tomato, coarsely chopped (about 1 cup)

1 *teaspoon thyme leaves*
2 *cups beef broth*
1 *cup dry red wine*
2 *tablespoons arrowroot diluted with ¼ cup*
    cold water

Heat the oil and butter in a large deep casserole with a cover. Brown the stuffed meat on all sides. Add the carrot, onion, bay leaves, tomato and thyme, allow to cook over moderate heat, uncovered, for 5 minutes. Add the broth and wine and bring to a boil, cover and braise on a very low heat on top of the stove or place in a 400° oven for 1 hour and 10 minutes. Lift the meat to a serving platter, remove the strings and keep warm. Stir the arrowroot-and-water mixture into the sauce. Bring up to a boil and cook until the sauce has thickened slightly. Stir in salt and pepper to taste. Strain the sauce or leave the vegetables in, according to your taste. Serve the carved meat with spoonfuls of the sauce.

Filet de Boeuf Périgourdine
Fillet of Beef with Périgueux Sauce

(*Serves 8*)

•

1 *whole fillet, about 7 pounds with fat*
1 *teaspoon salt*
½ *teaspoon freshly ground pepper*
¼ *cup* (½ *stick*) *sweet butter*

Trim the fillet of all the fat and sinews, including the "chain." Three and one-fourth to 3½ pounds of meat should be left. (Or, have the butcher trim it.)

Sprinkle the meat with salt and pepper. Melt the butter in a roasting pan over high heat and sear the meat on all sides (about 5 to 6 minutes). Place in a preheated 425° oven for 18 to 20 minutes, basting every 5 minutes. A meat thermometer should register approximately 115° internal temperature. Place the meat on a heated serving platter and allow it to rest for 10 to 15 minutes so the juices can settle, thus making carving easier and giving the meat a pink color throughout.

Sauce Périgueux

> ½ cup Madeira or dry sherry
> 2 cups brown gravy (homemade)
> ⅓ cup chopped black truffles
> juice from the truffles
> 1 tablespoon (approximately) arrowroot diluted
>   with ¼ cup cold water
> salt, depending on the saltiness of the brown
>   gravy
> freshly ground pepper
> 2 tablespoons sweet butter

Pour off the surplus fat from the roasting pan. Add the wine. Bring to a boil and stir to melt all the solidified juices. Stir in the brown gravy and bring to a boil. Strain into a saucepan. Add the truffles and their juices. If the sauce is very thin, add the arrowroot-and-water mixture to the hot sauce, stirring with a spoon. Add enough to reach the right consistency. Simmer for 5 to 6 minutes. Taste for seasoning. Finally, whip in the butter, bit by bit.

If the whole fillet is to be carved at the table, cover it with the sauce, reserving some on the side. If, on the other hand, it is to be carved in the kitchen, it is then served on individual dinner plates with the sauce poured *around* the slices.

Carbonnades de Boeuf Flamande
Carbonade of Beef Flamande

(*Serves 6 to 8*)

•

3 pounds sliced beef from chuck or round (slices
    should be about ¼ inch thick by 3 to 4
    inches in diameter)
½ stick sweet butter
1 tablespoon salt
1 teaspoon freshly ground pepper
½ cup flour
3 cups thickly sliced onions
⅓ teaspoon thyme
2 bay leaves
2 to 3 cans beer

Melt the butter in a frying pan. When it sizzles, add half the
meat, sprinkle with salt and pepper and brown lightly on all
sides. Stir in half of the flour and remove to a side tray. Repeat
the process with the remaining meat. Brown the onions in the
drippings of the meat. Place a layer of meat in an earthenware
kettle. Cover with onions. Then a layer of meat, then onions,
etc., until all the meat and onions are used. Put the thyme and
bay leaves on top and cover with beer. The meat should be
completely immersed. Bring to a boil, cover tightly, and simmer
for 1½ hours. It is usually served with boiled potatoes.

Choux Farcis
Small Stuffed Cabbages

(Serves 8)

•

Preparing the Leaves

Take 1 2-pound cabbage, Savoy or regular. Detach the leaves, trying not to break any. (You should have the heart left. Chop it finely and reserve. It should yield about 2 cups.) Plunge the leaves into boiling water, let come to a boil and cook for 5 minutes. Place the leaves under cold water. When they are cold, drain them in a colander. Place the leaves flat on the table and remove about 2 inches of the stem—the toughest part—of each leaf. You should have about 20 leaves. *If a leaf is too small, use it to patch bigger leaves, or use several small leaves together to form 1 stuffed cabbage.*

Stuffing

> 1½ *pounds chopped hamburger meat (it should*
> *not be too lean)*
> 5 *slices bacon, cut into small pieces*
> 1 *onion, chopped (¾ cup)*
> *reserved chopped cabbage heart*
> ¾ *cup water*
> 2 *eggs*
> 3 *to* 4 *cloves garlic*
> 1 *teaspoon salt*
> ½ *teaspoon ground black pepper*

Sauté the bacon in a large skillet until it is fried and has rendered all its fat. Add the onion to the bacon and sauté 1 minute. Add the chopped cabbage heart and the water and cook until all the liquid has evaporated and the mixture sizzles again (about 8 minutes). Transfer to a mixing bowl, add all remaining ingredients and mix thoroughly.

Braising

8 *slices bacon*
2 *medium carrots, peeled and sliced (1½ cups)*
1 *large onion, peeled and sliced (1½ to 2 cups, loose)*
½ *teaspoon crushed thyme (fresh is better)*
2 *bay leaves, broken into small pieces*
3 *large tomatoes, diced (about 2½ cups)*
2 *cups good brown gravy (see Basic Brown Sauce, page 31)*

Place about 2 ounces of stuffing on each leaf and fold the sides to make a nice neat package. Lay the bacon fat in an oven roasting pan (use a pan 10 inches by 12 inches by 2 inches deep). Sprinkle all remaining ingredients (except gravy) on top of the bacon and arrange the stuffed leaves side by side, with the folded side down, on top of this so they touch one another. Cover tightly with a piece of aluminum foil and cook in a preheated 375° oven for 2 hours. Remove the foil and pour the brown gravy on top of the cabbages. Place back in the oven for 30 minutes, uncovered. Then, arrange the cabbages on a serving platter. Taste the sauce, as it may need salt and pepper. Correct if necessary, then pour the sauce over the cabbages and serve immediately.

This dish is also excellent reheated.

Rognonnade de Veau Poêlée Matignon
Veal Roast Braised with Vegetables

(Serves 6 to 8)

•

1 loin of veal, about 4½ to 5 pounds oven-ready

You may prepare the roast yourself or ask the butcher to dress it. In any case, choose a pale rose meat with very white fat (*plume de veau* is the best grade of veal). The single loin of veal should be boned, trimmed of most fat, the tenderloin and the kidney placed back inside the loin instead of the bones, and the roast tied up with kitchen strings. Salt and pepper the roast with about ¼ teaspoon salt and ¼ teaspoon pepper.

½ stick (2 ounces) sweet butter
½ teaspoon salt
¼ teaspoon freshly ground white pepper
3 carrots (about 5 ounces), peeled and cut into
  a julienne*
2 leeks (the white part only), cut into a julienne
1 rib of celery, julienne
1 large, well-ripe tomato, peeled, seeded, and
  diced (about 1 cup) †

* *Julienne* refers to vegetables cut into long, thin, and narrow strips resembling hay. The vegetable may be shredded with a machine, but it looks nicer when cut by hand. To cut by hand, cut the vegetable in thin slices first. Then, stack the slices one on top of the other and cut into thin strips.

† Often, recipes require a pure pulp of fresh tomato. To peel and seed tomatoes, one can cut away the skin with a sharp paring knife retrenching as little flesh as possible. Slice the tomato in half and squeeze out the seeds. Tomatoes can also be plunged into boiling water for 20 to 30 seconds, cooled under cold water and peeled. The skin slides off easily.

2 cloves garlic, peeled, crushed, and chopped
¼ teaspoon crushed thyme (fresh is better)
¼ teaspoon crushed savory (fresh is better)
½ cup water

Melt the butter in a large casserole with a cover (it should be ovenproof). Cook the roast in the butter on medium heat until it is browned on all sides (about 12 minutes). Transfer the roast to a tray and add the carrots, leeks and celery to the casserole. Cook for 3 to 4 minutes on medium heat. Add the remaining ingredients to the casserole and cook slowly for 6 to 8 minutes. Let the mixture cool a few minutes.

1 cup dry white wine
1 tablespoon soft sweet butter

You need 1 large piece of *parchemin* (parchment) paper (waxed paper, although not as good, can be substituted). Lay the paper flat on the table and coat with the butter, using your fingers or a spatula. Spread half of the vegetable mixture on the paper, place the roast on top, and coat with the remaining vegetables. Fold the paper so that all the ingredients are secure inside. Fold the sides underneath. If your paper is not wide enough, place 2 overlapping strips side by side to have a wide piece. Place the wrapped roast carefully back in the casserole, pour the wine on top and bring to a boil on medium heat. Cover and cook in a preheated 375° oven for 1½ hours.

1½ tablespoons arrowroot
3 tablespoons dry sherry wine
salt and pepper to taste

Lift the roast, still wrapped, to a serving platter. Mix the arrowroot and the sherry together. Pour into the sauce, stirring with a large spoon, and bring to a boil stirring constantly. Salt and pepper to taste. Unwrap the roast, cut the strings off and add all the vegetables and the juices to the sauce. Bring to a boil. Slice the meat and serve with the sauce and the vegetables mixed together. Make sure that each guest gets a little piece of the veal kidney.

Jarret de Veau Provençale
Braised Veal Shank

(*Serves 6*)

•

2 *veal shanks* (*about 2 pounds each and 6 to 7
     inches long*), *cut across into 3 pieces each,
     with the bone*
1 *teaspoon salt*
1 *teaspoon freshly ground black pepper*
½ *cup all-purpose flour*
1 *stick sweet butter*
1 *cup water*

Sprinkle the shank pieces with salt and pepper and dredge with flour, shaking the pieces to remove excess flour. Melt the butter in 1 very large or 2 medium-sized skillets and place the veal pieces flat in the melted butter. Cook on medium to low heat for about 15 minutes, turning the pieces so they are browned on all sides. Transfer to a large casserole with a cover, pour the juices on top, and add the water to the skillet. Bring to a boil to melt the solidified juices and add to the veal.

2 *medium carrots, peeled and diced into a
     brunoise* (*¼-inch dices*) (*about 1 cup*)
3 *onions, peeled and coarsely chopped* (*1½
     cups*)

1 *leek, peeled, washed, and coarsely chopped*
    (1 cup)
1 *piece celery, diced small (½ cup)*
4 *tomatoes, cut into ½-inch dices (3 cups)*
1 *teaspoon salt*
½ *teaspoon freshly ground black pepper*
1 *cup dry white wine*
2 *bay leaves*
½ *teaspoon crushed thyme*

Add all the ingredients to the veal, bring to a boil, and simmer, covered, for 30 minutes.

4 *cloves garlic, peeled, crushed, and chopped*
    (1 tablespoon)

Add the garlic to the casserole and continue cooking for 20 minutes.

½ *cup fresh herbs, chopped (It may be a*
    mixture of any of the following: parsley,
    basil, chives, tarragon, chervil.)
½ *teaspoon grated orange rind*
1 *teaspoon grated lemon rind*

Add the above ingredients to the casserole and cook, uncovered, on medium heat for 25 minutes to reduce the juices. Let the dish "rest" for at least 30 minutes before serving.

Côtes de Veau aux Morilles
Veal Chops with Morels
(Serves 8)

•

2 ounces dried morels

Soak the morels in lukewarm water for 15 minutes. Lift them out of the water (*do not pour them into a sieve because the water will be sandy from the morels*). Change water and soak again for 15 minutes. Look to see if the stems need trimming. Squeeze the morels gently to extrude most of the water and cut the biggest into halves or quarters.

> *8 veal chops, lean and well-trimmed, about*
> *6 to 8 ounces each*
> *2 teaspoons salt*
> *1 teaspoon freshly ground white pepper*
> *2 tablespoons flour*
> *3 tablespoons sweet butter*
> *1 tablespoon vegetable oil*

Sprinkle the chops with salt and pepper and dust with the flour. Pat the chops to shake off the excess flour. Melt the butter in a large skillet or sauté pan (it should be large enough so that the chops do not overlap), add the oil and place the chops in the pan when the mixture is hot. Cook on medium heat for 7 minutes on each side. Cover and cook another 6 to 7 minutes on low fire.

> *2 tablespoons cognac*
> *½ cup dry white wine*
> *1¼ cups heavy cream*

½ *teaspoon salt*
½ *teaspoon freshly ground pepper*
1 *teaspoon flour*
1 *teaspoon butter*

Remove the chops to a serving platter and keep warm in a 180° oven. Place the skillet back on medium heat. Add the cognac and ignite. When the flames have died out, add the morels, wine, and mix with a wooden spoon so that all the coagulated juices melt. Cook 2 minutes. Add the cream, salt and pepper and bring to a boil. Mix the flour and butter to make a smooth paste (*beurre manié*), add to the pan and mix rapidly with a whisk to incorporate the mixture into the sauce. Taste for seasoning and add more salt and pepper if needed. Pour the sauce over the chops and serve immediately.

Fricadelles de Veau Smitane
Veal Patties with Sour Cream Sauce

(*Serves 6*)

•

Veal Patties

1¼ *pounds veal tenderloin, trimmed*
1¼ *cups heavy cream*
1½ *cups fresh white breadcrumbs (about 3*
    slices of white bread—trimmed, diced, and
    blended)
⅛ *teaspoon freshly grated nutmeg*
½ *teaspoon freshly ground white pepper*
1 *teaspoon salt*

You can have the meat ground by your butcher, but it is better if you chop it by hand with a big knife. Place the chopped meat in a clean vessel (not aluminum) over ice. The meat should be very cold. Mix ½ cup of the cream with ½ of the breadcrumbs to make a paste. Set aside. Start adding the remaining cream to the meat, 1 tablespoon at a time, beating with a wooden spatula after each addition to have the cream well incorporated into the meat. Keep adding the cream until it is all used. Add the nutmeg, pepper, and salt. *You will notice that the salt will tighten the mixture after it is added. This is why it is added only at the end.* Mix in the bread and cream mixture. Spread the remaining breadcrumbs on the table. Separate the mixture into 6 patties and flatten each portion into a round about 4 inches in diameter and ¾ inch thick. Dip into the breadcrumbs on both sides. Set aside.

Sauce

1 tablespoon sweet butter
½ cup finely chopped onion
¼ teaspoon crushed black peppercorns
1 bay leaf
⅓ cup white wine vinegar
1 teaspoon flour
1¼ cups heavy cream
¾ teaspoon salt

Melt the butter in a saucepan, add the onion, peppercorns, and bay leaf and sauté on low fire for about 8 minutes, until the onion is a golden color. Stir in the vinegar and reduce until the onions are just moist. Sprinkle with the flour, mix with a spoon and add the cream. Bring to a boil, stirring to avoid scorching. Add salt and reduce to about ¾ cup, until nice and smooth. Strain the sauce through a fine sieve and set aside.

3 tablespoons sweet butter
1½ tablespoons vegetable oil

Heat the butter and oil in a large skillet. When hot, place the *fricadelles* flat in the fat. Reduce heat to low and cook about 5 to 6 minutes on each side, until nicely browned.

Arrange on a serving platter and coat with the sauce. Serve immediately.

Escalopes de Veau Normande
Veal Scallopini with Cream, Calvados and Apples

(*Serves 6*)

•

This recipe calls for a rather large skillet. We tested it in a heavy paella pan, about 15 inches in diameter. Lacking a pan of that size, we suggest using 2 large skillets or even a heavy roasting pan and placing it over 2 burners.

> 12 *scallopini, ⅜ inch thick, not pounded* (*about*
>   *3½ to 4 inches in diameter*)
> 3 *medium-sized sweet apples* (*golden or red*
>   *Delicious are fine*)
> *juice of 2 lemons*
> 1 *teaspoon salt*
> 1 *teaspoon freshly ground pepper*
> ½ *cup flour*
> 4 *tablespoons* (½ *stick*) *sweet butter*
> 2 *tablespoons vegetable oil*
> ⅓ *cup* (*approximately*) *calvados or applejack*
> 1½ *cups heavy cream*

Peel and core the apples, then cut into small ½-inch cubes. Place in a bowl, add the lemon juice and mix thoroughly so the apples are well-coated. Set aside. Sprinkle the veal with salt and pepper, then flour. Shake off any excess. Heat the butter and oil in a large heavy skillet. When hot, add the veal, a few pieces at a time, and sauté until lightly browned on both sides (approximately 4 minutes on each side, over medium heat). When the veal is cooked, set aside in a warm place like a 180° oven. Add the apples and lemon juice and the calvados to the pan. Scrape up all the encrustations on the pan and cook over moderate heat, stirring frequently, for about 3 minutes. Add the cream and continue cooking until the mixture has turned to a rich ivory color. Reduce the heat and cook, stirring frequently, until the cream has reduced to about half and the sauce coats a spoon (almost 10 minutes). Taste for seasoning—you will probably need about ½ teaspoon of salt.

Do not cook the pieces of veal with the sauce. Further cooking will toughen the meat. Arrange the veal attractively on a heated platter and spoon the sauce over all.

Paupiettes de Veau Lyonnaise
Paupiettes of Veal Lyonnaise

(*Serves 6 to 8*)

•

A *paupiette* is always a thin piece of meat or fish, stuffed, rolled, secured with a string or a toothpick and braised. They are sometimes called headless birds—*oiseaux sans têtes*, because the neat little packages resemble stuffed quails or woodcocks.

The most delicate part of the recipe is to pound the scallopini properly. The meat should be without fat or gristle and is usually cut from the top sirloin or the loin. Each piece, approximately 2¼ to 2½ ounces, is pounded into a 6- to 8-inch wide, paper-thin slice. If you do not feel confident enough or if you do not have a good meat pounder, ask your butcher to prepare the scallopini for you.

> 8 pounded veal scallopini

Stuffing

> 1 pound ground pork shoulder
> 1 tablespoon sweet butter
> ½ cup chopped mushrooms (3 mushrooms)
> ½ cup chopped onion
> ¼ cup chopped celery
> 1 clove garlic, crushed and chopped
> 2 tablespoons chopped parsley
> ½ teaspoon salt
> ¼ teaspoon freshly ground pepper

In a saucepan, melt the butter, add the mushrooms and cook for 1 minute. Add the onion, celery and sauté for 2 minutes, remove from the heat and stir in the remaining ingredients.

Stuff each scallopini with 2 tablespoons of stuffing, roll into a little package and secure with string.

> 4 tablespoons sweet butter
> 1 pound onions, thinly sliced
> 3 cloves garlic, crushed and chopped
> 1 cup dry white wine
> 1 teaspoon salt
> ½ teaspoon freshly ground pepper
> 2 tablespoons water
> 1 teaspoon arrowroot
> 1 tablespoon chopped parsley

Melt 2 tablespoons of butter in a large casserole that has a cover. Brown the *paupiettes* on all sides and set aside. In a skillet, melt the remaining butter, add the onions and sauté for

3 to 4 minutes. Add the garlic and sauté 1 minute longer. Pour the onion mixture over the meat, deglaze the skillet with the wine and add to the meat with the salt, pepper and bring to a boil. Simmer, covered, on low heat for 25 minutes. With a slotted spoon, transfer the meat to a platter and remove the strings. Mix the water and the arrowroot together and stir into the braising liquid. Bring to a boil, add more pepper and salt if needed, pour the sauce over the meat, sprinkle with the chopped parsley and serve immediately.

Cervelles de Veau Provençale
Veal Brains Provence Style

(*Serves 4 to 6*)

•

Poaching the Brains

>2 *brains, fresh* (*approximately 1½ pounds*)

Soak in cold water for 1 to 2 hours. Then pull off the thin membrane (skin) covering the brain. Soak the brains in very cold water for another hour. This whitens and firms the meat.

>3 *cups water*
>⅓ *cup wine vinegar*
>1 *cup thinly sliced onions* (*about 2 onions*)
>2 *bay leaves*
>½ *teaspoon dried thyme*
>⅓ *cup* (*small bunch*) *parsley*
>2 *tablespoons crushed black peppercorns*
>1 *teaspoon salt*

Place all ingredients (except the brains) in a kettle and bring to a boil. Cook for 5 minutes on high heat. Add the brains, bring to a boil and simmer for 10 minutes. Remove from the heat and cool in the broth. *It is important to cool the brains in the broth as they will take on more flavor.*

Sauce

> 4 *tomatoes, peeled, seeded, and diced (approxi-*
> *mately 2½ cups)*
> 2 *tablespoons sweet butter*
> 1 *tablespoon olive oil*
> 1 *cup chopped onions (1 large or 2 medium*
> *onions)*
> ½ *teaspoon salt*
> ½ *teaspoon freshly ground black pepper*
> 3 *cloves garlic, peeled, crushed, and chopped*
> *fine (1 tablespoon)*
> 1 *cup pitted black olives, cut into pieces*
> 1 *tablespoon chopped fresh tarragon*

Melt the butter and add the oil and onions. Cook for 2 minutes on medium to high heat. Add the tomatoes, salt, pepper, garlic, and simmer, covered, for 10 minutes. Add the black olives and chopped tarragon and cook for 2 more minutes.

> ½ *teaspoon salt*
> ½ *cup flour*
> ½ *stick sweet butter*
> 1 *tablespoon oil*
> 2 *tablespoons fresh chopped parsley*

Remove the brains from the broth and dry on a paper towel. Separate the brains into halves. Split each half, sprinkle with the salt and dip into the flour. Pat the pieces to take off any excess flour. Melt half the butter in a large frying pan, add the oil and when the butter-oil mixture is hot, add the brains. You will probably be able to cook only half of the brains at a time. Cook 2 to 3 minutes on each side, until nicely browned, over medium heat. Arrange the tomato mixture on a large serving platter and place the pieces of brains on top when they are ready. Melt the remaining butter in a clean pan until it turns into a hazelnut color. Pour over the brains, sprinkle with the parsley and serve immediately.

Cervelles au Beurre Noir
Veal Brains with Black Butter

(*Serves 6*)

•

3 *calves' brains* (*about 2¾ pounds*)
1½ *cups sliced onion*
1 *tablespoon crushed black peppercorns*
1½ *teaspoons salt*
3 *bay leaves*
¼ *teaspoon thyme*
⅓ *cup red wine vinegar*
6 *cups water*

Place the brains in a pot under cold running water for 2 hours. Turn off the water and add 1 tablespoon of salt and leave the brains in the salted water for 1 more hour. This soaking will make the removal of the membrane easier. Slide your fingers into the crevices of the brains, pulling out the brown membranes. Some people do not bother to remove the membrane. If it is left on the brains will be darker in color when cooked. The membrane is a little tough, however, this will not change the taste.

Place all of the above ingredients, except the brains, in a casserole and bring to a boil. Simmer for 15 minutes. Add the brains to the boiling broth and allow to simmer slowly for 10 minutes. Remove from heat and *let the brains cool off in the broth*. This is the basic technique for poaching brains. They may be kept in the poaching liquid, refrigerated, for up to 2 weeks.

>   *salt, pepper and flour*
>   *1¼ sticks sweet butter (6 ounces)*
>   *4 tablespoons vegetable oil*
>   *3 tablespoons drained capers*
>   *2 tablespoons vinegar*
>   *3 tablespoons chopped parsley*

Halve the brains by cutting through with a knife. Split each half through the middle. You will have 12 pieces. Coat each piece with salt and fresh pepper. Dip in flour and pat the pieces to remove any excess flour. Use 2 large skillets. Place 1 tablespoon of butter and 2 tablespoons of oil in each skillet. When the mixture is hot, place the brains in flat. *Do not overlap.* Brown about 5 minutes on each side over medium heat. The pieces should be crusty and brown. Transfer to a serving platter; sprinkle with the capers. Melt the remaining butter in a clean skillet until it is black. *The butter should be smoking and be literally burnt.* Pour over the brains and immediately pour the vinegar into the hot skillet, shake the pan for a few seconds and pour this over the brains. (You will only have a few drops left.) Sprinkle with parsley and serve immediately.

You may also serve the brains heated from the broth, then placed on a platter, adding the black butter, capers and parsley as indicated, omitting the pan frying.

Pâte de Cervelles
Veal Brains in Pastry

(*Serves 6 to 8*)

•

⅓ recipe Puff Paste (*see page 52*)
3 *calves' brains, cooked as indicated* (see Veal
    Brains with Black Butter, *page 182*)
1½ *cups concentrated brown sauce* (*this may
    be done by reducing 3 cups by half*) (*see
    Basic Brown Sauce, page 31*)
1 egg, beaten (*for egg wash*)
2 *onions, sliced very thin* (*about 2 cups*)
2 *tablespoons sweet butter*
1½ *teaspoons salt*
⅛ *teaspoon freshly ground pepper*
⅓ *cup water*
1 *clove garlic, peeled, crushed, and chopped*
1 *eggplant* (*about ¾ pound*)
½ *cup vegetable oil*

Place the onions, butter, ½ teaspoon salt, pepper and water in a saucepan. Bring to a boil and let boil on medium heat until water has completely evaporated and the onions start sizzling in the butter. Brown lightly for 2 minutes, add the garlic and cook another 30 seconds. Set the mixture aside.

Peel the eggplant and cut lengthwise into ½-inch thick slices. You will have about 8 to 10 slices. Slash each slice with the point of a knife and sprinkle on both sides with the remaining salt. Place the slices flat on a toweled surface and put a tray on top weighted with a heavy object. This drains the bitter liquid out of the eggplant. *Eggplant has a tendency to absorb a lot of oil while frying; pressing the slices with salt exudes the liquid and the eggplant won't use as much oil.* Fry each slice in the oil about 1½ minutes on each side and drain on a paper towel.

⅓ cup freshly chopped mixed herbs (A mixture of chervil, chives or parsley will do. Do not use dry herbs.)

Roll the puff pastry dough into a rectangle 16 inches long by 12 inches wide. The dough should be rolled very thin, not thicker than ⅛ to ¼ inch thick. Place the dough on a wet cookie sheet. Leaving a 2-inch border from the edge of the rolled dough, arrange half of the eggplant slices down one side. Spread half the onion mixture on top of the eggplant and sprinkle with half of the chopped fresh herbs. Drain the brains from the broth and cut into large slices. Arrange on top of the eggplant, onion, etc. Sprinkle ½ cup of cold brown sauce on top of the brains. Top with the remaining onion, herbs, and finally arrange the remaining slices of eggplant on top. Brush the inside of the dough with egg wash 2 inches from the edge. Fold the dough over the brains, eggplant, etc., so that both edges meet on one side. Press so that both sides are well sealed together. Trim with a knife. Brush the loaf with egg wash and mark with the point of a knife. Make a hole on the top to let steam escape. Cook in a 375° oven for 35 minutes or until well browned. Slice and serve each slice with 1 tablespoon of the remaining hot brown sauce.

Ris de Veau au Madère
Sweetbreads with Madeira Sauce

(Serves 4 to 6)

•

When buying sweetbreads, insist on getting the large round chunks; these will be the juicier and more tasty pieces. Soak in cold water for 2 to 3 hours to whiten the meat. Cover with cold water, bring to a boil and let boil 1 minute. Place under cold running water until the meat is cold. Pull out the sinews—rubberlike pieces adhering to the meat. Place a towel on a flat tray, the sweetbreads on top, cover with another towel. Then, place a flat tray or a platter on top and press down by putting weight on the tray. Three or 4 pounds suffice (canned goods or a pot of water may be used as weight). *Pressing the sweetbread extrudes the undesirable pinky liquid and gives a white and compact sweetbread.* Keep pressed for a few hours. This can be done the day before.

> 2¼ pounds sweetbreads (about 2 pounds after
>   blanched and pressed)
> 2 tablespoons sweet butter

Melt the butter in a heavy casserole that has a cover. Sauté the sweetbreads for 5 to 8 minutes on medium or low heat so that they poach in the butter but do not take on any brown color.

> 1 small carrot, diced fine (¼ cup)
> 1 white of a leek, sliced fine (½ cup)
> 1 small onion, chopped (¼ cup)
> 1 large tomato, peeled, seeded, and chopped
>   (about ¾ cup)

1 *bay leaf*
1 *teaspoon thyme*
½ *cup good Xeres or Madeira wine (although*
   not as good, sherry is a substitute)
½ *teaspoon salt*
¼ *teaspoon freshly ground white pepper*

Add all ingredients to the sweetbreads except the wine. Cook for 4 to 5 minutes on medium heat and then add the wine. Cover and simmer slowly for 10 minutes. Add the salt and pepper.

1½ *cups homemade brown gravy*
1 *or 2 tablespoons arrowroot diluted in cold*
   water
salt and pepper to taste
2 *tablespoons sweet butter*
1 *tablespoon chopped parsley*

Add the brown gravy to the sweetbreads and place in a pre-heated 400° oven, uncovered, for 20 minutes. *Baste every 5 minutes. The sweetbreads will develop a nice golden color.* Remove the meat from the casserole and arrange on a serving platter. If the sauce is too thin—depending on your brown gravy and your personal liking, thicken it with the arrowroot by pouring in the diluted cornstarch with one hand and stirring with a spoon in the other. Taste for seasoning; you will probably need more salt and pepper. *Again, this depends on the seasoning of the brown gravy and how much the sauce has reduced during the cooking process.* Add the butter, bit by bit, stirring with a spoon to have it blend with the sauce. You may add a bit more wine if you feel the taste is not pronounced enough. Spoon the sauce over the sweetbreads, sprinkle with parsley and serve immediately.

Croûte de Ris de Veau à l'Estragon
Sweetbreads in Pastry

(*Serves 8 to 10*)

•

1 *pound sweetbreads*
4 *tablespoons sweet butter*
⅓ *cup coarsely chopped carrots*
½ *cup finely diced onion*
1 *medium-sized tomato, diced (about ¾ cup)*
½ *teaspoon freshly chopped garlic*
¼ *cup coarsely chopped parsley*
⅛ *teaspoon dried thyme*
2 *bay leaves*
¼ *teaspoon salt*
½ *teaspoon freshly ground pepper*
1½ *cups brown sauce (see Basic Brown Sauce,
    page 31)*

Place the sweetbreads in a saucepan and add cold water to cover. Bring to a boil, simmer for 1 minute and drain. Run under cold water until well-chilled. Pull out any sinews which adhere to the meat. Preheat the oven to 400°. Melt the butter in a saucepan and add the sweetbreads and the other ingredients. Cook, stirring occasionally, about 2 minutes. Cover with waxed paper and place in the oven. Bake 10 minutes. Add ½ cup brown sauce and bake about 15 minutes longer with the waxed paper removed. Remove the sweetbreads. Put the sauce through a sieve, pushing with the back of a wooden spoon to extract as much liquid as possible from the solids. There should be about 1 cup. Pour this into a saucepan and reduce to ½ cup. Cut the sweetbreads into 1-inch chunks; there should be about 8 to 10 pieces. Reduce the oven heat to 350° for the next step.

1 *recipe Pâte à Pâté (see page 51)*
1 *pound ground pork*
½ *pound ground veal*
1 *tablespoon butter*
1 *cup sliced mushrooms (5 to 6 mushrooms,*
     depending on size)
10 *shallots, peeled and thinly sliced (about ½*
     cup)
2 *black truffles, thinly sliced (optional)*
2 *teaspoons salt*
¾ *teaspoon freshly ground white pepper*
2 *tablespoons cognac*
10 *thin little slices of ham, about 3 inches wide*
     by 4 to 5 inches long

Melt the butter in a saucepan and sauté the mushrooms until slightly browned (about 4 to 5 minutes). Put the pork and veal in a mixing bowl and add the shallots, truffles, salt, pepper, and cognac. Blend well and add the hot sauce from the first step. Stir to blend thoroughly.

Roll the pastry into a circle and fit it into an 8-cup round mold, letting the dough hang over the edge about 1 inch all around. Wrap each piece of sweetbreads with a piece of ham. Add ⅓ of the pork mixture and arrange some of the sweetbread pieces over that with some mushrooms. Add another ⅓ of the pork mixture, the remaining sweetbreads and mushrooms and a fine layer of the remaining pork mixture. Pat down and smooth over. Fold the edges of the pastry over the mixture and brush with water. Roll out a piece of dough just big enough to cover the top of the pâté, and apply so that it overlaps and sticks to the dough already covering the pâté. (Scraps of dough may be rolled out and cut into fancy shapes for decoration.) Brush with water. If cut-outs of pastry are used, apply them and brush with water. Cut a small hole in the center to allow steam to escape. Bake on a tray in a preheated 325° oven for 1 hour and 45 minutes, until it registers 160° internal temperature. Let rest 30 minutes before unmolding. Serve lukewarm to hot with sauce.

Sauce

> 1 *cup brown sauce* (*from Step I*)
> 1 *tablespoon finely chopped fresh tarragon*
> *salt and pepper to taste*
> 1 *tablespoon sweet butter*

Bring the brown sauce to a boil, add the fresh tarragon and let simmer for 2 to 3 minutes. Add salt and pepper if necessary, and 1 tablespoon of sweet butter in bits, shaking the pan so that the butter blends well with the sauce. Slice the pâté and serve each slice with a tablespoon of the sauce.

Selle d'Agneau Provençale
Saddle of Lamb Provençale

(*Serves 6 to 8*)

•

> 1 4- *to 6-pound saddle of lamb, trimmed and*
> *oven-ready* (*it should be trimmed so that*
> *practically all the fat is removed*)
> *salt*
> *freshly ground pepper*
> ½ *cup fresh breadcrumbs* (1 *piece firm bread*
> *makes about* ½ *cup breadcrumbs*)
> 4 to 5 *sprigs parsley, chopped fine*
> 1 *shallot, peeled and chopped fine*
> 2 *cloves garlic, peeled and chopped fine*
> ½ *cup* (1 *stick*) *sweet butter, melted*
> 1 *cup brown beef gravy*

Rub the saddle all over with salt and pepper. Then tie it cross-wise in 3 places. Place in a roasting pan and roast in a preheated 425° oven for 25 to 30 minutes, basting every 10 minutes.

Meanwhile, mix the breadcrumbs, parsley, shallot, and garlic together. Melt the butter in a skillet and add the mixture. Mix so that the butter moistens the breadcrumb mixture well. At this point, remove the strings from the saddle and pat the crumb mixture on top. If necessary use some of the fat from the pan so all the bread is thoroughly moistened. Return the meat to the oven for 10 to 12 minutes longer or until nicely browned.

Lift the saddle to a heated serving platter. Pour off any fat in the pan, add the beef gravy and bring to a boil. Strain into a heated sauceboat. Serve with the meat carved at the table.

Note: The meat should "rest" for at least 15 minutes after it comes out of the oven to have a nice pink color throughout. It may be kept in a very low oven or on top of the pilot on the stove.

Noisettes d'Agneau Monégasque
Lamb Chops with Eggplant and Tomato Fondue
(*Serves 6 to 8*)

•

2 *single racks of lamb, oven-ready**
3 *to 4 large ripe tomatoes*
1 *tablespoon sweet butter*
½ *cup vegetable oil*
1 *tablespoon chopped onion*
1 *clove garlic, peeled, crushed, and chopped*
salt
freshly ground pepper
1 *tablespoon tomato paste*
1 *large eggplant*
1 *tablespoon flour*

* The racks are trimmed so that only a thin layer of fat remains on the meat. The ribs are trimmed off approximately 2 to 2½ inches above the center of the chop.

Dip the tomatoes in boiling water for 30 to 40 seconds, then cool under cold running water. Slide the skin off, cut in half, and press out the seeds. Chop coarsely.

Place 1 tablespoon of butter and 1 tablespoon of the oil in a heavy skillet. Add the onion and sauté it for 1 minute without allowing it to brown. Add the tomatoes, garlic, salt and pepper. Sauté for 5 to 6 minutes. Stir in the tomato paste and cook another 3 to 4 minutes. Set aside and keep warm.

Trim the eggplant on both ends, then cut into 6 thick slices with the skin on. *Sprinkle with salt and place the slices flat on a board. Place a cookie sheet on top of the slices with a weight on top to "bleed" the eggplant. This takes out the bitter liquid and prevents the eggplant from absorbing too much oil during cooking.* Pepper and flour the slices. Heat the remaining oil and fry the slices until lightly browned on both sides. Place in a shallow baking pan in a preheated 325° oven for 10 minutes to finish cooking.

Sprinkle the racks of lamb with salt and pepper. Place, fat side up, in a preheated 450° oven for 18 to 20 minutes. After 10 minutes, turn the racks over. Allow the meat to "rest" in a lukewarm place, such as a 180° oven or on top of the stove over the pilot, for 10 minutes before carving.

> ½ *cup brown gravy*
> 2 *tablespoons sweet butter*
> 1 *cup black Greek olives*
> 2 *tablespoons chopped parsley*
> 1 *tablespoon chopped fresh tarragon*

Heat the brown gravy in a saucepan; melt the sweet butter in a skillet until it is a nutty-brown color and set aside. Cut the racks of lamb into individual chops and arrange in the center of a large platter. Surround the chops with the cooked eggplant slices and pour a couple of tablespoons of the tomato mixture over the eggplant. Imbed a few olives in the tomato and sprinkle with the parsley and tarragon. Pour the brown gravy around the lamb chops and the melted butter over the eggplant. Serve immediately.

Porc Braisé aux Marrons
Braised Pork with Chestnuts

(Serves 8)

•

Peeling Chestnuts

When buying chestnuts, watch for little holes which indicate wormy chestnuts. With the point of a sharp paring knife, score each chestnut on both sides. The incisions help the skin release during cooking. Put on a flat cookie tray (the chestnuts should not overlap) and place in a preheated 400° oven for 30 minutes. Remove from the oven and, using a towel to avoid burning your hands, peel the chestnuts. Both inner and outer skins should come off. Discard the bad ones. You may lose up to ⅓ of the chestnuts. *If you don't want to go to the trouble of peeling chestnuts use the dried chestnuts rather than the canned ones.*

> 1 *oven-ready pork roast, about 6 pounds (use*
> *the shoulder or bottom round)*
> 1 *teaspoon salt*
> ½ *teaspoon freshly ground black pepper*
> 2 *onions, coarsely sliced (about 1½ cups)*
> 1 *pound peeled chestnuts*

3 rutabagas (sometimes called yellow turnips),
    about 3½ pounds
6½ cups water

Sprinkle the meat with the salt and pepper. Place in a large heavy kettle, fat side down. Add ½ cup of water and place on medium heat. Cook covered for 15 minutes. Uncover the meat and keep cooking until all the liquid has evaporated and the meat starts to brown. Brown all around. (This takes about 12 minutes.) Add the onions, 5 cups of water, cover and cook on medium heat for 1 hour. Add the chestnuts and cook covered for another hour. Meanwhile, peel the rutabagas and cut them into 2- to 2½-inch chunks. Shape the pieces with a small knife so that they are equal in size and cook uniformly. You will have about 2½ pounds left. Add the rutabagas, another cup of water and cook another 45 minutes covered. Taste for seasonings. It probably will need salt and pepper. By this time there should not be much liquid left. Remove the roast to a serving platter and using a slotted spoon, scoop out the chestnuts and rutabagas and place around the meat. *Tip the kettle to one side so that all the juices accumulate in one corner and skim out as much fat as you can.* If you have less than 1 cup of juice left, add ¾ to 1 cup of water to the kettle and boil on high heat for 1 or 2 minutes to melt the solidified juices and to emulsify the juices together. Pour over the meat or in a sauceboat and serve immediately.

Côtes de Porc Charcutière
Pork Chops with Mustard and Pickles

(*Serves 6*)

•

6 *pork chops, approximately 8 to 10 ounces each,*
   or lean pork steaks (from the shoulder or
   the leg), 6 to 8 ounces each
salt and pepper
2 *tablespoons sweet butter*

Sprinkle the meat with salt and pepper on both sides. Melt the butter in a large skillet and add the pork chops. *They should be placed in the skillet so that they don't overlap.* Cook for about 8 minutes on medium heat. Turn the chops with a fork, cover, and cook another 10 minutes on low heat. *You should cover the meat at this stage so that it absorbs moisture and becomes tender.* Remove the meat and arrange on a serving platter. Keep warm.

1 *onion, peeled and chopped fine (about ⅓ cup)*
1 *large or 2 small cloves garlic, peeled, crushed,*
   and chopped
2 *tablespoons chopped fresh chives (if unavail-*
   able, use parsley)
½ *cup dry white wine*
1 *tablespoon tomato paste*
1 *tablespoon French mustard*
½ *cup brown gravy (see Basic Brown Sauce,*
   page 31)
15 to 18 *small sour gherkins* (cornichons),
   sliced thin

After you have removed the meat from the skillet, pour out all the fat but about 2 tablespoons. Add the onion, garlic, and chives to the skillet and sauté for about 1 to 2 minutes. Add the wine and let it boil down until there is only 2 to 3 tablespoons of liquid left. Add the tomato paste, the mustard, and the brown gravy, bring to a boil and simmer for 2 minutes. Taste for seasonings (you might have to add salt and pepper). Add the *cornichons* and pour over the meat. Serve immediately. Excellent with plain fried potatoes.

Grenadins de Porc Normande
Pork Chops with Cream and Calvados

(*Serves 6*)

•

6 *individual loin pork chops, boned and tied,*
  about 10 ounces each (The chops should
  be tied if the chop is composed of the loin
  and tenderloin. After it is boned it separates
  and should be secured with a string.)
1 *package (12-ounce size) large pitted prunes*
2 *tablespoons sweet butter*
1 *teaspoon salt*
1 *teaspoon freshly ground white pepper*
2 *shallots or green onion bulbs, chopped*
  (1 tablespoon)
2 *tablespoons calvados (applejack)*
½ *cup chicken broth*
1 *cup heavy cream*
1 *tablespoon flour*
juice of ½ lemon (about 1 tablespoon)

Place the prunes in a saucepan. Cover with cold water and bring to a boil. Take off the heat, cover, and allow to cool in the juices.

Melt 1 tablespoon of the butter in a large heavy skillet.* Sprinkle the chops on both sides with salt and pepper. Cook each chop 10 minutes on each side, on medium to high heat, then place on a warm platter. Keep warm in a 160° oven.

Pour most of the fat from the pan, add the shallots and cook 1 minute. Add the calvados and the chicken broth. Bring to a boil. Add the cream and bring to a boil again. Cook for 1 minute. Mix the flour into the remaining butter to make a *beurre manié*. Add to the sauce, bit by bit, whipping hard with a wire whisk. Cook 5 to 6 minutes on low heat. Taste for seasoning and add salt and pepper if needed. Stir in the lemon juice, then strain through a fine sieve.

Place 2 prunes on top of each *grenadin* and arrange the remainder around the meat. Coat generously with the sauce and serve at once.

Note: If the sauce seems too thick, add a little more chicken broth to thin it. If it is too thin, reduce a few more minutes until it reaches the right consistency.

Cayettes de Cochon
Pork Dumplings with Spinach
(Serves 6 to 8)

•

The *cayette* or *caillette* is a kind of sausage made with pork, pork liver, and some greens. In some parts of France cabbage is used, in Lyon we use *blettes* (Swiss chard), and in Dauphine,

---

* Be sure that the skillet is large enough to accommodate the 6 chops. If not, use 2 skillets. Be sure the meat cooks slowly or it will be tough and dry.

spinach. The mixture of meat, greens, and seasonings is formed into patties and each patty is wrapped in a piece of caul fat (*crépinette* in French). The caul fat is a very thin, beautifully lacy, membranous part of the peritoneum. Even though it is readily available in France, it is not in the United States (especially outside New York). The little meat patties are arranged in neat rows and cooked in the oven. They are sold cold in French *charcuterie* and may be eaten as is or reheated in the oven and served with mashed or fried potatoes. If caul fat is available use it, however, it can be omitted in this recipe for those who cannot obtain it.

1 *pound fresh ground pork*
1 *package fresh spinach* (*usually 10 ounces*)
½ *cup water*
1 *medium leek, peeled, washed, thinly sliced,
    with most of the green removed* (*about ¾
    cup*)
2 *tablespoons chopped celery stalk*
2 *tablespoons chopped parsley*
2 *cloves garlic, peeled, crushed, and chopped fine*
3 *ounces pork liver or 2 chicken livers, cleaned
    and chopped*
3 *tablespoons flour*
2 *tablespoons red wine*
1½ *teaspoons salt*
1 *teaspoon freshly ground black pepper*

Wash the spinach under cold water and chop it very coarsely. Place in a pan with ½ cup of water, bring to a boil and cook covered for 5 minutes. Add the sliced leek (*when washing the leek be sure to split it open with a knife because it is usually sandy in the middle*), the celery, parsley, and garlic and cook another 5 minutes on medium heat. The water should have completely evaporated by that time. Remove from the heat and add the pork, liver, flour, wine, salt and pepper. Mix carefully.

Divide it into 10 meatballs and wrap them in the caul fat, if available. Place the patties in a large skillet approximately 10 inches in diameter. Place in a preheated 400° oven for 30 minutes. They should have an internal temperature of 160°. Discard the fat accumulated in the pan. Serve the patties immediately. The patties can also be eaten cold with French mustard, *cornichons* (small sour gherkins), and crusty French bread.

Pâté de Foie en Brioche
Pork Liver Pâté in Brioche

(*Serves 8*)

•

2 *tablespoons sweet butter*
1½ *cups chopped onion*
1 *small clove garlic, peeled, crushed, and*
    chopped fine
¼ *teaspoon crushed thyme (fresh if possible)*
¾ *pound pork liver, ground very fine*
½ *pound ground pork*
1 *whole egg*
1 *egg yolk*
⅓ *cup dry white wine*
1 *tablespoon salt*
1 *teaspoon freshly ground white pepper*

Melt the butter in a saucepan, add the onion and sauté for 5 minutes without letting the onion brown. Add the garlic, thyme and cook for ½ minute. In a bowl, mix all the remaining ingredients with the sautéed onion until well mixed. Pour the mixture into a round mold—a charlotte mold is good—and place the mold in a double boiler. Cook in a 325° oven for 2 hours. Remove the mold from the *bain-marie* and when cool enough to handle, unmold the pâté by turning upside down on a tray. Some fat and juices will run. Dry the pâté with paper towels.

> ½ recipe Brioche Dough (see page 48)
> 1 egg, beaten (for egg wash)

Flour your board very lightly. With your hands, spread the dough so that the center is about ½ inch thick. Brush the dough with the egg wash. Place the lukewarm pâté in the middle (on the thinnest part) and fold the dough so that it joins on top of the pâté. Press all the edges together so that they do not separate during cooking. Butter a mold or a cheesecake pan (about 8 to 9 inches in diameter by 3 inches deep) and place the pâté and dough in it upside down. *The edges should be on the bottom and the thin part on top. This is important because the pâté will sink a little bit during cooking. It is also important that the pâté be lukewarm. This will prevent the dough from separating from the pâté during cooking.* Brush with egg wash and let the dough rise for about 30 minutes in a lukewarm place. Do not let it rise for a longer period; the dough should just start to "work up" when it goes into the oven. Cook in a preheated 400° oven for about 30 minutes. Let the brioche rest about 5 minutes before unmolding. Place it on a tray (you may line the tray with a towel) and cut at the table. Serve plain or with a Périgueux, Bordelaise, or mushroom sauce.

Boudins Noirs aux Pommes
Blood Sausage with Apples

(*Serves 8 to 10*)

•

The most difficult part of making *boudins* is finding the pork blood. Calf blood is only a fair substitute and beef blood, readily available, will not work at all. There are many regional recipes for *boudins*—with leek in Ardèche, pork head in Alsace, spinach in the Creuse, chestnut in Berry, and apple in Bresse—each region claiming to have the best and the original.

> ½ *stick sweet butter*
> 2½ *pounds onions (about 10 to 12 medium*
>   *onions), peeled and sliced very thin (about*
>   *8 cups)*
> 1 *cup water*
> 2 *teaspoons salt*
> 1 *teaspoon freshly ground white pepper*
> 1 *teaspoon Spice Parisienne**
> 1 *teaspoon fresh chopped savory (if available)*
> 10 *ounces leaf lard cut into small ¼-inch dices*
> ¾ *cup heavy cream*
> 1 *pint fresh pork blood*
> *hog casing, ready to be used (see page 100,*
>   *Saucisson de Campagne)*

Melt the butter in a skillet, add the onion and water and cook on high heat until all the water has evaporated (about 10 to 12 minutes). By this time the onion should be cooked. Remove from the heat, add the salt, pepper, spices, savory, and leaf lard.

---

* Spice Parisienne, called *quatre épices* in France, is usually a mixture of pepper, nutmeg, cloves, and cinnamon or ginger.

Mix and let cool to lukewarm. Mix in the cream and blood. Using a funnel, pour the mixture into the casing. When all the mixture has been used, you may cook the *boudins* in a large kettle and pour boiling water on top until the water reaches about 2 inches above the *boudins*. Poach on low heat (do not let the water go above 180° or the casing will burst) for about 30 minutes. By this time the *boudins* will rise to the surface of the water and when punctured with a tiny needle, only a small amount of the mixture will run out of the casing; then the running will stop. Remove the *boudins* from the water to a tray and cool to room temperature. Cover and refrigerate. *Yield:* About 12 pieces.

Serve 1 piece of *boudins* as a first course or 2 pieces as a main course. For 6 pieces of *boudins:*

> 3 *red or golden Delicious apples, peeled, cored,*
>   *and cut into ¾-inch chunks*
> 5 *tablespoons sweet butter*
> 1 *tablespoon sugar*
> ¼ *teaspoon salt*

Melt 3 tablespoons of butter in a skillet, add the apples and cook on medium heat for 4 to 5 minutes or until all the liquid rendered by the fruit evaporates and the slices start to brown. Add the sugar and salt and continue sautéing for a few minutes until nicely browned. Meanwhile, melt the remaining butter in a heavy skillet, prick the *boudins* 5 or 6 times with a regular fork, and cook in butter on low heat for 8 to 10 minutes until nicely crisp and very hot. Arrange on a platter with the apples on the side and serve immediately.

Jambon en Croûte au Madère
Ham in Crust with Madeira Sauce

(Serves 12 to 15)

•

1 *ham, about 12 pounds (buy a fully cooked*
ham with bone and skin)

Place the ham in a large kettle and cover with cold water. Bring to a boil slowly and simmer slowly for 1 hour and 45 minutes to 2 hours. (*There is a small bone parallel to the big bone of the shank. It should come out when pulled. If so, the cooking is right.*) Let the ham cool in the liquid. This step may be done the day before you plan to use the ham.

> ¾ *cup Madeira wine or dry sherry*
> 2 *cups brown gravy (see Basic Brown Sauce,*
> *page 31)*
> 2 *tablespoons sugar*
> 1 *tablespoon arrowroot or cornstarch*
> *salt and pepper to taste, according to the*
> *saltiness of the brown gravy and the ham*

Remove the ham from the water. Trim the skin and the fat, leaving just a thin layer of fat about ¼ inch thick. Trim around the bone near the shank to have the bone sticking out about 2½ to 3 inches. Remove the flat hipbone opposite the shank on the bottom side of the ham. Place the ham, fat side up, in a roasting pan. Add the wine, brown gravy, and sprinkle the ham with the sugar. Place in a preheated 500° oven for 35 to 45 minutes, until the top is nicely glazed and brown. Place the ham on a carving board until cool enough to handle. Pour all the liquid in a saucepan. Mix the arrowroot with ¼ cup cold water and add to the sauce, stirring constantly. Bring to a boil, add salt and pepper if needed, and strain the sauce. Set aside, covering the top with plastic wrap to prevent a skin from forming.

Carve the ham until you have the bone completely exposed. Be sure that as you carve the slices you place them in order next to you on the table. When carved, place all the slices back on the bone, remaking the ham in its original form.

> 1 recipe *Pâte à Pâté* (see page 51)
> 1 egg, beaten (for egg wash)

Divide the dough in half. Roll out one half, not too thin (it should be almost ¼ inch thick), except at the edges, which should be very thin. Place the ham, sliced side up, on the dough and bring the dough up around the ham so that it clings to the meat. It will wrap about half of the ham. Roll the remaining dough out ⅛ inch thick. Wet the dough on one side with water and place on top of the ham so that it covers it and overlaps the first dough. Trim the edge if it hangs too far down. It should come at least ¾ of the way down the ham. Press both layers of dough together. Roll the trimmed-off dough to make a long flat strip about 1 inch wide. Wet on one side and place on top of the ham in a circle to imitate the rim of a lid. You can make little leaves of dough and stick them around the ham under the "rim." Score the inside of the rim with the point of a knife in any pattern you like. Make a hole in the middle of the lid to let the steam escape and place a little chimney of aluminum foil through the hole. Brush the dough with egg wash. Let dry for 15 minutes. Place in a 400° oven for 1 hour and 5 minutes until nicely browned. Remove from the oven; let cool 10 minutes and cut out the lid inside the rim. Remove and pour about ½ cup of sauce inside. Put a *papillote* or frill on the end of the bone for decoration. Replace the lid and serve with sauce on the side.

Tomates Farcies à l'Ancienne
Braised Stuffed Tomatoes

(*Serves 6 to 8*)

•

10 *large ripe tomatoes* (*about 4 pounds*)
3 *tablespoons olive oil*
1 *large onion, chopped fine* (*about 1 cup*)
4 *ounces mushrooms, chopped fine* (*about 3
   cups*)
3 *cloves garlic, peeled, crushed, and chopped
   fine* (*1 tablespoon*)
10 *ounces good boiled ham, diced very small or
   coarsely chopped* (*2½ cups*)
⅓ *cup chopped fresh parsley*
1 *teaspoon chopped fresh basil*
3 *hard-boiled eggs, coarsely chopped*
1½ *teaspoons salt*
1 *teaspoon freshly ground white pepper*

Wash the tomatoes, remove the stems and cut the tops off about ⅜ inch down to make a nice "hat." Empty the tomatoes with a spoon ¾ of the way down. You should have about 1½ pounds of pulp removed, set it aside. Sprinkle the cavities of the tomatoes with ½ teaspoon salt. Place the tomatoes side by side in a gratin dish.

Heat the oil in a saucepan and add the onion. Cook for 1 to 2 minutes. Add the mushrooms and cook until all the liquid has evaporated (about 6 minutes). Add the garlic and mix well. Add the ham and cook for 1 minute. Remove from the heat and add the chopped parsley and basil, the chopped eggs, ½ teaspoon salt (salt content may change depending on the saltiness of the ham), and ½ teaspoon pepper. Stuff the tomatoes with the mixture so that about ½ inch of the stuffing is showing above the tops of the tomatoes. Place the "hats" back on the stuffed tomatoes.

Meanwhile, chop or blend the tomato pulp. Place in a saucepan with ½ teaspoon salt and ½ teaspoon pepper and cook on high heat until the tomato pulp reduces to 2 cups. Pour the sauce on the tomatoes. Place the gratin dish on a cookie sheet and place in a preheated 375° oven for 45 minutes. Remove from the oven and let the tomatoes "rest" for 10 to 15 minutes. Transfer the tomatoes to a serving platter and reduce the liquid remaining in the gratin dish a few minutes to bring it to the right consistency. Pour over the tomatoes and serve immediately.

Selle de Chevreuil Poivrade
Saddle of Venison with a Red Wine Sauce

•

This recipe may be used with a piece of the leg instead of the saddle. I have also used a saddle of lamb with considerable success. The marinade, explained in the first part of the recipe, is often done differently. The meat is allowed to macerate with the wine, vinegar, vegetables, and seasonings for several days, but everything is mixed together cold. This recipe is faster and by pouring the hot marinade onto the meat, it accelerates the process and the meat requires only a few hours of maceration.

> 1 4- to 5-pound saddle of venison (*This meat
> has practically no fat. However, you should
> still trim it or have it trimmed. Reserve the
> trimmings; you should have at least 2 cups.*)

Marinade

> 2 cups good dry red wine
> 1 cup good wine vinegar
> 1½ cups diced leek
> ¾ cup diced carrot
> ¾ cup diced celery
> 1½ cups diced onion
> 4 cloves garlic, crushed with skin on
> 2 bay leaves
> 1 teaspoon crushed black peppercorns
>   (mignonnette)
> 1 teaspoon dried thyme (1 tablespoon fresh
>   thyme, if available)
> 1 teaspoon dried tarragon (1 tablespoon fresh
>   tarragon, if available)
> 1 teaspoon salt

Place all the ingredients, including the trimmings, in a kettle and bring to a boil. Boil for 2 minutes and pour over the saddle. Let the meat macerate for at least 4 hours, turning it every 30 minutes in the marinade.

> 2 tablespoons sweet butter
> 2 tablespoons flour
> 2 cups homemade brown gravy (see Basic
>   Brown Sauce, page 31)

Melt the butter in a heavy saucepan. Remove the trimmings from the marinade, add to the butter and let it brown 5 to 8 minutes. Sprinkle with the flour and mix with a large spoon. Add the marinade (vegetables and all) and bring to a boil, stirring once in a while with a spoon. Cook slowly for 35 minutes or until the liquid is almost completely reduced. Add the brown gravy and simmer slowly for another 25 minutes. Strain the sauce through a fine sieve, pressing the vegetables with a spoon to extract all the juices. Cover and set aside.

½ *stick sweet butter*
2 *tablespoons currant jelly*
½ *cup heavy cream*
salt and pepper to taste

Sprinkle the saddle all around with salt and pepper. Rub with the soft butter and place in a baking dish in a preheated 425° oven for about 35 minutes for medium-rare. Baste the saddle every 5 minutes during cooking.

Remove the saddle from the baking dish and set aside in a warm place. It should "rest" at least 15 minutes before being carved. Pour the sauce in the baking dish, add the currant jelly and bring to a boil. Be sure to stir with a spatula in order to melt all the solidified juices. Boil 2 to 3 minutes and strain through a sieve. Add the cream, salt and pepper to taste, and bring to a boil. It should be peppery, sour and sweet at the same time. Pour a few tablespoons on top of the saddle and bring to the dining room to carve in front of the guests. Serve the rest of the sauce on the side. Excellent with a puree of chestnuts or a puree of carrots. The greatest wines of Burgundy or Bordeaux can be served with this dish.

Lapin Farci
Stuffed Rabbit

(*Serves 6*)

•

Domestic rabbit, like game, is not often featured on American tables; the housewife who will happily cook a chicken will hesitate to cook a rabbit. In France it is served almost as often as chicken and it is just as delicious.

1 2½- to 3-pound fresh rabbit, cleaned
¼ pound fresh salt bacon, dried (lardons, see
    page 237)
½ cup chopped onions
2 cloves garlic, chopped
dash freshly ground white pepper
½ tablespoon freshly chopped chives
1 tablespoon freshly chopped parsley
½ tablespoon freshly chopped tarragon
1 egg
½ cup fresh breadcrumbs
½ cup cognac or brandy
1 teaspoon salt
4 tablespoons (½ stick) sweet butter
4 medium-sized potatoes, peeled and coarsely
    sliced (about 2½ to 3 cups)
1 cup dry white wine or cider

Remove the liver and kidneys from the rabbit and chop fine. Place the bacon in a saucepan and cook until it sizzles. Add the onions and sauté for 1 minute. Add the garlic, the liver and kidney mixture, pepper, chives, parsley, and tarragon. Mix together and cook for 2 minutes. Take off the heat and add the egg, breadcrumbs, and cognac. Mix carefully.

Stuff the rabbit with the mixture and tie it up to hold the stuffing inside. Sprinkle the rabbit with salt and pepper. Melt the butter in a wide enameled iron casserole. When hot, brown the rabbit on all sides. Add the potatoes and wine or cider. Cover. Cook on a low heat for approximately 65 to 80 minutes, depending on how tough the meat is. When cooked, remove the rabbit from the casserole, untie, and cut into portions. Place on a platter and surround with the pan juices and potatoes.

Lapin aux Pruneaux
Rabbit with Prunes

(Serves 6 to 8)

•

1 4½- to 5-pound rabbit *(approximately* 3¼
    *pounds after it has been skinned and
    cleaned)*
¼ *pound bacon, cut into small dices*
20 *very small onions, peeled (they should not
    be larger than an extra-large olive)*
2 *tablespoons flour*
2 *cups dry white wine*
1 *cup chicken or beef stock*
2 *teaspoons salt*
1 *teaspoon freshly ground white pepper*
2 *cups large unpitted prunes*
¼ *cup sugar*
3 *tablespoons wine vinegar*

Cut the rabbit into 12 pieces (split each hind leg in half; the
2 front legs; 3 pieces from the back and 3 pieces from the front,
ribs and neck). Chop the liver and kidney into a paste. Sauté
the bacon in a large pot until it turns crispy and brown. Pour all
the liquid fat into a frying pan. Add the onions to the frying pan
and brown on all sides. Add to the bacon. Brown the rabbit on
all sides in the same manner and add to the pot. Mix the flour
with ½ cup of the wine and add to the pot. Pour in the remaining wine, stock, salt, pepper, and chopped liver mixture and
bring to a boil. Simmer for 1 hour and 10 minutes. Add the
prunes and cook, simmering, for 10 more minutes. Meanwhile,
combine the vinegar and the sugar in a saucepan and cook on
high heat until it turns into a caramel. Pour directly into the

rabbit stew and mix carefully. Simmer for 10 more minutes and serve with boiled potatoes.

Canard aux Pommes
Duck with Apples

(*Serves 6 to 8*)

•

2 3½- to 4-pound ducks, eviscerated and oven-
    ready (*that is, cleaned and trussed*)
2 *teaspoons salt*
1 *teaspoon freshly ground white pepper*
½ *cup water*
3 *pounds McIntosh apples* (*about 10 to 12*),
    peeled, cored, and quartered
¼ *cup sugar*
¼ *cup red wine vinegar*
½ *cup water*

Salt and pepper the ducks inside and out and place in a large baking pan breast side up. Add the water to the pan and place in a preheated 400° oven for 65 minutes. Meanwhile, combine the apple pieces, sugar, and vinegar. Remove the ducks from the oven and pour out all the fat accumulated in the pan. Be sure not to pour out the juices, but only the clear fat. Take out as much fat as you can. Add the apple mixture and place back in the oven for 15 minutes. Add the ½ cup water and cook for another 15 to 20 minutes. Remove the ducks from the oven. Let "rest" for 10 minutes and then cut into quarters or smaller pieces. Arrange on a platter with the apples and juices mixed around.

Canard à l'Orange
Roast Duck with Orange Sauce

(Serves 6 to 8)

•

2 4- to 4½-pound ducks
1 teaspoon salt
½ teaspoon freshly ground pepper

Cut the wings off each duck, salt and pepper the ducks inside and out. Truss. Place the ducks, breast side up, in a large roasting pan with 1 cup cold water. Bake in a preheated 400° oven for 1 hour. After 1 hour of roasting, pour off all the fat that has accumulated in the pan or suck it up with a bulb baster. Continue roasting another 45 minutes for a total of 1 hour and 45 minutes. Pour off all the fat and set the roasting pan aside to use later.

Place the ducks in a large skillet, breast side down. Cook over a high heat for 2 to 3 minutes to melt any remaining fat. Keep warm. (Do this only if the ducks are still fatty and not crisp enough.) While the ducks are roasting, make the sauce.

Sauce

neck, wings, heart, and gizzard of the ducks
    (Do not use the liver.)
4 tablespoons sweet butter
1 leek, diced (¾ cup)
1 carrot, diced (¾ cup)
1 large onion, peeled and diced (½ cup)
1 large tomato (1 cup), coarsely chopped
1 rib celery, diced (½ cup)
½ cup parsley sprigs

2 *bay leaves*
1 *teaspoon dried thyme*
2 *cloves garlic, crushed*
2 *tablespoons tomato paste*
3 *tablespoons flour*
1 *cup dry white wine*
4 *cups beef or chicken broth (or 3 10½-ounce*
    cans)
5 *navel oranges*
⅓ *cup sugar*
⅓ *cup white vinegar*
juice ½ lemon (about 4 tablespoons)
2 *tablespoons currant jelly*
2 *tablespoons Grand Marnier*

Cut the neck, wings, heart, and gizzard into small pieces. Melt 2 tablespoons of the butter in a heavy kettle, add the pieces and sauté for about 10 minutes or until they are starting to brown. Add all the vegetables and herbs. Cook for 5 to 8 minutes. Then stir in the tomato paste and flour, mixing well. Finally, add the wine and broth. Bring to a boil, reduce heat and simmer slowly for 1 hour. Strain. Pour into the pan in which the ducks were roasted. Bring to a boil to melt all the solidified juices, then strain.

Take 1 of the oranges and peel with a vegetable peeler, taking care not to pick up any of the white skin. Cut the skin strips into a *julienne* (see page 170). Blanch in boiling water for 1 minute, then refresh under cold water. Squeeze the orange and set the juice aside. Squeeze another of the oranges. Using a paring knife, peel the 3 remaining oranges right down to the flesh. Separate the segments by cutting along the fibers which separate the segments, so that you have only pure flesh sections.

Combine the sugar and vinegar in a large heavy saucepan. Bring to a boil and boil for 3 to 4 minutes. Add the orange juice, lemon juice, and currant jelly. Bring to a boil and add the strained sauce. Simmer for about 5 minutes, then taste for seasoning. It probably will need salt and pepper, depending on the saltiness of the broth. Stir in the Grand Marnier. Finally, add the remaining butter, bit by bit, shaking the pan as you add the butter so it blends into the sauce. Place the ducks on a heated serving platter, spoon sauce over each one. Sprinkle the top with the orange peel and surround with the orange sections as garnish. Serve extra sauce on the side.

Ballottine de Canard Braisée
Braised Duck Ballottine

(*Serves 8*)

•

The first 3 steps should be done the day before the dish is served.

> *2 ducks, 4½ pounds each, wings cut at the first joint*

Take the nicer of the ducks and make an incision on the back. Remove the skin, following the carcass of the duck. Remove the bones from the legs and the wings by pulling out and breaking the bones as closely as possible from the joint. *It is important to avoid cutting the skin open, or the stuffing will run during cooking.* Remove the breast meat in 2 pieces; butterfly each breast to have 4 flat pieces of duck. Remove all the other meat and set aside. You should now have a large flat piece of skin on the table. Try removing as much fat as possible where the fat is the most lumpy, without tearing the skin. Set aside for later use. Bone the other duck any way you like, because you won't use the skin. Butterfly also the 2 breast pieces of the second duck. You now have 8 flat pieces of duck. Place them flat on the skin; they should practically cover it all. Set aside. Remove all the meat from the second duck.

Stuffing

Grind the reserved pieces of duck meat and fat (you should have about 1¼ pounds).

> 1¼ *pounds ground pork* (*from the shoulder*)
> 2 *slices white bread, trimmed and cubed*
> ½ *cup milk*
> 10 *shallots, peeled and finely chopped* (½ *cup*)
> 3 *tablespoons finely chopped chives*
> 1 *small clove garlic, peeled, crushed, and*
>   *chopped*
> 2 *eggs*
> ½ *cup dry white wine*
> ½ *teaspoon dried thyme, chopped into powder*
> 2 *bay leaves, crushed and chopped with a knife*
>   *into powder**
> 1½ *tablespoons salt*
> 1½ *teaspoons freshly ground white pepper*

Soak the bread cubes in the ½ cup of milk to make a puree. Add all of the remaining ingredients to the puree and mix together in a bowl with your hands.

> ¼ *pound fatback* (*unsalted, if possible*), *cut*
>   *into 8 long strips about ½ inch thick and*
>   *8 to 10 inches long*
> ½ *pound ham* (2 *or 3 thick slices*), *cut into*
>   *½-inch strips*

* Chop the thyme and bay leaves together because the pieces of bay leaf have a tendency to "jump."

Place the skin covered with the breast meat on the table. Fill the cavities of the wings and legs with some stuffing. Spread about ⅓ of the remaining stuffing over the breast meat. Arrange the strips of fatback and ham alternately, lengthwise down the duck. Spread ⅓ more of the stuffing on top, layer the rest of the strips, then cover with the rest of the stuffing. Bring the skin of the neck back over the stuffing. Slide about 6 lengths of butcher's string crosswise under the skin of the duck. Tie the strings so that they bring the edges of the skin together to remake the form of the duck. You may also roll the duck together and sew the opening back up with butcher's string. Place 1 or 2 large pieces of parchment or waxed paper on the table and roll the *ballotine* in it, folding the ends underneath to have the *ballotine* tightly enclosed. Chill overnight. (*Letting it stand overnight will greatly improve the flavor of the stuffing, and hence, of the whole dish.*)

> 6 *cups light brown gravy* (*see Basic Brown Sauce, page 31*)
> 2 *cups chicken broth*
> 2 *tablespoons arrowroot or cornstarch*
> ⅓ *cup dry sherry wine*
> 1 *tablespoon freshly chopped tarragon or parsley*

Place the wrapped *ballotine* in a large, deep roasting pan (the same as you would use for ham). Add the brown gravy and chicken stock and bring to a boil on top of the stove. Place in a preheated 425° oven for 1¼ hours, covered. Take the meat from the oven and remove the paper and strings. Scoop out as much fat as you can from the juices. Place the roast back in the oven for 45 minutes, basting every 10 minutes. It should be nicely browned. Remove to a serving platter and keep warm. Strain the juices and de-grease again. Mix the arrowroot with the sherry and add to the juices, stirring constantly. Bring to a boil. (*If the sauce is thick enough, do not add the arrowroot. This depends on your brown gravy.*) Yield: About 3 cups.

Slice some meat onto a platter. Place the roast next to it. Cover with some of the sauce and chopped tarragon, and serve with the remaining sauce on the side.

Canard Montmorency
Braised Duck with Cherries

(Serves 4 to 6)

•

1 4- to 5-pound duck, oven-ready
1 pound Bing cherries, pitted (about 50 to 60)
½ cup Madeira or sherry wine
½ cup cherry brandy

Macerate the cherries with the Madeira and the cherry brandy at room temperature for 2 to 3 hours.

Sauce

neck, giblet, heart, and wing tips of the duck,
    coarsely chopped
1 tablespoon sweet butter
½ carrot, washed, unpeeled, and coarsely sliced
    (½ cup loose)
1 medium-sized onion, unpeeled and coarsely
    sliced (¾ cup loose)
1 large tomato, coarsely chopped
1 teaspoon black peppercorns, crushed
1 clove garlic, unpeeled and crushed
4 sprigs parsley, coarsely chopped
2 bay leaves
1 teaspoon thyme leaves
3 cups beef broth
3 tablespoons arrowroot or cornstarch

Melt the butter in a large saucepan and add the neck, giblet, heart and wings. Sauté for 2 to 3 minutes and add the vegetables and seasonings. Add the broth and bring to a boil. Simmer for 1 hour. You should have 2 cups of liquid left. If not, adjust with some water. Put the strained liquid into a clean saucepan and add the cornstarch diluted with ½ cup of water, stirring with a wooden spoon. Bring to a boil and set aside.

Duck

> 1 *teaspoon salt*
> 1 *teaspoon freshly ground white pepper*
> ½ *carrot, coarsely sliced* (½ *cup*)
> 1 *onion, coarsely sliced* (¾ *cup*)
> 3 *sprigs parsley, coarsely chopped*

Salt and pepper the duck inside and out. Place in an oven dish and cook in a preheated 400° oven, breast side up, for 1 hour. Pour off the fat which has accumulated in the dish and add the carrot, onion, and parsley. Cook again for 30 minutes. Remove the duck to a warm platter, take the trussing string out, and keep warm. Pour the fat from the oven dish and put the duck back into it, breast side down, and cook on top of the stove for a few minutes so that any excess fat left on the breast will melt. Remove the duck and set aside. Pour the fat out of the dish and add the sauce. Cook, stirring for a few minutes, making sure that you melt all the solidified juices sticking in the bottom of the oven dish. Strain the sauce and add the cherries and wine mixture. Cook slowly for approximately 20 minutes, until the sauce has reduced to about 2½ cups. Season with salt and pepper if needed, and pour over the duck. Serve immediately.

Note: The duck can be cut in the kitchen and the sauce poured around, but it is not as dramatic as serving it whole and carving it in the dining room.

Oie Farcie Rôtie
Roast Stuffed Goose

•

1 10 to 12 pound goose, either fresh or frozen,
    thawed
6 tablespoons (¾ stick) sweet butter
5 cooking apples, peeled, cored and cut into
    ½-inch dice
3 yellow onions, peeled and chopped (about 2
    cups)
1 large clove garlic, crushed, peeled and chopped
    fine (about 1 teaspoon)
1 pound ground pork shoulder
goose liver, chopped very fine
1 tablespoon salt
½ teaspoon freshly ground white pepper
¾ teaspoon dried thyme
¼ cup Armagnac or Cognac
2 large eggs

To Make Stuffing

Melt 4 tablespoons of the butter in a large skillet. Add the apples, cover, and cook slowly for 20 minutes. Stir occasionally to prevent scorching.

Place the onions, 1 cup of water and the remaining butter in a heavy pan. Cook, uncovered, over high heat until all the water has evaporated and the onions start to sizzle (about 25 minutes). Add the garlic and cook another minute over low heat. When the apple and onion mixtures are cool enough to handle, combine them and mix with the pork, liver, salt, pepper, thyme, Armagnac and eggs.

To Roast the Goose

6 *tablespoons (¾ stick) sweet butter*
salt
giblets of goose
wing tips of goose
2 *carrots, peeled and coarsely chopped (¾ cup)*
1 *rib celery, coarsely chopped (½ cup)*
2 *cups chicken broth*
2 *cups dry white wine*
½ *teaspoon thyme*
1 *bay leaf*

Remove the neck and giblets from the cavity and any excess fat. Refrigerate these if not used immediately. Cut off the two wing tips at the second joint and set aside. Wash and dry the bird, fill the cavity with stuffing, sew up the opening with string or white thread. Melt the butter in a large roasting pan over medium heat. Sprinkle the bird with salt. Place in the pan and brown all over in the hot butter. Add all the remaining ingredients, including neck and giblets, and bring to a boil over a good heat. Roast in preheated 400° oven for 1 hour, basting every 10 to 15 minutes. Reduce oven heat to 350° and roast another 1½ hours, basting every 15 minutes, by which time the goose should be nicely browned and the liquids reduced to a rich sauce. Lift the goose to a heated serving platter. Remove the trussing strings. Keep warm.

Strain the juices through a fine sieve, pushing hard with the back of a wooden spoon or spatula to extract the vegetable pulp. Then scoop off as much fat as you can (approximately 4½ cups of juice will yield about 2½ cups of rich sauce and 1½ cups of fat). Allow the goose to rest at least 1 hour before serving.

Cassoulet
Bean and Meat Casserole

(*Serves 8*)

•

The *cassoulet* is an excellent dish, but as the *Dictionnaire de l'Académie des Gastronomes* points out, "It is first of all a peasant dish," sturdy country fare. How the *cassoulet* is made varies according to whoever is preparing it. In this recipe duck and pork are used. Often goose and lamb are used. A *cassoulet* always has one kind of poultry, some sausage, and one or two kinds of other meat, including pork.

> 2 pounds white pea beans or navy beans
> 1 tablespoon salt
> 1 medium leek, well washed and split
> 1 medium onion, stuck with 2 cloves
> 1 medium carrot, scraped and cut in half
> 2 large fresh tomatoes, peeled, seeded, and
>   chopped (2 cups)
> 3 cloves garlic, crushed
> 1 tablespoon tomato paste
> 1 bay leaf
> 1 teaspoon dried thyme
> 4 or 5 sprigs parsley
> ¾ pound pork skin, tied in 3 or 4 bundles (pork
>   rind)
> 1 pound lean, cured bacon, all in 1 piece
> 4 cups chicken broth (3 10½-ounce cans)
> 6 cups cold water
> 1 pound garlic sausage (see page 104), or use
>   keilbasa (Polish sausage) or Genoa salami

Cover the beans with cold water and allow to soak for 2 to 3 hours. Lift the beans from the water to an 8- to 10-quart heavy, enameled casserole. (You can also wash the beans and cook them directly in cold water with the seasonings. *It is important that the beans start in cold water and come slowly to a boil, otherwise they will harden and not cook properly.*) Add the salt, leek, onion, carrot, tomatoes, garlic, tomato paste, *bouquet garni* (bay leaf, thyme, and parsley tied in a piece of cheesecloth), pork skin, bacon, broth, and 6 cups of cold water. Bring to a boil slowly, reduce heat, cover, and simmer for about 1¼ hours. At this point, prick the sausage with a fork and add to the casserole. Cook another ½ hour.

> 1 4- to 5-pound duck, oven-ready
> 2 to 3 pounds pork shoulder, boned, rolled, and
> tied (or fresh pork butt)
> 2 teaspoons freshly ground pepper
> 2 teaspoons salt

Meanwhile, salt and pepper both the duck and the pork. Place each in a separate roasting pan and roast in a preheated 375° oven for 1½ hours.

When the beans are cooked (they should be tender, but not mushy), turn off the heat. Lift the sausage, pork rind, bacon, onion, carrot, leek and *bouquet garni* from the casserole onto a flat sheet and let cool until cool enough to handle. Discard the *bouquet garni* and the cloves from the onion.

When the duck and pork are cooked, pour ½ cup fat from the roasting pans into a measuring cup and set aside. Discard any extra fat from the duck and pork pans. Deglaze both pans by adding ½ cup of the juice from the beans into each pan. Bring to a boil, then simmer, stirring together all the coagulated cooking juices. Add to the beans. Chop the onion, carrot, and leek into a puree and return to the beans. Prepare the meats to combine with the beans. Remove the skin from the sausage and slice into ¾-inch slices. Slice the pork rind and fresh bacon into strips ½ inch wide by 3 inches long. Slice the pork in half lengthwise, then into 1-inch slices. Cut the duck in half with a heavy sharp knife, then cut each half into 5 pieces, bones and all (cut each leg in half and the wing and breast pieces into thirds).

4 slices bread, made into fine crumbs (1½ cups)
½ cup reserved fat from the pork and/or duck

Pour the beans into another container. Then rinse out the casserole. Layer the various ingredients in the casserole starting with about ⅓ of the beans, followed by layers of each of the 5 meats and the beans, the remaining meats, ending with the beans. Spread the breadcrumbs over the entire surface, then spoon the ½ cup of fat over the top. Place in a preheated 350° oven for about 1½ hours. After 30 minutes, when a crust has formed on top, break the crust by pushing it into the beans with a large spoon. It will brown again, leaving a crust intact for serving. *Pushing the first crust into the dish gives a crunchy, nutty taste to the beans.* At the end of the cooking time the *cassoulet* can "rest" out of the oven for 20 to 30 minutes before serving. Serve straight from the casserole, giving each one at the table a serving of the various ingredients.

Pigeon Bressane
Braised Squab

(Serves 6)

•

1½ cups finely diced mushrooms (4 to 5
    ounces)
1 tablespoon sweet butter
¼ teaspoon salt
⅛ teaspoon ground black pepper
liver and heart of the squab, cut into small
    pieces

Melt the butter in a saucepan, add the mushrooms and sauté
for 5 to 6 minutes until all of the liquid from the mushrooms
has evaporated. Add the salt, pepper, liver, and heart and sauté
for 2 minutes on medium heat. Set aside.

2 tablespoons sweet butter
¾ cup chopped onions
¾ cup converted rice
1½ cups good chicken stock

Melt the butter in a saucepan, add the onions and cook for
1 minute. Add the rice and mix well so that all of the grains are
coated with the butter. Add the stock (salt and pepper if necessary, depending on the seasoning of your stock) and bring to a
boil. Cover and simmer slowly on the top of the stove for 20
minutes. Combine with the mushroom mixture and stuff the
squab with this.

6 squab (about ¾ pound each) cleaned,
    stuffed, and tied

1 *teaspoon salt*
1 *teaspoon freshly ground white pepper*
1 *tablespoon butter*
1 *diced carrot (½ cup)*
1 *diced onion (1 cup)*
½ *cup dry white wine*
½ *cup water*

Melt the butter in a large casserole (with a cover). Salt and pepper the squab and brown on medium heat for about 10 minutes; until they are browned on all sides. Add the carrot and onion, cover, reduce the heat and simmer for 15 minutes. Add the wine and water, cover and simmer for another 30 minutes. Arrange the squab on a large serving platter, remove the string, strain the juices and pour over the squab. Serve immediately. One per person.

Faisan Rôti sur Canapés
Roast Pheasant on Canapés

(*Serves 4*)

•

It is hard to get good fresh pheasant nowadays, unless one goes hunting or has a friend who does. The female is more tender than the male and they are both best under a year old. If you plan to eat the bird without aging it, it is better to pluck soon after it has been shot because the feathers come off very easily. If you age it a few days or freeze it, leave the feathers on and the meat will be protected and remain moist and tender. Aging the meat 4 or 5 days under refrigeration will tenderize the bird and give the meat a slight gamy taste, more desirable, I believe, for a pheasant. Before plucking the pheasant, drop into boiling water for a few seconds, otherwise it will be hard to pluck and pulling the feathers will tear the skin, especially around the neck and breast.

Whether you freeze the pheasant or age it, it has to be eviscerated within the hour after it has been killed or it will taste bitter and sour. Using your finger, or a hook made of a piece of wire, pull out the intestines until you see the liver. Cut the gut at the end of the liver and discard. The liver, heart, lungs, and giblet remain in the cavity of the bird. If you freeze the pheasant, defrost under refrigeration. Cut the wings at the second joint with the feathers and discard. Drop the pheasant in boiling water for a few seconds and pluck. When the pheasant is "nude," hold the neck in one hand and the feet in the other hand and rotate the bird over the flame of the gas burner so that all the little fuzz still adhering to the flesh is burnt. Cut the neck off and make a large opening, then cut off the tail to empty the pheasant. Cut out the bile (the little green sac) from the liver, being careful not to puncture it or the liver will taste bitter. Take out the giblet and reserve with the heart and the neck for stock or soup. Remove the 2 lumps of fat on both sides of the opening and chop it fine. Cut the liver into 3 or 4 pieces.

Canapé Farce

> 1 *tablespoon sweet butter*
> *the chopped fat and liver of the pheasant*
> *dash of salt and freshly ground white pepper*
> ¼ *teaspoon good cognac*
> 4 *slices French bread, about* ½ *inch thick*

Melt the butter in a skillet, add the chopped fat and cook slowly over low heat until all the fat is melted. Increase the heat and add the liver pieces and salt and pepper. Cook over high heat for 30 to 40 seconds. *Be careful not to burn yourself because the fat will splash during cooking.* Pour the mixture in a metal sieve and push through with a metal spoon into a bowl.

Add the cognac, more salt and pepper if needed, and cool in the refrigerator, mixing the mixture as it cools off. You should have a smooth, well-seasoned liver mixture (about 3 to 4 table-spoons). Just before serving the pheasant, toast the bread and spread with the mixture.

> 1 *teaspoon salt*
> ¼ *teaspoon freshly ground white pepper*
> 2 *tablespoons sweet butter*

Salt and pepper the pheasant inside and out. Truss it with a needle and string or simply tie it up with a string. Melt the butter in a heavy skillet and brown the pheasant on all sides on top of the stove for 6 to 8 minutes on medium heat. Place in a preheated 425° oven and cook for 25 minutes, basting every 5 minutes. Place the pheasant on a serving platter and remove the string. Add ¼ cup of water to the cooking skillet and *bring to a rolling boil for 10 seconds. This will emulsify the juices and the water.* After the pheasant has "rested" for 5 minutes, quarter it, remove the bone from the breast, and place each piece on the canapés. Pour the juices over and serve immediately.

The flesh will be slightly pink inside, especially near the leg joint, and it should be served this way. Older pheasant, especially the male, have a very tough skin; if you are using one of these, remove the skin before serving.

How to Bone a Chicken into Quarters

•

There are innumerable ways to bone and serve chicken. With such great dishes as Galantine de Volaille and Ballotine de Volaille, the meat is completely separated from the carcass, left in one piece, then stuffed, sewed, and poached or roasted. But one of the simplest and more usual ways is to bone and quarter the bird. Customarily sautéed, it can also be served *à la crème* or in a stew, such as chicken fricassee or *coq au vin*. Allow one 3- to 3¼-pound broiler-fryer for 4 people.

Place the chicken on its side. With a small, sharp-pointed knife, cut the skin all around the leg. Pull the leg away from the body to expose the joint where the thigh joins the body. Cut at the joint, holding the body firmly, and pull the leg until it is completely separated. Cut off the end of the drumstick and cut into the joint where the thigh and leg join, but do not cut completely through. Separate the other leg the same way.

With the chicken still lying on its side, pull back the wing. With the point of your knife, find the joint where the wing joins the body, then sever. Repeat with the other wing.

Follow the wishbone and along the breastbone with your knife, loosening the breast from the bones. Then pull it away from the body in one piece. Remove the second side of the breast in the same manner.

Now completely disjointed, there are 2 breasts, 2 legs, 2 wing tips, and the carcass. The wing tips, carcass, neck, and gizzard are used as the base for a good chicken stock. The delicate liver is never used to make stock. If the parts are not used immediately, they should be frozen for future use. Freeze the liver separately. Obviously, all should be freezer-wrapped.

Poulet Grillé aux Herbes
Charbroiled Chicken with Herbs

(*Serves 6*)

•

1 3- to 3½-pound chicken, cut into eighths
1 teaspoon salt
¾ teaspoon freshly ground black pepper
1 tablespoon oil

Mix all ingredients together and let macerate while the charcoal is burning. Be sure to use real charcoal or use pieces of wood. Wait until there is no more flame and all the charcoal or wood is transformed into hot coals or red ashes. *Be sure the broiler rack is clean and hot when you place the chicken on it. Set the wire rack far from the coals, otherwise the chicken will cook too fast and be burned on the outside by the time it is cooked inside.* Place the pieces of chicken skin side down on the barbecue and cook for 45 minutes. Turn the chicken after 15 minutes and every 10 minutes after that. (Start taking the smaller pieces and the breast off after 35 minutes.) If the heat is too great and the meat is cooking too fast, push the ashes to one side of the barbecue and keep the chicken on the other side.

¾ stick sweet butter
2 to 3 cloves of garlic, peeled, crushed, and
    chopped fine
⅓ cup fresh, chopped herbs (any mixture of the
    following: parsley, thyme, rosemary, savory,
    tarragon)
¼ teaspoon salt
¼ teaspoon freshly ground pepper
⅓ cup Brown Sauce (see page 31)

Melt the butter in a large skillet, add the garlic and sauté a few seconds. Then add the herbs, salt and pepper, and brown sauce. Bring to a boil. As the pieces of chicken are cooked, turn them in the sauce to coat each piece. Keep warm in the sauce until all the chicken is cooked, then serve immediately.

Poulet Fine Champagne
Chicken with Cognac

(Serves 6 to 8)

•

1 3½-pound roasting chicken
½ teaspoon salt
½ teaspoon freshly ground pepper
¼ cup (½ stick) sweet butter, softened

Sprinkle the chicken with salt and pepper and rub all over with the butter. Place in a roasting pan and roast in a preheated 400° oven for 15 minutes on one side, basting occasionally. Turn on the other side and continue roasting for another 15 minutes. Turn breast side up and roast, still basting every 5 minutes, for 15 to 20 minutes longer. Remove the trussing string and place on a warm platter. Keep warm.

Pour off all the fat that has accumulated in the pan. Deglaze the pan with 1 cup of water. Melt all the solidified juices and pour through a fine strainer into a saucepan. Allow the liquid to reduce until it is as thick as a jam. This is a meat glaze. Place aside and keep warm in a double boiler. It will yield about 1 tablespoon of glaze.

Sauce

2 *cups fresh or canned chicken stock*
½ *cup diced onion*
½ *teaspoon whole black peppercorns*
8 to 10 *sprigs parsley, coarsely chopped*
4 *tablespoons flour*
3 *tablespoons sweet butter*
¾ *cup dry white wine*
1 *cup heavy cream*
salt
freshly ground white pepper
¼ *cup good cognac*

Combine the stock, onion, peppercorns, and parsley in a heavy saucepan. Bring to a boil and reduce to half. Work the flour into the butter to make a mixture called *beurre manié*. Add to the sauce, bit by bit, beating constantly with a wire whisk. Then simmer slowly for 10 minutes. Add the wine, bring to a boil, and reduce for another 3 to 4 minutes on medium heat. Stir with a spatula or spoon every so often because the mixture, being thick, has a tendency to scorch. Stir in the cream and reduce again for a few minutes until the sauce reaches a nice smooth consistency and coats the spoon. Strain the sauce. Taste for seasoning; add salt and pepper if needed (this will depend on the seasoning of the chicken stock). Stir in the cognac.

To serve, coat the chicken with the sauce and "sprinkle" the meat glaze over the top. Serve immediately.

Poulet au Vinaigre
Chicken in Vinegar

(*Serves 6*)

•

1½ *chickens* (*about* 4½ *pounds*), *cut into 12
  pieces* (*each quarter is cut into halves*)
1½ *teaspoons salt*
¾ *teaspoon freshly ground black pepper*
⅓ *stick sweet butter*

Sprinkle the chicken pieces with the salt and pepper. Melt the
butter in two heavy skillets. When the butter is hot, place the
pieces skin side down and brown for a few minutes on medium
heat. Turn the pieces and brown on the other side (the pieces
should be browned all around). This takes about 8 to 10
minutes.

⅓ *cup good red wine vinegar*
⅓ *cup water*

Add the vinegar and water equally divided between both
skillets. Cover tightly and cook on medium heat for 20 minutes.
Remove the chicken to a serving platter. As soon as it cools
somewhat, you may remove the bone from the breast (it pulls
off easily) and the piece of backbone from the legs. It may be
considered a little more elegant to remove the bones, but it can
certainly be served unboned. Keep the chickens warm on the
corner of the stove or in a 180° oven. *Do not cover, or the
chickens may taste slightly reheated.*

3 *cloves garlic, peeled, crushed, and chopped fine*
⅓ *cup good red wine vinegar*

1 *tablespoon tomato paste*
salt and freshly ground pepper to taste
⅓ *stick sweet butter*
1 *tablespoon chopped parsley*
2 *teaspoons freshly chopped tarragon* (*if fresh*
   tarragon is not available, omit altogether)

After removing the pieces of chicken from the skillets, add the garlic to one skillet and sauté for 1 minute. *Be careful not to burn the garlic or the sauce will be ruined.* Add the wine vinegar and boil, making sure that you melt all the solidified juices. Transfer the liquid to the second skillet and add the tomato paste to thicken the sauce. Add salt and pepper to taste; the sauce should be peppery. Remove the skillet from the heat and add the butter, bit by bit, with one hand. *At the same time, shake the skillet with the other hand so that the butter blends with the sauce.* It should yield only 1 to 1¼ cups of sauce. Pour the sauce over the chickens, sprinkle with the herbs and serve immediately.

Note: You may omit the freshly ground pepper in Step III and replace it with 1 teaspoon of crushed green pepper. If sauce breaks down, emulsify with some warm water.

Yassa de Poulet
Chicken African Style

(*Serves 4 to 6*)

•

Chicken and Marinade

1 2½- *to 3-pound chicken, cut into 8 pieces*
2 *cups onions, very thinly sliced* (2 *large*
   onions)

> 4 to 6 *cloves garlic, depending on size, peeled,*
> *crushed and chopped fine*
> ½ *teaspoon hot chili-pepper flakes*
> ½ *tablespoon grated fresh ginger*
> 1 *teaspoon salt*
> ¼ *teaspoon freshly ground black pepper*
> ¼ *cup lime juice*

Mix all ingredients together and let macerate overnight in the refrigerator or 4 to 5 hours at room temperature, mixing every hour. Cut the little pieces of fat which usually cling to the thighs of the chicken into small pieces. Melt in a saucepan and brown the pieces of chicken in this fat. When the chicken is browned, place in a large kettle. Deglaze the saucepan with the marinade and add to the chicken. Bring to a boil, cover and simmer slowly for 15 minutes. Take the cover off and boil on high heat for 5 minutes to reduce the sauce.

Couscous

> 1 *cup couscous (granulated wheat or semolina)*
> 2 *tablespoons sweet butter*
> 1 *cup boiling water*
> *dash salt*

Melt the butter in a saucepan. Add the couscous and mix carefully so that all the grains are coated with butter. Pour the boiling water on top, add salt, cover and let stand for 15 minutes at room temperature. Stir with a fork to separate the grains. Serve hot with the chicken in one dish.

Poulet Lyonnaise
Chicken Lyonnaise
(Serves 6 to 8)

•

Whenever the adjective *lyonnaise* is used in a French recipe it implies that onions are part of the recipe.

> 2 3½-pound chickens
> 3 teaspoons salt
> 1½ teaspoons freshly ground black pepper
> 4 tablespoons butter, softened
> 1 tablespoon vegetable oil
> 3 cups sliced onions
> 2 cloves garlic, peeled, crushed, and chopped
> 1 cup breadcrumbs (fresh if possible)
> ½ cup water

Trim the chicken wings by removing the tips at the last joint. Split the chickens through the back and flatten them until they lay even on the table. Sprinkle on each side with 2 teaspoons of salt and 1 teaspoon of pepper. Rub 2 tablespoons of the butter on the skin of the chicken and place them on a tray, skin side up, in a 425° oven for 25 minutes. Turn the chicken over and cook an additional 15 minutes on the other side. Meanwhile, melt the remaining butter and the oil in a saucepan and add the onions, 1 teaspoon of salt, and ½ teaspoon of pepper. Cook on medium heat on top of the stove for 12 minutes, turning the onions once in a while. Add the garlic and cook another 2 minutes. The onions should be cooked through and light brown in color. Arrange the onion mixture on top of the chicken (*i.e.*, the onions go on the skin of the chicken). Top with breadcrumbs and moisten the topping with the fat accumulated in the pan. *Tip the pan to one side and use a spoon or a baster to pick up the juices and coat the bread mixture with it.* Place the chicken back in the oven for 25 minutes, or until nicely browned. Place the chicken on a serving dish and add the water to the cooking pan. Melt all the solidified juices and bring to a boil. You may serve the chicken cut into quarters with the sauce poured on top.

A nice Beaujolais like Morgon, Chiroubles or Moulin-à-vent would be excellent with this dish.

Poulet Grandmère
Chicken Grandma Style
(*Serves 6 to 8*)

•

Garnishes

> 30 to 35 *very small pearl onions, about the size*
> *of a large olive*
> *water*
> ½ *teaspoon salt*
> 1 *tablespoon sugar*
> 3 *tablespoons sweet butter*

Place onions in a skillet in 1 layer. Add water, just enough to cover the onions, and the rest of the ingredients. Bring to a rapid boil and cook hard to evaporate all the liquid, about 8 to 10 minutes. Reduce heat and continue cooking. Shaking the pan, brown the onions over the flame. Or, put the pan under the broiler for 1 or 2 minutes. Set onions aside.

> ¾ *pound salt pork* (*bacon before it is smoked;*
> *also called pork belly or sweet pickle. It is*
> *cured but not smoked.*)

Cut pork into *lardons,* approximately ½ inch by ½ inch by ¾ inch. Cover with cold water, bring to a boil, and boil 2 minutes. Run cold water into the pan for several minutes. Drain. Cook in pan over medium heat to brown, tossing frequently, about 6 to 7 minutes. When brown, strain the pieces in a metal sieve and set aside. Discard the fat.

> *½ pound cultivated mushrooms*
> *2 tablespoons sweet butter*

Clean the mushrooms and cut into halves, or quarters if very large. Toss in butter over high heat to brown lightly, until all the mushroom liquid has evaporated and the mushrooms start to brown. Set aside.

Pommes Cocottes

> *4 large Idaho potatoes*
> *water*

Cut potatoes into large slices crosswise. Discard the ends. Cut each slice into several pieces lengthwise (each slice about ½ inch wide and 2 inches long). *The important thing is to trim all the pieces so that they are about the same size and the same shape. That way they will cook very evenly.* Cover with cold water, bring to a boil and drain. *Do not refresh or rinse the potatoes under cold water after cooking.* The heat will dry the potatoes.

The 4 steps above can be done a couple hours ahead.

Preparation

> *2 2½-pound chickens*
> *2 teaspoons salt*
> *1 teaspoon pepper*
> *3 tablespoons sweet butter*
> *1 cup dry white wine*

Cut chickens into eighths (see page 227), and salt and pepper the chicken pieces on all sides. Melt 3 tablespoons of butter in a large sauteuse pan and add the chicken, skin side down. Brown for approximately 9 minutes; turn and cook 2 more minutes; then cover for 2 more minutes. Remove breast pieces, cover pan, and cook dark meat 7 to 8 minutes more. Replace the breast meat, add wine, cover, and cook 5 minutes more on high heat.

> 1 *tablespoon sweet butter*
> 1 *tablespoon vegetable oil*
> *potatoes*
> *mushrooms*
> *onions*
> lardons
> 1 *cup Brown Sauce (see page 31)*
> 1 *tablespoon freshly chopped parsley*

In separate skillet, heat butter and oil. Add potatoes and toss until brown, about 6 to 7 minutes on high heat. This must be done at the last minute, otherwise the potatoes won't be crunchy. Add the mushrooms, onions, *lardons*, and heat.

Put chicken on a serving dish. Add brown sauce to sauteuse pan and reduce liquid to approximately ¾ cup over high heat. Taste for seasoning and add salt and pepper if needed. Pour sauce over chicken and spoon garnishes over all. Sprinkle with chopped parsley and serve immediately.

This dish is also excellent done with veal chops instead of chicken.

Poulet Sauté Boivin
Sautéed Chicken with Artichokes

(Serves 6 to 8)

•

1 3½- to 4-pound chicken, cut into 8 pieces
3 medium-sized artichokes
1 lemon, cut in half
½ cup (1 stick) sweet butter
salt
freshly ground pepper
15 to 20 small white onions, peeled
¾ pound potatoes, peeled and shaped into
    small balls
1 clove garlic, crushed and chopped fine
1 cup homemade veal stock or brown beef gravy
    (see Basic Brown Sauce, page 31)
minced parsley

Trim the artichokes right down to the bottom, then cut away the hairy choke (see page 258). Cut each bottom into about 6 pieces. Then rub with the cut side of the lemon.

Melt half the butter in a large, heavy skillet. Salt and pepper the chicken pieces. Then sauté each piece until brown all over. As you finish browning the pieces, place in a large enameled casserole or Dutch oven. Add the onions to the skillet and brown them (they will not brown evenly), then combine with the chicken. Brown the potatoes and artichokes the same way, using more butter as it is needed. As each vegetable is finished, add to the casserole. Sprinkle with salt and pepper, then add the garlic. Cover tightly and place in a preheated 425° oven for 30 minutes. Remove from the oven and arrange the chicken pieces with the vegetables on a heated serving platter. Keep warm.

Using a large spoon, remove any superfluous fat from the casserole. Stir the brown gravy into the solidified juices and bring to a boil. Strain over the chicken and vegetables. Garnish with the parsley. Serve at once.

Poulet aux Topinambours
Creamed Chicken with Jerusalem Artichokes

(*Serves 4*)

•

1 chicken about 3½-pounds, cut into 8 pieces
   (*you may buy it quartered and cut each
   piece in half*)
1¼ pounds Jerusalem artichokes (*about 1
   pound after they are peeled*)
1 tablespoon sweet butter
¼ teaspoon crushed thyme
¼ teaspoon oregano
¾ cup dry white wine
¾ cup heavy cream
1 teaspoon salt
½ teaspoon freshly ground pepper

Break the artichokes into segments so that they may be peeled more easily. Cut each segment into 2 or 3 pieces, depending on size, and trim each piece with a knife or a vegetable peeler. *The peeled pieces should be about the same size and shape* (about 1½ to 2 inches in diameter). Put the artichoke pieces in a casserole and cover with cold water, add ½ teaspoon of salt, and bring to a boil over high heat. Simmer for 8 minutes. By this time, the pieces should be half-cooked and floating on the surface of the water. Drain in a colander.

Salt and pepper the pieces of chicken. Melt the butter in a large heavy saucepan with a cover. Sauté the chicken on all sides, starting skin side down, until all the pieces are nice and brown (about 6 to 8 minutes on medium heat). Add the thyme, oregano, the wine and the artichokes. Bring to a boil and simmer for 15 minutes. Add the cream, ½ teaspoon of salt, ½ teaspoon of ground pepper, and boil on high heat for 5 to 6 minutes, uncovered, to reduce and thicken the sauce. Place the pieces of chicken on a serving platter, taste the sauce for seasoning as it might need more salt and pepper. Pour the sauce and artichokes over the chicken and serve immediately.

Mayonnaise de Volaille
Chicken Mayonnaise

(*Serves 6*)

•

1 3½- to 4-pound chicken, poached
Mayonnaise (see page 35)
1 large head Boston lettuce, outside leaves
    cleaned and cut into julienne (*see page*
    170); the center heart (about 2 inches
    high) kept whole
juice ¼ lemon (about 1 tablespoon)
salt
freshly ground pepper

Garnishes

2 *hard-cooked eggs, quartered*
2 *ripe tomatoes, cut into wedges*
1 *small can anchovy fillets in oil*
2 *tablespoons well-drained capers*
5 to 6 *sprigs parsley, minced*

Poach the chicken with 1 carrot and 4 cloves in salted water (start in cold water) for 50 minutes. Allow to barely simmer during cooking. Cool the chicken in the broth. Make the mayonnaise. Prepare the garnishes the day you will serve the chicken and *julienne* the lettuce shortly before serving.

Skin the chicken and pull the meat off the bones in large pieces, then cut into thin slices. Place the *julienne* of lettuce in a large crystal bowl, sprinkle with lemon juice, salt, and pepper. Toss lightly with a fork and spoon. Arrange the sliced chicken on top of the lettuce and coat with mayonnaise, spreading it with a metal spatula so that all the chicken is equally coated with the mayonnaise. Place the lettuce heart standing in the center of the mayonnaise (you may have to push the pieces of chicken to make a hole so that the heart can stand up) and arrange the garnishes all around. Sprinkle with minced parsley. Serve at once.

Gâteau de Foies de Volaille à la Tomate
Chicken Liver Custard
Served with a Tomato Sauce

(Serves 6 to 8)

•

This is one of the most typical dishes of Bressan cooking and there are many variations for it. One of the most refined versions utilizes a Nantua sauce, crayfish, and truffles to complement the *gâteau*. A very unsophisticated rendition is a simple mixture of livers, milk, eggs, flour, and parsley, baked and served in a gratin dish. Our version is not complicated but can be made more elegant by the addition of pike quenelles and wild mushrooms such as meadow mushrooms (*Agaricus campestris*), which grow in fields during July and August. Our recipe for the sauce is made with cultivated mushrooms—the counterpart of the meadow mushrooms which, if not quite as fragrant, are still quite satisfactory.

Custard Mixture

4 *trimmed chicken livers*
1 *tablespoon chopped parsley*
1 *large or 2 small cloves garlic*
½ *teaspoon dried thyme, pulverized (1½ teaspoons chopped fresh thyme would be better)*
1 *teaspoon butter*
2 *cups heavy cream*
6 *eggs*
½ *teaspoon freshly ground white pepper*
1 *teaspoon salt*

Chop the livers, parsley, and the peeled garlic with a large knife until it is reduced into a nice puree. Add the thyme. Melt the butter in a metal 1½-quart charlotte mold. Add the pureed mixture and cook on medium heat, stirring with a spoon, for 1 or 2 minutes until the liver mixture changes color and firms up. *This is important because if you add the liver to the liquid without cooking it, it will go down to the bottom of the mold during cooking. By precooking it, it helps to distribute it properly throughout the whole gâteau.* Mix the cream, the eggs, salt, and pepper together until smooth, and strain it through a fine sieve. Combine with the liver mixture, pour everything into the charlotte mold, place in a pan with cold water around it and cook in a 400° oven for 45 minutes to 1 hour, until a knife inserted in the middle of the *gâteau* comes out clean. Let "rest" 10 minutes before inverting on the serving tray. If any liquid comes out of the *gâteau*, remove it with a baster or paper towels.

Tomato Sauce

This tomato sauce can be used for several different dishes and is a basic sauce.

A.

1 tablespoon butter
2 tablespoons olive oil
1 large onion, peeled and diced (about 1 cup)
2 carrots, peeled and diced (about 1 cup)
¾ cup diced leek
½ cup diced celery
3 cloves garlic, crushed with skin on
1 can (6 ounces) tomato paste
3 tablespoons flour
1 quart beef broth
1 teaspoon salt
½ teaspoon whole black peppercorns crushed.
    You may crush them with a heavy skillet or
    a saucepan directly on your chopping block.
    (This is called mignonnette in French.)
2 cups water
1 teaspoon sugar
¼ cup coarsely chopped parsley
½ teaspoon dried thyme (If available, fresh is
    better; double proportion.)
½ teaspoon dried oregano (If available, fresh is
    better; double proportion.)
½ teaspoon dried tarragon (If available, fresh is
    better; double proportion.)

Melt the butter in a large kettle, add the oil and when the mixture is foaming, add the onion, carrots, and leek. Sauté for 5 minutes. Add the celery and garlic and sauté for 1 or 2 minutes. Mix in the tomato paste and the flour and add the beef stock, salt, and pepper. Bring to a boil, mixing with a whisk once in a while to avoid scorching. When boiling, add the 2 cups of water and the rest of the ingredients. Bring to a boil and simmer slowly for 45 minutes uncovered. Skim every 5 minutes to remove the foam which accumulates on top of the sauce. *The carrots give a good sweet taste to a tomato sauce and should not be omitted.* Strain the sauce through a fine sieve and set aside covered with plastic wrap.

B. (This should be done while the tomato sauce is cooking.)

> 4 *well-ripe, medium-sized tomatoes (about 1¼*
> *pounds)*
> 1 *tablespoon olive oil*
> 1 *small green or red hot pepper, split, seeded,*
> *and chopped (optional)*

Remove the core of the tomatoes and dip them into boiling water for 30 or 40 seconds. Transfer them with a slotted spoon to a bowl of cold water. Remove the skin, which will slide off easily, split them lengthwise into halves and squeeze the seeds out. Add the cores, skins, and seeds to the cooking sauce. Dice the tomatoes, then heat for about 10 minutes, or until most of the liquid is evaporated. You should have approximately 1½ cups of pulp left over. Add the pulp to the strained tomato sauce and bring to a boil. *Yield:* About 5½ cups of sauce. *Be sure to apply pressure to the vegetables when straining the sauce so that you get as much of the flavor of the seasonings and vegetables as possible.* At serving time, add 1 tablespoon of fresh butter in bits to each cup of sauce and mix it well to have the butter blend with the sauce and smooth it.

Note: You need about half of the recipe to serve with the chicken liver *gâteau.* The remaining sauce may be kept in the refrigerator for up to 10 days, covered, or it may be frozen.

> ½ *pound mushrooms, washed and thickly sliced*

Sauté the mushrooms with 1 tablespoon of butter until the juices from the mushrooms is evaporated. Add 2½ to 3 cups of sauce to the mushrooms and bring to a boil. Pour over the *gâteau* and serve immediately.

Vegetables

Salade à la Crème
Salad with Cream Dressing
(*Serves 6*)

•

This dressing is particularly good with tender salad greens such as Bibb lettuce, Boston lettuce, oak-leaf lettuce, and the like. The dressing should be prepared ahead but not tossed with the salad until serving time, as the greens will wilt very fast after the dressing is added. Take care when washing and drying the salad greens not to bruise the leaves.

> 2 or 3 *heads Boston lettuce, depending on size,*
>   *or 5 to 6 heads Bibb lettuce*
> ½ *teaspoon salt*
> ½ *teaspoon freshly ground white pepper*
> 4 *teaspoons good wine vinegar*
> 6 *tablespoons heavy cream*
> 2 *tablespoons vegetable oil*

In a bowl, combine the salt, pepper, vinegar, and cream. Beat with a whisk or a spoon for about 20 seconds. *The mixture should be foamy and creamy in consistency.* Add the oil and mix with a spoon to blend it. Toss the salad gently in the dressing at serving time.

Salade de Betterave et Doucette
Salad of Beets and Field Salad

(Serves 6 to 8)

•

4 medium beets (about 1¼ pounds)
salt
¾ pound field salad or lamb's tongues
½ cup rich vinaigrette

Cut the tops off the beets leaving about 2 inches. Drop in a pot of boiling salted water, cover and cook for about 1½ hours or until tender when pierced with the point of a sharp knife. Drain and cool. When cool enough to handle, peel and slice into large *julienne* slices (see page 170). Mix with Rich Vinaigrette. Wash the field lettuce thoroughly because it is usually sandy, and drain. At serving time, add the field lettuce to the beets and toss together well.

Rich Vinaigrette

1 egg yolk
2 tablespoons wine or tarragon vinegar
1 tablespoon Dijon mustard
1 tablespoon chopped shallots (about 1 or 2
    shallots) or green onion bulbs
½ teaspoon salt
½ teaspoon freshly ground white pepper
¾ cup vegetable oil (or a mixture of olive oil
    and vegetable oil)

Combine the egg yolk, vinegar, mustard, shallots, salt and pepper to taste. Whip together with a whisk for about 1 minute. Add the oil very slowly, beating constantly with a wire whisk. Makes 1 cup. This may be considered a light mayonnaise.

Salade de Pissenlits au Lard
Dandelion Salad with Bacon and Croutons

(*Serves 5 to 6*)

•

Dandelion comes from the French *dent-de-lion*, meaning lion's tooth, undoubtedly because of the dandelion's jagged-edged leaves. Wild dandelions, plentiful from April to August, should be picked before the flowers open. They may be eaten raw in a salad or cooked like spinach. The wild species has more "bite" than the cultivated one available commercially in Italian stores. When a salad is served with a vinegar dressing, wine is omitted because it would conflict with the vinegar. However, this salad, originally from the Lyonnaise region, is the exception. With it should be served a light, cool Beaujolais, and the salad is served on lukewarm plates.

> 4 *tablespoons vegetable oil*
> 15 to 20 *slices* (½ *inch thick*) *French bread.*
> *If the loaf is large, cut only 10 slices and*
> *split them into halves.*
> 1 *large clove garlic, peeled*
> 4 *ounces bacon in 1 piece*
> 6 *anchovy fillets in oil, chopped*
> 1 *large clove garlic, peeled, crushed, and*
> *chopped fine*
> *salt and pepper to taste*

1 *pound dandelion greens (wild preferably),*
   washed and dried
2 *tablespoons good wine vinegar*
3 *hard-boiled eggs, peeled and quartered*

Heat the oil in a large skillet and brown the bread on both sides. Let cool enough to handle and rub each piece with the whole clove of garlic. Cut the bacon into strips ½-inch thick, and cut each strip across into ½-inch long sticks. Place the bacon *lardons* (the name of the little sticks in French) into a saucepan. Cover with cold water and bring to a boil. Let simmer 3 to 4 minutes. Cool under cold water and drain. Place in a skillet and cook the *lardons* over medium heat until they are crisp and brown. Meanwhile, mix the anchovies, chopped garlic, and some salt and pepper in the bottom of a large salad bowl. Add the dandelion greens and pour the hot *lardons* and the fat on top of the salad. Immediately, pour the vinegar into the hot skillet and shake it back and forth. Pour over the salad. Toss the salad, then add the egg quarters and the croutons. Serve immediately.

Tomato Salad

(Serves 6)

•

1½ *pounds ripe tomatoes (about 5 medium size)*
1 *teaspoon salt*
½ *teaspoon freshly ground white pepper*
1½ *tablespoons of good red wine vinegar*
⅓ *cup oil (preferably half olive, half peanut)*
½ *tablespoon minced fresh basil (about 6 to 8*
   leaves; if fresh basil is unavailable, use fresh
   tarragon, chervil, or parsley; do not use
   dried herbs.)

Wash the tomatoes, remove the cores and cut into thin slices, arranging the pieces attractively on a platter as you go along. Sprinkle with the salt and pepper, then with the vinegar, the oil, and finally the herbs. Keep in a cool place until ready to serve.

Salade d'Endives
Endive Salad

(*Serves 6*)

•

6 to 8 *firm white endives*
1 *egg yolk*
1 *tablespoon Dijon mustard*
2 *tablespoons wine or tarragon vinegar*
1 *large shallot or green onion bulb, minced*
salt
freshly ground white pepper
¾ *cup vegetable oil*

To prepare the endives, wash, then trim off any dark color on the ends. Cut crosswise into 1-inch chunks. Place the cut endive in ice-cold water until serving time. Then drain thoroughly, pat dry, and toss in the dressing.

To make the dressing, combine the egg yolk, mustard, vinegar, shallot, and salt and pepper in a salad bowl. Whip together vigorously. Then begin to add the oil very slowly, beating constantly. Makes about 1 cup of dressing. For this salad, use about ½ cup.

Note: The endives can also be cut into a *julienne* (see page 170). Separate the leaves and stack a few together and cut in long, thin strips. Place in water with a lot of ice. *The strips will curl up in the ice-cold water and be deliciously crisp.* Drain and dry carefully before tossing in the dressing at serving time.

Endives Braisées
Braised Endive

(*Serves 6 to 8*)

•

8 to 10 *medium-sized Belgian endives*
2 *tablespoons butter*
1 *teaspoon salt*
½ *tablespoon sugar*
juice of ½ lemon, strained
⅓ *cup water*
minced parsley

Trim the base of the endives and remove any bruised leaves. Wash carefully under cold running water. Drain.

Arrange the endives in an enameled, ovenproof casserole. Dot with the butter, sprinkle with salt and sugar, then pour over the lemon juice and water. Cover with a piece of waxed paper, then place a saucer or plate on top to keep it in place. Add the cover and bring to a boil. Reduce heat and braise on top of the stove or in a preheated 325° oven for 35 to 40 minutes, or until tender when pierced with a paring knife.

At this point, the endives can be placed in a tureen with their juices and refrigerated, covered, for 1 to 2 weeks. Or, they can also be served just as they are, hot from the broth. To serve, drain the endives, flatten with a large knife, then cut the large ones in half lengthwise.

Heat butter in a large skillet and sauté the endives for 5 to 6 minutes until golden. Garnish with minced parsley. You may also pour 1 or 2 tablespoons of brown gravy on top at the last moment, 2 to 3 tablespoons of melted butter, and top with chopped parsley.

Laitues Braisées
Braised Lettuce

(Serves 8)

•

Although lettuce is customarily braised with carrots, onions, herbs, etc., if you have a good brown sauce it is easier to blanch the lettuce and finish it with the sauce, and the result is just as good.

8 medium to small heads Boston lettuce

Remove any bruised leaves from the lettuce and wash in cold water, spreading the leaves gently to remove any sand. Drop the lettuce in a large pot of boiling water, preferably salted, and cover until it comes to a boil again. Remove the cover as soon as it boils (if it is cooked covered, the lettuce will turn yellow) and place a piece of cheesecloth, towel, or even paper towel on top of the water. *This helps the lettuce to cook evenly all around.* Let boil for approximately 20 minutes, or until the cores of the lettuce are tender when pierced with a knife. Immediately place the lettuce under cold running water. *Place a large spoon or a skimmer across the kettle containing the lettuce so that the cold water does not hit the tender leaves directly.* When cold, remove the lettuce and squeeze each one gently, being careful to keep the shape of the lettuce. You will have long, narrow, even shapes. Split each lettuce lengthwise. Lay the halves of lettuce, cut side up, flat on a board. Flatten each half with the flat blade of a knife. Fold the leafy end approximately ¼ of the way over the cut end. Turn the lettuce half so that the folded side is underneath and trim the core off. You should have nice little bundles resembling triangles.

> 4 *tablespoons sweet butter*
> *salt*
> *freshly ground black pepper*
> 1 *cup brown sauce (see Basic Brown Sauce,*
> *page 31)*

In a large skillet, melt the butter and place the lettuce pieces next to one another, folded side up. Sprinkle with salt and pepper. Cook on medium heat 6 to 8 minutes until the lettuce is slightly brown. Turn on the other side and cook for 4 to 5 minutes on medium heat. Add the brown gravy, cover with a piece of waxed or *parchemin* (parchment) paper, and place in a preheated 400° oven for 6 to 8 minutes.

> 2 *tablespoons sweet butter*
> 1 *tablespoon chopped parsley*

At serving time, arrange the lettuce on a serving platter and coat each "bundle" with a small spoon of gravy. Melt the butter in a frypan; when it turns hazelnut in color, pour over the lettuce. Place a little dot of chopped parsley on each lettuce and serve immediately.

Concombres Persillés
Parsleyed Cucumbers

(Enough garnish for 6 to 8)

•

4 *medium-sized cucumbers*

Cut each cucumber into 4 chunks or cylinders. Place each cylinder, flat side down, on the board and quarter it. With a small paring knife, cut off the seeds and the skin. With your knife, shape the little cucumber pieces as you go along. All the pieces should be about the same size and shape. Drop the cucumbers in salted boiling water and boil on high heat for 6 to 7 minutes. The pieces should be tender when pierced with the point of a knife. Immediately place under cold water to stop the cooking and cool off the cucumbers. *Be careful that the spray of water is not too strong, or it will break the cucumbers. You may place a spoon across the saucepan so that the cold water does not hit the cucumbers directly.* When cold, drain and set aside.

> 3 *tablespoons sweet butter*
> ½ *teaspoon salt*
> ¼ *teaspoon freshly ground white pepper*
> 1 *tablespoon chopped parsley*

Melt the butter in a skillet, add the cucumbers, salt and pepper and sauté on medium heat for 4 to 5 minutes. Add the parsley and serve immediately.

Concombres à la Crème
Cucumbers with Cream

(Enough garnish for 6 to 8)

•

Follow Basic Recipe (see page 255)

> 4 *cooked cucumbers in pieces*
> 1 *tablespoon sweet butter*
> 1 *teaspoon salt*
> ¼ *teaspoon freshly ground white pepper*
> ¼ *cup heavy cream*
> 1 *tablespoon chopped parsley*
> 1 *tablespoon chopped tarragon (If you do not*
>   *have fresh tarragon, omit.)*

Melt the butter in a large skillet and add the drained cucumbers, salt and pepper. Sauté for 1 minute on medium heat. Add the cream and boil it down on medium to high heat until it is reduced and thick enough to coat the cucumbers (about 5 to 6 minutes). Sprinkle with the herbs and serve immediately.

Poireaux au Gratin
Gratin of Leeks

(Serves 6 to 8)

•

> 8 to 10 *large leeks*
> ½ *pound bacon*
> 1 *cup water*

salt
freshly ground white pepper
dash of ground thyme
2 tablespoons butter
2 tablespoons flour
1 cup milk
1 egg yolk
½ cup heavy cream
2 tablespoons grated Swiss cheese

Cut the leeks into 2-inch pieces, using only the white and light green parts. Trim off the roots. Split the pieces into fourths (measured, there should be about 6 cups), and wash very thoroughly to get rid of any sand. Lift them out of the water rather than draining them, or you may get some of the sand you have washed off.

Cut the bacon into 2-inch pieces and sauté in a frying pan until nicely brown. Add the leeks, water, salt and pepper to taste (this will change depending on the saltiness of the bacon), and thyme. Cover tightly and cook for 20 to 25 minutes, or long enough so the leeks are tender and all the water has evaporated.

Melt the butter in a small saucepan, stir in the flour until smooth, add the milk and cook, whipping constantly with a wire whisk, until the *béchamel* comes to a boil. Continue to cook for 5 minutes. Stir yolk and cream together, mix into the white sauce, then combine with the leeks, stirring constantly with a wooden spatula.

Pour into a shallow ovenproof dish, sprinkle with the cheese, and bake in a preheated 375° oven for about 20 minutes, until golden brown.

Leeks, like onions, are delicious with beef or fowl. They are widely used in France and are sometimes called "the asparagus of the poor" because they are much less expensive than asparagus, and they are eaten cold with a vinaigrette sauce like asparagus. In the United States it is the contrary because leeks are the more expensive.

Artichokes and Artichoke Bottoms

•

The artichoke, which has been cultivated in France since the beginning of the sixteenth century, is now a common vegetable on the table of the American housewife. The small artichoke can be served raw and eaten with butter and salt. Cooked, it can be served cold as a first course with oil and vinegar; lukewarm, as a vegetable with hollandaise or melted butter; or hot, stuffed with meat or vegetable. A good-sized artichoke weighs about 8 ounces (*i.e.*, 32 to the case), it takes approximately 40 to 45 minutes to cook (uncovered, to keep it green) in a lot of boiling, salted water. To check for "doneness," pull out a leaf; if it comes out easily it is cooked. Add the artichokes to the water only when the water is boiling. Cool them off under cold water as soon as they are cooked, otherwise they will turn yellowish very rapidly. It is better not to refrigerate them, but if you have to (you may cook them a day ahead), take them out of the refrigerator 1 hour before serving. If you serve them lukewarm, drop them in boiling water for 2 minutes and choke them just before serving.

1. Trim the stem with a knife or break it off—this helps to pull out of the heart the stringy fibers that artichokes develop when they get too old. Cut approximately 1½ inches off the top leaves.

2. Trim the points of the rest of the leaves with scissors (for esthetic purposes). Secure a slice of lemon to the base of the artichoke and cook it with the artichoke. This is done only when the artichoke is to be kept a few days in the refrigerator. The lemon keeps the bottom white.

3. At serving time, pull out the center leaves, which should come out together like a small funnel. Keep them in one piece.

With a teaspoon, remove the choke from the cavity and replace the center leaves upside down. Garnish the center with curly parsley.

Artichoke Bottoms or Hearts—Basic Technique

Artichoke bottoms are used in countless recipes, cold or hot, stuffed with different ingredients from smoked salmon to stewed tomatoes to poached beef marrow. Many restaurants use canned bottoms, but the difference is quite evident. Although it takes some practice to shape or "turn" the artichoke properly, it is quite worth the effort.

1. With a sharp knife, cut the leaves all around the artichoke heart, as close as you can without taking too much "meat" out of the heart.
2. Cut the leaves at the point where they attach to the choke or the "hay."
3. With a small knife, trim the remaining greenish leaves and smooth the bottom as well as you can. Rub each heart with lemon. For 6 bottoms add:

> 1 *quart water*
> 2 *tablespoons vegetable oil*
> *the juice of 1 lemon*
> *½ tablespoon salt*

Bring all the ingredients to a boil and simmer for 40 to 45 minutes, or until tender when pierced with the point of a small knife. When cool enough to handle, remove the "hay" with a spoon, then place the hearts in a container with enough of the cooking liquid to cover. They can be kept for at least 1 week in the refrigerator in the broth.

Artichauts au Beurre Moussant
Artichokes in Butter Sauce

(Serves 6 to 8)

•

6 good-sized artichokes (see page 258 for
  instructions)
¼ cup water
dash salt
freshly ground white pepper
juice of ½ lemon
½ cup (1 stick) sweet butter, cut into
  pieces

Place artichokes in a large kettle with boiling, salted water.
Bring to a boil again, covering the kettle to hasten the process,
and then cook, uncovered, at a rolling boil for about 45 minutes,
or until a leaf will pull out easily. Cool immediately under cold
running water to stop the cooking. When cold, spread the leaves
apart so you can reach the interior easily. Then pull out the
center cone of leaves, all in one piece. This will expose the
choke. Scrape out the choke with a teaspoon. Turn the cone of
leaves upside down and replace in the hollow of the artichoke.
Place a sprig of parsley on the artichoke. To serve, arrange on
folded napkins. It is better to serve the artichokes lukewarm or
cool, but not cold. They lose some flavor if they are cooled in
the refrigerator.

Butter Sauce

Bring the water, salt, pepper, and lemon juice to a rolling boil.
Add the butter, bit by bit, shaking the saucepan back and forth
until all the butter has been absorbed and the mixture starts to

foam and rise. *At this point the butter will homogenize with the water and thicken. It is important to stop the cooking at this particular moment because if the butter heats longer it will break down and clarify again.* This is a kind of *beurre blanc.* Pour into a heated serving boat and serve immediately.

How to Prepare and Cook Cauliflower

•

In choosing cauliflower, be sure the heads are very white and very firm, with small compact flowers squeezed together.

With a good heavy knife, cut off the leaves from the stem. Separate the flowerets from the central core by cutting around each one with a knife.

Next, with a small paring knife, pull off the hard skin around the stem of each floweret.

Have ready a large pot of boiling, salted water. Add the cauliflower. Bring to a boil again and cook, uncovered, for 10 to 12 minutes, or until the stems can be pierced easily with the point of a knife. Refresh immediately under cold running water to stop the cooking. To prevent the tender flowerets from breaking under the stream of cold water, rest a large spoon across the kettle so the water will hit the handle of the spoon and fall gently onto the cauliflower. When cold, drain thoroughly, arrange on a platter, cover with a clean towel wrung out in cold water or with plastic wrap, and refrigerate.

The cooked cauliflower can be sautéed in butter and garnished with parsley; reheated in boiling water and served with melted butter or hollandaise; added to a hot cream sauce (*béchamel*); or served au gratin (that is, mixed with a rich *béchamel*, sprinkled with grated Swiss or Parmesan cheese and then browned under the broiler).

Choux Fleurs au Gratin
Cauliflower au Gratin
(*Serves 6 to 8*)

•

2 *small or 1 large head cauliflower* (*1¾ pounds*
without the leaves), *cooked in water* (*see*
page 261)
3 *tablespoons sweet butter*
3 *tablespoons flour*
1½ *cups milk*
¾ *cup heavy cream*
½ *teaspoon salt*
¼ *teaspoon freshly ground white pepper*
⅛ *teaspoon freshly ground nutmeg*

Melt the butter in a saucepan and add the flour. Cook on low heat for about 1 minute, stirring with a whisk. Do not let the mixture brown. Add the milk and bring to a boil on medium heat, stirring constantly to avoid scorching. Simmer on low heat for 3 to 4 minutes. Add cream, salt, pepper, nutmeg, and bring to a boil. Set aside, covered with plastic wrap to avoid a skin forming on top.

1 *tablespoon sweet butter*
1½ *tablespoons grated Parmesan cheese or*
grated Swiss cheese (*or a mixture of both*)

Butter well a gratin dish about 1¼ inches deep. Place the flowerets in the dish stem side down and coat with the white sauce. Sprinkle with cheese, place on a cookie sheet and cook in a preheated 400° oven for 20 minutes until golden brown. Serve immediately.

Purée Freneuse
Puree of White Turnips
(Serves 6)

•

1¾ *pounds white turnips* (*about 4 or 5, which*
    yield 1½ pounds peeled)
2 *potatoes* (*about ½ pound peeled*)
1 *teaspoon salt*
¼ *teaspoon freshly ground white pepper*
¾ *cup heavy cream*
3 *tablespoons arrowroot or cornstarch*
2 *tablespoons sweet butter*

Cut the peeled turnips and potatoes into large chunks, place
in a pot with enough water to cover, add ½ teaspoon of salt and
bring to a boil. Cover and simmer for 30 minutes. They should
be tender when pierced with the point of a knife. *Certain
periods of the year the turnips are very tough and fibrous and
impossible to cook. If you have such turnips you will not get
good results and it is advisable to substitute another dish.* Drain
in a colander and push the mixture through a fine metal sieve
with a metal spatula or use a food mill. Place the puree back in
a pot, add the rest of the salt, pepper and butter and mix well.
At that point the puree is very liquid. I do not like to strain the
puree in a cloth to remove the excess water because if the puree
is too concentrated, it is bitter. Mix the arrowroot with the
cream using a whip to blend both ingredients together. Add the
cream mixture to the puree and stir with a whisk until it comes
to a boil.

Carottes Vichy
Steamed Carrots

(*Serves 6 to 8*)

•

2½ *pounds fresh carrots (about 16 to 20,*
    depending on size), peeled and sliced very
    thin (about 8 cups sliced)
½ *stick sweet butter*
2 *teaspoons salt*
4 *teaspoons sugar*
4 *cups water*
1 *tablespoon fresh chopped parsley*

Place all ingredients except parsley in a kettle (the water should just cover the carrots). Boil uncovered for about 35 minutes, or until all the liquid has evaporated and the carrots are just moist. Serve sprinkled with chopped parsley.

Petits Pois à la Francaise
French Style Peas

(*Serves 6*)

•

8 *ounces fresh tiny white onions (about 30 to*
    35), peeled (these onions are the size of
    large olives)
1 *large head Boston lettuce, sliced crosswise into*
    ½-inch slices

1 *tablespoon sweet butter*
2 *teaspoons sugar*
1 *teaspoon salt*
1 *cup water*
1 *pound fresh small shelled peas (frozen will do)*

Place all of the ingredients, except the peas, in a large casserole (not aluminum); bring to a boil, cover and simmer for 15 minutes. Add the peas and simmer for an additional 10 minutes.

1 *tablespoon sweet butter, softened*
1 *tablespoon flour*

Mix the flour and butter together until well blended (this is called a *beurre manié*). Pour the liquid from the peas on the butter mixture and mix with a whisk to blend together. Pour the sauce back onto the peas, cover and simmer for 5 to 6 minutes. Taste for seasoning, you may need a dash of sugar.

Petits Pois Paysanne
Stewed Peas

(Serves 6)

•

1½ *pounds shelled fresh peas (or frozen small*
   young tender peas)
1 *6-ounce piece of cured pork or bacon. Cut into*
   ½-inch slices. Cut each slice across into
   little strips ½-inch wide. These little pieces
   of cured pork are called lardons *in French.*
   (About 1 cup lardons.*)*
2 *dozen tiny white onions, peeled (or 2 cups*

> cubed onions; 1-inch cubes)
> 2 dozen small baby carrots, peeled (or 1½ cups
>   small carrot sticks)
> 1 tablespoon flour
> 1½ cups water
> 1½ teaspoons salt
> ¼ teaspoon fresh pepper
> 1 teaspoon sugar

Place the *lardons* in a saucepan, cover with cold water and bring to a boil and boil for 1 minute. Cool under cold running water and drain. Place in a heavy casserole and cook the *lardons* over medium heat for about 8 minutes, or until they have rendered most of their fat and are well browned. Add the onions and sauté for 1 minute. Mix in the flour, add the water and bring to a boil, stirring constantly to blend the flour with the liquid. Add the carrots, cover tightly and cook over medium heat for 10 minutes. Add salt, pepper, sugar, and the peas. Bring to a boil, cover tightly and simmer slowly for 20 to 25 minutes. The peas may be reheated for the next day.

Timbale d'Epinards
Spinach Mold

(Serves 6)

•

1 pound fresh spinach
1 teaspoon salt
½ teaspoon freshly ground pepper
⅛ teaspoon freshly grated nutmeg
3 tablespoons sweet butter
2 teaspoons flour

¾ cup milk
½ cup heavy cream
3 eggs
6 slices firm white bread, cut into rounds about
    2½ inches wide*

Butter thoroughly 6 or 7 small *dariole* or *baba* molds measuring approximately 2¼ inches in diameter and 2 inches high. Set aside.

Remove the stems from the spinach. Fold the leaves vertically, underside up, in one hand. Grasp the stem with the other hand and rip it off. Wash the spinach carefully. Then drop into boiling salted water and boil, uncovered, for 5 to 6 minutes. Cool under running water. Drain and press to get rid of all the moisture. Chop the spinach coarsely, it will yield about 1 loose cup. Then sprinkle with salt, pepper, and nutmeg.

Melt the butter in a heavy saucepan and let it cook until it is black and smoking. Add the spinach and mix with a fork. Sprinkle with the flour, mixing it in well. Add the milk and cream and bring to a boil, stirring constantly. Take off the heat and cool to lukewarm. Beat the eggs and stir into the spinach. Fill the prepared molds and place in a pan of cold water. Bake in a preheated 375° oven for 25 to 30 minutes, or until set.

To serve, run a knife around the inside of the mold to loosen the *timbale*. Unmold each *timbale* on a round of bread and arrange around a roast, or serve separately as a vegetable course.

* Combine 2 or 3 tablespoons butter and vegetable oil in a skillet. When hot, brown the rounds of bread until golden.

Soufflé aux Epinards
Spinach Soufflé

(*Serves 6*)

•

6 eggs poached

To poach the eggs, use a wide, shallow pan (8 inches wide, 3 inches deep). Pour 4 to 6 cups water and ½ cup white vinegar (vinegar helps to "firm" the whites) into the pan and bring to a boil. Break the eggs, 1 at a time, into a saucer or plate and slip each egg into the boiling water. Turn the heat down, allowing the water barely to simmer or "shiver" (*fremir*). As the eggs cook, drag the cup of a large metal spoon or skimmer across the surface of the water to move the eggs and to keep them from sticking to the bottom of the pan. Cook for 1½ to 2 minutes only, because the eggs are going to cook again in the soufflé and they should be cooked only to a minimum. For regular poached eggs, cook for about 3 to 3½ minutes. At this point, the whites should be set and the yolks soft to the touch. Lift from the hot water with a slotted spoon and place in a bowl of ice water. This washes off the vinegar and stops the cooking. When cool enough to handle, trim. Cover your left hand with a clean dry cloth, lift the egg with the slotted spoon into the palm of this hand, and trim with a sharp knife or a pair of scissors. Place back in the ice water. Once cold, poached eggs can be kept in cold water, refrigerated, for several days.

½ tablespoon sweet butter
1 tablespoon flour

Butter a 2-quart soufflé mold and sprinkle with the flour. Pour off any excess flour. Refrigerate the mold. By having the coating on the mold very cold, it helps the soufflé to rise straight up.

1 *pound fresh spinach*
1½ *cups milk*
4 *tablespoons all-purpose flour*
1 *teaspoon salt*
¼ *teaspoon pepper*
⅛ *teaspoon nutmeg*
4 *eggs, separated*
2 *extra white eggs*

Preheat the oven to 375°. Wash the spinach and drop into salted boiling water. Boil for 8 to 10 minutes. Remove from the heat and put immediately under cold running water. When cold, drain the spinach and press with your hands to extract as much water as possible. You will have approximately 1 to 1½ cups of cooked spinach. Place the spinach in the blender with 1 cup of milk and blend until you have a smooth puree. Pour this into a saucepan. Rinse the blender with the remaining milk and add it to the saucepan. Add the flour, salt, pepper, and nutmeg and mix with a whisk. Turn on the heat and bring to a boil, stirring frequently with the whisk. Cook for 5 minutes. Remove from the heat and let cool, stirring with the whisk for 5 to 6 minutes. Add the 4 egg yolks and mix well. Whip the 6 egg whites until they are stiff, but not dry. Whip about ⅓ of the beaten whites into the spinach vigorously with a whisk. Gently fold (see page 296) in the remaining egg whites. Pour ⅓ of the soufflé mixture into the prepared mold. Carefully remove the poached eggs from the water and dry them with a paper towel. Arrange the poached eggs on top and cover with the remainder of the soufflé mixture. Smooth the top with a spatula and place in a preheated 375° oven for 20 to 25 minutes. Do not overcook. Serve at once.

Note: By the time you serve the soufflé, the eggs will be almost cooked in the center.

Beignets d'Aubergines
Eggplant Fritters

(Makes about 15)

•

This recipe is extremely simple and quite good. The eggplant can be substituted with corn (fresh kernels sliced from the cob), artichoke bottoms, cauliflower, etc. The fritters are best when they just come out of the fryer. *If they are kept too long they will soften. If they are too thick they will be mushy in the middle.*

> 1 *eggplant, peeled and cut into* ⅛-*inch slices*
> *in a* julienne *(i.e.,* thin, long strips. *About*
> 3½ *loose cups of* julienne.)
> 1½ *cups flour*
> 1 *tablespoon baking powder*
> 1½ *cups water*

Mix the flour, baking powder, and 1 cup of water in a bowl. Mix with a whip until smooth. Add the remaining water and mix again until smooth. *If you add all the water at once it might get lumpy.* (By adding only 1 cup at first, the batter is easily worked into a smooth, thick mixture. Then there is no more danger of lumps forming and the rest of the water may be added.) Mix the eggplant *julienne* in with a spoon.

> 2 *tablespoons vegetable oil*
> *salt*

Heat the oil in a large skillet. When hot, drop about 2 table-spoons of the eggplant batter in the oil and spread it. It should be about 3 to 4 inches in diameter. Cook for 2 minutes on medium heat on the first side and about 1½ minutes on the other side. You should be able to make 3 to 4 fritters at one time, depending on the size of your skillet. Drain on paper towel and sprinkle lightly with salt.

Pommes Persillées
Parsleyed Potatoes

(Serves 6 to 8)

•

3 *pounds small potatoes (If big potatoes are*
   used, cut them into large chunks and trim
   the pieces so that you have about 30 pieces,
   approximately 1½ inches in diameter.)
1 *teaspoon salt*
½ *stick sweet butter*
4 *tablespoons freshly chopped parsley*

Cover the potatoes with cold water, add the salt and bring to a boil. Boil slowly, about 15 to 18 minutes, or until tender when pierced with a small knife. Drain the potatoes, place them back in the saucepan and over medium heat to evaporate all remain-ing water. *This step is important as it will give you a very moist and rich-textured potato.* Add the butter and parsley and cook just long enough for the butter to melt and coat the potatoes. Serve immediately.

Pommes Savonnettes
Potatoes Savonnettes

(Serves 6)

•

6 *Idaho potatoes, peeled*
½ *teaspoon salt*
½ *teaspoon freshly ground pepper*
4 *tablespoons* (½ *stick*) *sweet butter*
1 *tablespoon vegetable oil*

Cut each potato into thick slices, approximately 1½ inches thick. Trim each slice into a round or oval so that all the slices have the same shape and lie flat in a big iron skillet. *The slices must not overlap. Use 2 skillets.* You should have about 20 to 25 slices. (Save the trimmings to make soup or mashed potatoes.) Sprinkle with salt and pepper. Add the butter, bit by bit, the oil, and just enough water to barely cover the slices. Bring to a rolling boil on top of the stove, then place in a preheated 425° oven for 35 to 40 minutes, or until all the water has evaporated and the slices are sizzling in the oil-and-butter mixture. Take out of the oven and check to see if the potatoes are nicely browned underneath. If not, place over direct heat on top of the stove for 2 to 3 minutes.

To serve, turn the slices upside down on a serving tray and brush with melted butter to "shine" the potatoes.

Note: While cooking, the potatoes absorb the water and remain very moist inside while browning on the outside.

Pommes Biron
Biron Potatoes

(Serves 8)

•

2½ pounds (5) Idaho potatoes
½ teaspoon salt
¼ teaspoon freshly ground pepper
⅛ teaspoon grated nutmeg
5 tablespoons sweet butter
1 tablespoon oil

Place the potatoes in a preheated 425° oven and cook for 1 hour. When cool enough to handle, scoop the pulp from the potatoes. Mix the salt, pepper, nutmeg, and 4 tablespoons of butter into the pulp. (*The potato mixture should still be lumpy.*) Melt the remaining butter and oil in a *pommes Anna* pan (you may substitute an 8-inch iron pan about 2 inches deep). Pack the mixture into the pan. Place in a preheated 425° oven for 45 minutes, pressing the potatoes with a skimmer every 10 or 15 minutes. Remove from the oven and let cool a few minutes. Turn upside down on a serving platter. It should slide out easily. At this point, you have what is called *pommes macaire.* It looks like a nicely-browned cake.

3 tablespoons heavy cream, slightly beaten with
a whisk to make foamy
¼ cup grated Gruyère cheese

Spread the cream on top of the "cake," sprinkle with cheese, and place under the broiler for 1 or 2 minutes until nicely glazed. Serve immediately.

Gratin Dauphinois
Scalloped Potatoes in Garlic and Cream

(Serves 8)

•

Gratin dauphinois, one of the simplest potato preparations, might very well be the most sublime manner of treating this lowly vegetable. A specialty of Grenoble, a town bordering the Alps, it is well-known in the eastern part of France, particularly around the Rhône Valley, and is made in many restaurants with varying degrees of success. In Grenoble it is considered heretical to sprinkle the dish with cheese, but it is accepted in Lyon. The cheese is necessary if the dish is made mostly of milk, for it will help the gratin to achieve a beautiful golden color. However, many fine restaurants use a large amount of cream, or often only cream is used. In these cases, the potatoes will color beautifully without the help of the cheese. *It is essential that the potatoes, once sliced, are not soaked or rinsed in water as they would lose the starch needed for the dish to be smooth and creamy.*

Around the Grenoble area any leftover *gratin dauphinois* is eaten without reheating, accompanied by a green salad seasoned with oil, vinegar, and a generous amount of chopped garlic.

> 2 pounds boiling potatoes, peeled (about 5 to 6
>   cups)
> 2 cups milk
> 1½ cups heavy cream
> 1 large or 2 small cloves garlic, peeled, crushed,
>   and minced to puree
> ¾ teaspoon salt
> ½ teaspoon freshly ground white pepper

1 *tablespoon butter*
½ *cup grated Swiss cheese (about 2 ounces)*

Wash the potatoes well and dry them thoroughly. Slice the potatoes ⅛ inch thick into a large saucepan. Add the milk, cream, garlic, salt, and pepper and bring the liquid to a boil over moderate heat, stirring with a wooden spatula to prevent scorching. Remove the pan from the heat. Pour the potato mixture into a well-buttered gratin dish or a shallow baking dish. Sprinkle the grated cheese over the mixture and bake on a baking sheet in a preheated 400° oven for about 1 hour. The potatoes are done when they are nicely browned and the tip of a knife pierces a potato easily.

Let the dish stand for 15 to 20 minutes before serving.

Gratin Savoyard
Baked Sliced Potatoes with Cheese

•

The Gratin Savoyard is traditionally made with Beaufort, a cheese from Savoy. If Beaufort is unavailable, use a good Swiss cheese.

3 *pounds good mealy potatoes (about 2¼*
    pounds peeled) sliced very thin (about 7
    cups sliced)
¾ *stick sweet butter*
1 *teaspoon salt*
¾ *teaspoon freshly ground white pepper*
⅛ *teaspoon grated nutmeg*
2 *cups grated Beaufort cheese*
1¼ *cups chicken stock*

Place the thinly sliced potatoes in cold water to cover. Butter a gratin dish heavily (we used one measuring 11¼ inches long, 7½ inches wide and 1¾ inches deep). Mix the salt, pepper and nutmeg together. Drain the potatoes and set the oven at 425°. Place a third of the potatoes in the bottom of the dish. Sprinkle with a third of the seasonings, a third of the cheese and a third of the butter. Repeat the same procedure twice more until all the ingredients have been used up. Add the chicken stock and place the dish on a cookie sheet (this allows good transfer of heat during cooking and catches any spillage). Place in oven and bake at 425° for about seventy minutes. By this time, all the liquid (except for the butter) should be evaporated from the potatoes and the top should be nicely browned. Remove from oven and let the gratin stand for 10 or 15 minutes before serving.

Pommes Dauphine
Puff Potatoes

(*Serves 6 to 8*)

•

¾ *pounds firm potatoes* (*about 3 to 4, depending on size*)
1 *teaspoon salt*

Wash the potatoes, cover with cold water, add the salt and bring to a boil. Cook, boiling slightly, about 20 to 25 minutes until done. Be sure the potatoes are always covered with water during cooking. As soon as the potatoes are cooked, drain in a colander. When cool enough to handle, peel the potatoes, cut into chunks and push through a fine metal sieve. *Yield:* About 1½ cups of pulp.

1 *cup water*
½ *teaspoon salt*
⅛ *teaspoon freshly ground white pepper*
⅓ *stick sweet butter, cut into pieces*
1 *cup all-purpose flour*
4 *large eggs*

Place the water, salt, pepper, and butter in a heavy saucepan. Bring to a boil. As soon as the water boils, remove from the heat and add all the flour at once. Work the mixture with a wooden spatula. Place back on the stove and cook 3 to 4 minutes on low heat, stirring the mixture, which will form into a shiny, homogeneous mass. Transfer to a clean bowl and let cool for 10 minutes. Add the eggs, 1 at a time, beating well after each addition. Stir in the potato pulp.

Heat fresh vegetable oil in a deep skillet (you should have 1½ to 2 inches of oil) to about 350°. Place 1 tablespoon of the mixture at a time in the oil, pushing the dough out of the spoon with your finger. Make about 10 to 20 pieces at a time. Cook for 8 to 10 minutes, turning the potatoes in the oil to have them brown evenly on all sides. As soon as one batch is done, remove with a slotted spoon and place in a tray lined with paper towels. Keep hot in a 200° oven while you are cooking another batch. *Yield:* 55 to 60 potato puffs. Sprinkle lightly with salt and serve as soon as possible. If the potatoes sit too long they will soften and lose their delicious crispness.

Pommes Soufflées
Puffed or Inflated Potato Slices

(Serves 6)

•

Pommes soufflées are still made in most of the classic French restaurants. It is a delicate operation because the potatoes have to be just right; if they have too much moisture like new potatoes, it does not work. If they are soft or marbled like old potatoes, it does not work either. In any case, it is customary to have 10 to 20 percent of the potatoes stay flat. These are served as regular fried potatoes. The recipe was discovered, according to the *Larousse Gastronomique*, in 1837 on the inauguration day of the railroad in a small town near Paris. A meal had been prepared, which included fried, sliced potatoes, by a restaurant for the official delegation. However, the train was late and the chef had removed his potatoes from the frying pan half-cooked and had set them aside. When the guests finally arrived, the potatoes were dipped into the hot oil and, to the chef's amazement, started to puff up. Later on a recipe was worked out from that first experiment.

> 3 to 4 big Idaho potatoes
> 1 gallon vegetable oil

Trim the potatoes all around to shape a "tube" 2½ to 3 inches in diameter. With a slicer, or by hand, slice the potatoes into ¼- to ⅜-inch thick slices. Wash in cold water and dry with a paper towel. Heat vegetable oil in 2 different saucepans. One to 325° and the other to 375°. Drop approximately 15 to 20 slices in the 325° fryer and shake the pan back and forth on top of the heat for 6 to 7 minutes. An asbestos pad makes the saucepan slide easier and helps the shaking. This is a delicate part of the operation (be careful not to splash your hand or the stove with the hot oil), but the potatoes have to be agitated to puff up. After 4 to 5 minutes some blisters should start to appear on the slices. Keep shaking the pan for another minute.

Lift a few slices at a time onto a skimmer and dip into the 375° fryer. The slices should swell instantly. As they puff, transfer the slices to a towel to drain. They will collapse, but pick out the ones that puffed and arrange them in a tray before final cooking. At this point the potatoes can be kept, covered with a towel, for several hours. At serving time, drop the slices into the 375° fryer and cook them for approximately 1 minute, moving them with a skimmer to have them brown evenly. They should be crisp enough to stay puffed. Sprinkle with salt and serve immediately on a folded napkin.

Note: During the first cooking, the surface of the slices becomes watertight. When the slices are dropped into the hot oil, the water imprisoned inside the slices tries to escape and pushes from the center, making the potatoes puff up.

Beignets de Pommes de Terre
Potato Fritters

(*Serves 6*)

•

4 to 5 *potatoes (about 1⅓ pounds)*
3 *eggs*
2 *tablespoons flour*
1 *medium onion, peeled and grated (about ½*
cup)
1 *tablespoon chopped parsley*

1 *teaspoon salt*
⅛ *teaspoon freshly ground white pepper*
2 *tablespoons heavy cream*
1 *cup (approximately) vegetable oil*

Peel, wash, and grate the potatoes. The potatoes should be liquid. Press the mixture in a towel to extrude some of the juices. Mix with the eggs, flour, grated onion, parsley, salt, pepper, and cream. Heat 3 tablespoons of oil at a time in a large skillet and drop 2 tablespoons of the batter for each fritter. Make 3 or 4 fritters at a time, depending on the size of the skillet. Cook about 2 minutes over medium heat on the first side; turn over and cook 1 minute on the other side. Repeat until you use all the batter. *Yield:* About 12 to 14 fritters. *Serve as quickly as possible because the fritters will eventually soften and lose their crispness.*

Crêpes Mère Blanc
Potato Pancakes

(Serves 6)

•

This is a small potato pancake originated by Mrs. Blanc, an innkeeper in a small village near Bourg-en-Bresse called Vonnas. Her grandson is still there maintaining the same tradition, and her son runs the celebrated Chapon Fin, one of the best tables of France, in a town nearby called Thoissey. The crêpes are usually served as a garnish with meat, and more rarely sprinkled with sugar and served for dessert. They are approximately 3½ inches in diameter and ¼ inch thick in the center. As you see, they are quite different from the extra-thin and lacy pancake usually made in French cooking.

2 *medium potatoes* (*14 to 16 ounces*)
1½ *tablespoons flour*
1 *small teaspoon salt*
⅛ *teaspoon freshly ground white pepper*
3 to 4 *eggs, depending on size*
⅓ *cup heavy cream*
1 *stick sweet butter*

Place the potatoes in cold water, bring them to a boil, and cook them until they are tender, boiling gently for 35 to 40 minutes. Remove from the water and when cool enough to handle, peel the potatoes and push them through a food mill or potato masher. This gives you approximately 1½ cups of smooth paste. Add the flour and mix with a whisk. Add the salt and pepper and the eggs 2 at a time. Mix until smooth before adding more eggs. Add the cream and mix until smooth again. Refrigerate. *If, on the following day, the mixture is too thick, add 1 or 2 tablespoons of milk to thin it down. It should have the consistency of a Russian or French dressing.* Place 1½ tablespoons of butter in a large skillet. When the butter turns to a nutty color, drop 1½ tablespoons of batter into the skillet, letting it spread by itself. You should be able to make 3 pancakes in each batch, allowing enough space in between crêpes so that each one takes on a nice round shape. Cook on medium fire for approximately 50 to 60 seconds on the first side, turn over and cook about 30 seconds on the other side. Remove to a platter and keep warm. *Yield:* About 20 crêpes; enough for 6 persons.

Rizotto Piémontaise
Risotto with Cheese and Saffron

(Serves 6)

•

1 cup Carolina rice (or any unconverted rice, or
    rice that is not par-boiled)
2 tablespoons sweet butter
1 medium onion, peeled and sliced very thin
    (1 cup)
1 teaspoon real saffron pistils
2 cups chicken broth
½ cup dry white wine
½ teaspoon freshly ground white pepper
salt, depending on the saltiness of the chicken
    broth

Melt the butter in a heavy pot with a cover, and add the
onion. Cook on low heat for 3 to 4 minutes, stirring with a
wooden spoon. Do not allow the onion to take on any color.
Add the rice and mix well so that all the grains are coated with
the butter. Add the saffron, broth, wine, pepper, and salt and
bring to a boil, stirring to avoid scorching. Reduce heat to a
very low temperature, cover the pot, and let cook for 25 minutes.

⅔ cup good grated Swiss cheese
2 tablespoons grated Parmesan cheese
1 tablespoon sweet butter

Five minutes before serving, add the above ingredients to the
rice and mix in with a fork. *The mixture will become quite
sticky and mushy, similar to potatoes, but quite delicious.*

Riz Pilaf
Rice Pilaf

(Serves 6 to 8)

•

1½ *cups converted or par-boiled rice*
1 *tablespoon sweet butter*
½ *onion, peeled and minced*
3 *cups chicken broth, your own or canned*
salt
freshly ground white pepper
dash dried thyme
1 *bay leaf*

Heat the butter in a deep saucepan. Add the onion and sauté for 2 minutes on medium to low heat. Keep stirring with a spoon. Do not allow the onion to brown. Add the rice and mix with the butter well, so that all the grains are coated with butter. Then add the broth and the seasonings. Bring to a boil on top of the stove. Cover tightly and place in a preheated 400° oven for 20 minutes.

Riz Valencienne
Rice Valenciana

(Serves 6 to 8)

•

2 *cups par-boiled or converted rice*
3 *tablespoons olive oil*
½ *cup chopped onion* (1 *onion*)

1 *cup diced fresh green pepper (1 pepper,*
      seeded)
1 *cup diced fresh tomato (1 tomato)*
¼ *teaspoon fresh or dried thyme leaves*
¼ *teaspoon freshly ground black pepper*
4 *cups beef or chicken bouillon*

Pour the oil into a thick enameled pot and place on the fire. Add the onion and sizzle for 1 minute. Add the green pepper and tomato and cook for another 2 minutes. Add the rice, thyme, pepper, and stir to have the rice well coated with the oil. Add the stock and bring to a boil, stirring to avoid scorching. Taste for seasoning; you might need salt, depending on the saltiness of the broth. Cover and place in a preheated 400° oven for 20 minutes. Stir with a fork to separate the grains and serve.

Nouilles Fraîches
Fresh Noodles

(Serves 6)

•

Making fresh noodles is easier when one uses a small rolling machine available in most gourmet shops. If one has to roll the noodles by hand with a rolling pin, the dough cannot be as stiff and the proportion of water has to be increased.

2 *cups all-purpose flour*
1 *teaspoon salt*
1 *egg*
2 *egg yolks*
1 *tablespoon olive oil*
2 *tablespoons water if rolled by machine;*
     4 tablespoons water if rolled by hand

Combine all ingredients and knead the dough for 2 to 3 minutes, until it is well-blended and smooth. If using the machine, cut the dough into 3 pieces and roll through the machine from the largest to the smallest opening. When the dough is stretched, place through the cutter and spread the noodles flat on a table or tray to dry for a few minutes. If rolled by hand, use as little flour as possible. Roll not thicker than ⅛ inch. Then, roll the dough to form a roll and slice in about ⅜-inch slices. Unroll the slices and let the noodles dry for 5 to 10 minutes.

> ½ stick sweet butter
> ½ teaspoon salt
> ½ teaspoon freshly ground white pepper
> grated Parmesan or Swiss cheese

Cook the noodles in about 4 to 5 quarts of salted, boiling water for 4 to 5 minutes. Drain and toss with ½ stick of sweet butter cut into small pieces, then salt and pepper. Serve with Parmesan or grated Swiss cheese.

Gnocchi Parisienne Sauce Aurore
Dumplings Baked in a Tomato and Cream Sauce

(Serves 8)

•

Dumplings

> 1 cup water
> 4 tablespoons butter
> 1 teaspoon salt
> ¼ teaspoon freshly ground white pepper

1⅓ cups sifted flour
4 eggs
1½ tablespoons grated Parmesan cheese

Combine the water, butter, salt, and pepper in a small saucepan. Bring to a boil and add the flour, all at once, stirring rapidly with a wooden spoon. Work the mixture, stirring round and round with the spoon, until it becomes smooth and shiny and the mixture does not stick to the bottom. Transfer to a clean bowl and let cool 10 to 15 minutes. Add the eggs, 1 at a time, beating thoroughly and briskly after each addition until each egg is well incorporated. Stir in the cheese until just blended.

Half fill a large pan with water. The pan we use measures about 12 inches in diameter and is 3 inches deep. Bring the water to a simmer and add salt to taste. Fit a pastry bag with a round tube. The tube should have an opening about ½ inch in diameter. Spoon the dough into the bag. Rest the tube on the side of the pan. Squeeze the bag with one hand, and as the dough is pushed out about 1 inch, cut it off with the blade of a paring knife, running the knife smoothly against the tip of the tube. This should make very neat 1-inch cylinders of dough that fall into the simmering water. With a little practice squeezing with one hand and slicing with the other, this should go quite fast. When half the dough has been shaped and dropped into the simmering water, let the dumplings cook 3 to 4 minutes, with the water just simmering. With a slotted spoon, transfer the dumplings into a large bowl of water and ice. When the dumplings are very cold they will fall to the bottom of the bowl. Drain, cover and set them aside. Continue making dumplings with the remaining dough, repeating this procedure.

Sauce

3 tablespoons sweet butter
3½ tablespoons flour
3 cups milk

¾ *cup heavy cream*
⅛ *teaspoon nutmeg*
1 *teaspoon salt*
¼ *teaspoon freshly ground pepper*
2 *tablespoons tomato paste*
2 *tablespoons grated Parmesan cheese*

Melt the butter in a saucepan and add the flour, stirring with a wire whisk. When blended, add the milk, stirring rapidly with the whisk. Bring to a boil, still stirring to avoid scorching. When thick and smooth, stir in the cream, nutmeg, salt, pepper, and tomato paste. Bring to a boil again.

Preheat the oven to 400°. Butter a baking dish (we use an oval dish measuring about 10 by 16 by 2 inches). Arrange the *gnocchi* in 1 layer and spoon the sauce over. Smooth it over. Sprinkle with grated Parmesan cheese and bake 30 minutes. As the *gnocchi* cook, shake the pan occasionally to make sure the dumplings do not stick to the bottom of the gratin dish. They should at least double in volume. Serve piping hot.

Gnocchi Romaine
Gnocchi Roman Style

(*Serves 8 to 10*)

•

3 *cups milk*
2 *tablespoons sweet butter*   ᵗ ᵒᵘⁿᶜᵉ
2 *teaspoons salt*
½ *teaspoon freshly ground white pepper*
⅛ *teaspoon freshly grated nutmeg*
1 *cup semolina or farina*

Place the milk, butter, salt, pepper, and nutmeg in a large heavy kettle and bring to a boil. Pour in the farina, mixing vigorously with a strong whisk. Reduce the heat and cook for 2 to 3 minutes, stirring with the whisk, until the mixture becomes very thick.

> 1 *cup heavy cream*
> 3 *large eggs*
> 1 *teaspoon vegetable oil*

Beat the eggs and cream together in a bowl. Add the farina mixture and mix thoroughly with the whisk. Bring to a boil and remove from the heat. Oil an oven tray with an edge about 1 inch high (we use a tray about 12 inches by 12 inches). Pour the mixture on the tray and spread it out. *It should be about ¾ inch thick all around. Use a wet spatula to spread the mixture.* Cover with plastic wrap and refrigerate until cold and set (at least 3 to 4 hours).

> ⅓ *stick sweet butter, melted* 2T + 2t
> ¾ *cup grated Swiss cheese* circa 3 ounces
> 1½ *cups heavy cream*

Using a round cookie cutter about 2½ inches in diameter, cut rounds from the cold semolina mixture. Gather the trimmings into a solid flat piece so that you can cut rounds from it. You should have about 18 rounds. Roll each round into the melted butter and arrange in an au gratin dish, slightly overlapping the pieces. The dish should be at least 8 by 12 inches by about 1½ inches deep. Sprinkle the cheese on top and place on a tray in a preheated 425° oven for 25 minutes, or until slightly browned. Pour cream on top and place back in the oven for 10 to 12 more minutes, until glazed and beautifully browned. Let the dish rest for 5 to 6 minutes before serving.

Desserts

Gâteau Chocolat
Chocolate Cake

(Serves 8)

•

8 1-ounce squares semisweet chocolate
1½ sticks sweet butter, softened
8 large eggs
1 cup sugar
1 teaspoon grated orange rind
2 cups almonds, ground in the blender (yields
    2¼ cups ground)
½ cup fresh breadcrumbs (about 1 slice bread)

Melt the chocolate on top of boiling water or in a 180° oven. Work the butter, eggs, sugar, and orange rind for 2 to 3 minutes with a wire whisk until creamy and smooth. Add the melted chocolate and almond powder and mix until smooth. Fold in the breadcrumbs.

Using ½ teaspoon of soft butter and 2 tablespoons of flour, butter and flour a round mold 10 inches in diameter by 2 inches high. (A spring mold will make your work easier.) Pour the mixture in the prepared mold, place on a cookie sheet and cook in a preheated 375° oven for 30 minutes. Let cool to room temperature and unmold.

> 4 1-ounce squares semisweet chocolate, melted
> 1 cup heavy cream, whipped

Split the cake horizontally into halves. Usually the bottom of the cake is the flattest and smoothest part. Coat the smoothest part with the melted chocolate. Place the whipped cream on the lowest layer and place the chocolate-coated half on top. Decorate the top with some whipped cream or whole nuts. Serve very cold in wedges.

Paris-Brest
Paris-Brest Cake

(Serves 8 to 10)

or more if cake is made 10" in diam.
For 16 per LaTechnique

•

Butter and flour a cookie sheet and make a mark with a 10-inch ring. Set aside.

(This is enough pate a choux for 14 – 16 chouf or eclairs)

> 1 cup all-purpose flour
> 1 cup water
> ½ stick (2 ounces) sweet butter
> ¼ teaspoon salt
> 4 large eggs
> 1 egg, beaten (for egg wash)
> 1 tablespoon sliced almonds

Place water, butter, and salt in a heavy saucepan and bring to a boil. When boiling, remove from the heat and add the flour all at once. Mix with a wooden spatula. You should not have any lumps of flour; the dough should be smooth and not sticking to your fingers. Place back on medium heat and cook for 4 to 5 minutes, stirring with the spatula to dry the dough. A whitish crust should form at the bottom of the saucepan. Place the dough in another bowl and let cool for 10 minutes. Add the eggs, 1 at a time, beating between each addition until the mixture is smooth. *If you add the eggs when the basic dough is too hot, you will cook the eggs and the dough will not cook in the oven.* Place the dough in a pastry bag with a plain tube (Number 6 is good). Make a ring of dough following the mark on your cookie sheet. Make another ring inside and against the first one. Make the third ring on top and in between the first 2 rings. You now have 3 rings, one against the other, shaped like a pyramid. Brush with egg wash. Let the cake dry for 10 minutes before putting in the oven. The egg wash will dry and give a beautiful glaze during cooking and a shiny cake. Sprinkle with the almonds and place in a preheated 400° oven for 50 minutes. *During the last 5 minutes of cooking, keep the oven door open about 2 inches (stick a spoon in the door to keep it open) so that the steam escapes and the cake does not soften up too much after cooking.* Remove from the oven and let cool at a lukewarm temperature. *If the cake is cooled too fast, it will also soften up.* When cold, cut the top off (about ⅓ of the way down the cake) so that it may be filled. *use a long blade knife*

Nougatine

> 1 cup confectioners' sugar
> ½ cup shredded, sliced, or whole almonds

or combine + after over heat to melt sugar

Put the sugar in a heavy casserole and place on a medium fire, mixing with a wooden spatula. Keep stirring and cooking until the mixture turns into caramel. *This caramel is made without water and it makes a dry, hard, shiny caramel used for nougatine.* It will take a few minutes (6 to 8) before it starts to melt. After it starts, *it will turn almost right away into caramel.*

Add the almonds and mix with the caramel for a few seconds. *Beforehand,* Rub a cookie sheet with a few drops of oil and pour the mixture on top. Spread with an oiled spatula (if you do not oil it, it will stick). Let cool for about 10 to 15 minutes and then break into pieces into a blender. Blend into a coarse powder. Set aside.

Crème Patissière

From La Technique
yield: about 3 cups

    4 egg yolks   *6 yolks*
    ⅓ cup sugar   *⅔C sugar*
    1 teaspoon vanilla extract   *or 1t vanilla*
    2 tablespoons cornstarch   *½C flour*
    1¼ cups milk   *2 cups milk*

Combine the yolks, sugar, and vanilla extract in a bowl and work together with a whisk for a few minutes until the mixture forms a ribbon (see page 346). Add the cornstarch and mix until blended. Meanwhile, bring the milk to a boil in a heavy saucepan. Pour half of the hot milk into the yolk mixture and mix with a whisk until smooth. Pour the whole thing back into the saucepan and bring to a boil on medium heat, stirring constantly to avoid scorching. Bring to a good rolling boil. Pour into a bowl, cover with plastic wrap and cool. When cold, mix in the nougatine mixture. Spoon the cream into the large bottom part of the cake. It should be ½ to ¾ full.

    2 cups heavy cream
    3 tablespoons confectioners' sugar
    2 tablespoons dark rum

Whip the cream and when it starts to thicken, add 2 tablespoons of sugar and the rum. Keep whipping until stiff. Place in a pastry bag with a fluted tube and pipe the whipped cream over the nougatine cream. It should come about 1 inch above the cake. Replace the top part of the cake carefully and lightly on the cream, sprinkle with the remaining powdered sugar, and the cake is ready to be sliced.

Keep in a cool, not too cold, Dry place.
Cut into small wedges with a serrated knife

Bûche de Noël
Christmas Yule Log

(Serves 8)

•

Years ago it was the custom in France to burn a Christmas log of great size that, once lighted, would last through Christmas Eve and Christmas Eve supper. Apparently, this was the inspiration for Bûche de Noël, one of the most charming traditional French holiday cakes.

Biscuit Roulé (Cake Roll)

3 eggs, separated
½ cup sugar
⅓ cup plus 1 tablespoon all-purpose flour
2 tablespoons cornstarch
1 tablespoon sweet butter, melted

Line an 11-by-16-inch jelly-roll pan with parchment paper or buttered and floured waxed paper. Set aside.

Combine the egg yolks and sugar in a large bowl and beat until very light and the mixture makes "ribbons" (see page 346). Mix in the flour and cornstarch. Beat the whites with a rotary or electric beater until they hold firm, shiny peaks when the beater is held straight up. With a wire whisk, beat about ⅓ of the whites into the batter vigorously. Then, using a rubber spatula, fold in the remainder. *Go as fast as you can when adding the whites or they will be grainy.* Finally, fold in the melted butter. Pour into the prepared pan, smoothing the batter evenly so that it touches all sides.

Bake in a preheated 400° oven for 12 to 15 minutes, or until the *roulé* begins to shrink from the sides of the pan. Let cool for 30 minutes, *cover with a wet towel and refrigerate until ready to use. Be sure the towel is kept damp.*

Crème au Beurre (Butter Cream)

> ⅓ cup sugar
> ¼ cup water
> 3 egg yolks
> ¾ cup (1½ sticks) sweet butter, at room
> temperature

Combine the sugar and water in a saucepan. Bring to a boil. Boil for 4 minutes on medium heat.

Place the egg yolks in a bowl. Add the syrup very gradually, beating constantly with an electric beater. After the syrup has been added, beat another 5 minutes to give texture and consistency to the mixture. Place the bowl in a pan of cold water and continue beating until cool. At this point, begin to add the butter, bit by bit, beating in each addition thoroughly. When all the butter has been added, the *crème* should be firm enough to hold a shape. If not used immediately, cover and refrigerate. Bring to room temperature before using. *If the* crème *curdles during the addition of the butter, heat it slightly over hot water and work with a whisk to combine together again.*

To finish the Bûche de Noël you will need a 10-ounce jar of currant jelly, 2 tablespoons of kirsch, green food coloring, powdered instant coffee, and 3 squares (1-ounce size) of unsweetened chocolate, plus the *crème au beurre.*

Spoon the currant jelly into a bowl and beat with a fork. Mix the kirsch with 1 tablespoon of water and sprinkle all over one side of the *biscuit roulé.* Spread the jelly over the entire surface of the *roulé.* Roll up tightly with the seam side down. Take 1½ tablespoons of the *crème au beurre;* add a few drops of the green food coloring, and mix well. Set aside. Dissolve 1 tablespoon powdered instant coffee in ½ teaspoon water. Stir into ⅓ cup of *crème au beurre.* Set aside. Melt the chocolate over hot, not boiling, water. When melted, stir into the remaining *crème*. With a spatula, spread the chocolate *crème* thickly over the top and sides, but not the ends. Then draw the tines of a fork down the full length of the roll, sides and top, to simulate bark. Coat the ends of the "log" with the coffee-flavored *crème*. With a paper cornet make a trimming of ivy with green *crème* over the "bark." Scatter chopped pistachios over the top to make moss. The log may be garnished with meringue mushrooms.

Cake Anglais
Fruit Cake

(*Serves 12*)

•

This is an excellent cake customarily done around the Christmas holiday in France. The cake is best a few days old. Wrapped in plastic wrap and refrigerated, it will keep for over a month. *For a rich pound cake, follow the same procedure omitting the glazed fruits, raisins, and the rum.*

> 1½ *ounces dark raisins*
> ⅓ *cup good dark rum*
> 1 *pound fresh sweet butter at room temperature*
> 1 *pound sugar*
> 7 *large eggs*
> 1 *pound all-purpose flour* (3½ *cups loose flour*)
> *grated rind of 1 lemon*
> *grated rind of 1 orange*
> 14 *ounces glazed or candied mixed fruits*

Place the raisins and the rum in a bowl and let macerate for 1 hour. Meanwhile, work the butter and sugar together with a whisk until the mixture becomes light, fluffy, and smooth. Add 2 eggs at a time, mixing vigorously after each addition. Add the flour, mixing with the whisk until it is blended and no lumps show. Do not overmix or the cake will be too "tight." With a wood or rubber spatula, fold in the remaining ingredients, including the rum-raisin mixture. *"Folding" means that instead of stirring the ingredients in a circular movement from side to side, you stir the mixture in a circular up-and-down movement. The spatula cuts going down through the ingredients, and is kept flat coming up to lift up the mixture. This gentle technique helps to give cakes and soufflés the light texture which is peculiar to this kind of dessert.* Butter a piece of waxed paper and line a cake mold. The amount of mixture will make 1 large or 2 small cakes. Use one 10-inch long, 5-inch wide and 4-inch high mold, or two smaller molds. Place the mold on a cookie sheet and cook in a preheated 350° oven for 10 minutes. Reduce the heat to 325° and cook for another 1¼ hours. (If you choose to make 2 cakes the time should be adjusted accordingly.) When done, a thin knife-blade inserted in the middle of the cake should come out without any runny batter adhering to it. However, some sticky mixture will adhere to it. Let cool at room temperature at least overnight before cutting. *Yield:* 18 to 20 slices.

Vacherin aux Pêches
Meringue Cake with Peaches

(*Serves 8*)

•

Butter and flour 2 large cookie sheets. Mark 2 8-inch circles on each sheet using a flan ring or a tart ring by pressing the ring on the butter-and-flour mixture coating the sheets.

6 egg whites
1¼ cups superfine sugar, dash of salt

Beat the egg whites with an electric mixer and a whip until they are almost holding a peak. Pour in half the sugar, still whipping. When the egg whites hold a peak, remove them from the electric mixer immediately and fold in (see page 296) the remaining sugar. (*Folding the sugar in will give a crunchy, light meringue.*) Place the meringue in a large pastry bag with a plain tube with about a ½-inch opening. Fill up one of the marked rings by piping several concentric circles of meringue, smaller and smaller, until one ring is filled. This is the base of the cake. Pipe 3 rings, 1 on each of the other 3 delineated circles. These rings will be stacked on top of the base after they are cooked, forming the wall of the *vacherin*. Place the meringue in a 180 to 200° oven for 60 to 70 minutes. *Let cool slowly at room temperature. If you cool fast in a cool place the meringue will soften and "bleed."*

2 egg whites
½ cup sugar
5 or 6 broken candied violets

Make more meringue, following the above instructions. Place 2 or 3 dots of meringue on the outside ring of the base. Place one of the baked rings on top. Dot the ring with meringue and place the second ring into place. Repeat for the third ring. With a spatula, smooth the outside of the *vacherin* using some of the meringue—jut enough to fill the space between the different rings. Place some of the meringue in a pastry bag with a small fluted tube (about ¼-inch opening). Decorate the smoothed outside of the *vacherin* to your own liking, make leaves or stars or dots. Stick some pieces of candied violets into the dots. Place in a 200° oven for 45 minutes. Cool slowly. The shell is usually made at least 1 day ahead.

> 1 *cup fresh raspberries*
> ⅓ *cup sugar*
> 5 *tablespoons good raspberry preserves*
> 3 *tablespoons raspberry alcohol or kirsch*

Place the raspberries, sugar, and preserves in a blender and reduce to a puree. Place in a saucepan and bring to a boil. Then strain through a fine metal sieve. When cold, add the alcohol.

> 1 *cup heavy cream*
> 1 *tablespoon confectioners' sugar*
> 1 *teaspoon vanilla extract*
> 1 *quart good vanilla ice cream* (*not too cold*)
> 8 *peach halves, poached fresh or canned*
> 1 *tablespoon roasted sliced almonds*

Whip the cream and add the sugar and vanilla. Place in a pastry bag with a fluted tube. Place the empty meringue shell on a large round serving platter. Place half the ice cream in the bottom of the shell. Cut 4 peach halves into sections and cover the ice cream. Place the remaining ice cream on top. Place the 4 other peach halves on top with the hollow sides down. Coat with some of the raspberry sauce. Sprinkle with sliced almonds. Decorate with whipped cream on the top and around the base of the *vacherin*. Serve with the remaining sauce. Cut the *vacherin* with a serrated knife and serve the inside with a spoon.

Dacquoise au Chocolat
Chocolate and Meringue Cake
(*Serves 8*)

•

1 *teaspoon sweet butter, softened*
2 *tablespoons flour*

Butter and flour a cookie sheet and 2 tart rings 9 inches in diameter by 1 inch in height. Place the rings on the prepared cookie sheet.

¾ *cup sugar*
1½ *tablespoons cornstarch*
½ *cup hazelnuts*
½ *cup almonds*
6 *egg whites*

Mix the sugar and cornstarch together. Blend the almonds and hazelnuts in a blender and add to the sugar. Whip the egg whites until they hold a nice peak and immediately fold into (see page 296) the almond mixture. Pour the mixture into the 2 prepared rings and cook in a preheated 350° oven for about 20 to 25 minutes. You may also cook the mixture in a floured and buttered 10- by 12-inch sheet cake pan and cut the cooked cake in half. You will have a rectangular *dacquoise*. Let cake cool before finishing.

Crème au Beurre (Butter Cream)

½ *cup sugar*
¼ *cup water*
3 *egg yolks*
2 *sticks sweet butter* (8 *ounces*)
3 *ounces semisweet chocolate*

Mix the sugar and water and cook on medium heat for a few minutes (about 3 to 4) until it reaches the thread stage on a candy thermometer. Place the yolks in the bowl of a mixer, turn on medium speed and pour the syrup slowly on the yolks. Keep working the mixture for 6 to 8 minutes. It should be as thick as a light mayonnaise and very pale yellow. Add 1 stick of butter, cut into pieces. Add the chocolate (previously melted on top of a double boiler or in a 180° oven). Mix well. Add the remaining butter, bit by bit. Refrigerate. *If the cream starts to break down, the butter is probably too cold. Place the bowl of cream in hot water for a few seconds and let it start to melt around the edges. Work again with the mixer or a hand whip. It should smooth out.*

> *3 tablespoons chopped almonds or hazelnuts*
> *1 tablespoon confectioners' sugar*

Remove the rings from the 2 "disks" of meringue. One side (the side which touched the cookie sheet) will be very flat. Place 1 layer, flat side down, on a serving tray. Spoon all but 2 tablespoons of the butter cream on top. Place the other layer, *flat side up,* on top of the cream. Using a spatula, smooth around the cake with the remaining butter cream. Press the chopped almonds in the cream all around the cake. Place the powdered sugar in a sieve and sprinkle over the cake so that the top is covered with a white blanket. Refrigerate. Serve cold, cut into little wedges.

Meringues Chantilly
Meringue Shells with Chantilly Cream
(Serves 8 to 10)

•

4 egg whites
1 cup granulated sugar
7 tablespoons sifted confectioners' sugar
2 cups heavy cream
dash of vanilla extract
powdered cocoa or granulated sugar

Grease 2 cookie sheets and coat with flour, knocking off any excess. Set aside.

Place the egg whites in a medium-sized bowl and beat with an electric or rotary beater until they begin to hold a shape (about 3 minutes). At this point sprinkle half of the granulated sugar over the surface of the whites and continue beating hard (at high speed, if you are using an electric beater or mixer) for about 1 minute. Stop the beating and fold in the remaining granulated sugar. *This will give you a tender and crunchy meringue.* The finished meringue should be very shiny and stiff enough to stand in peaks when you hold up the beater. "Wet," as the saying goes, but not dry.

Spoon the meringue into a pastry bag fitted with a Number 7 tube and press out oval shells 1½ inches wide and 4 inches long. Sprinkle with confectioners' sugar. This amount of meringue should yield about 20 shells.

Bake in a preheated 200° oven for 2½ to 3 hours. The baked shells should be pure white, but if your oven isn't constant, they may turn a pale yellow. Once you take them from the oven, lift with a spatula from the sheets and cool on wire racks immediately.

Whip the cream until it begins to hold a shape, add the remaining confectioners' sugar and the vanilla, and continue to whip until the cream is stiff. Take care not to overwhip, otherwise your cream will become granular and turn to butter. Spoon the cream into a pastry bag. To serve, press about 3 tablespoons of the cream onto the flat side of a meringue shell, put another shell on top, and sprinkle the top with a little shower of cocoa or sugar.

Mont Blanc aux Marrons
Chestnut Puree with Meringues

(Serves 8)

•

about 20 meringues
1½ pounds chestnuts
3 cups milk
dash of vanilla extract
¼ pound butter, softened
1 cup granulated sugar
1 cup water
2 cups heavy cream
1 tablespoon confectioners' sugar

Make the meringues as in Meringues Chantilly (see page 301).

With a sharp knife, make an incision on the flat side of each chestnut. Drop the nuts into boiling water for 5 minutes, then peel while still warm. Place in a saucepan with the milk and vanilla and cook over moderate heat until tender (about 1 hour).

Push the chestnuts through a fine sieve to make a very compact and smooth puree. Mix in the softened butter thoroughly.

Combine the granulated sugar with the water and bring to a boil over moderate heat, stirring constantly until the sugar has dissolved; boil for 8 minutes. Stir the hot syrup into the chestnut mixture. Taste for sweetness. If not sweet enough according to your taste, add a bit more sugar.

To make the *crème chantilly*, whip the heavy cream until it begins to get stiff, add the confectioners' sugar and continue to whip until the cream is stiff. Take care not to overwhip, otherwise your cream will become granular and turn to butter.

To compose the Mont Blanc, place a meringue broken into large chunks in a wide glass, spoon 2 to 3 tablespoons of the chestnut puree on the meringue, cover with a second meringue and pipe *crème chantilly* over the top.

Oeufs à la Neige
Meringue Balls Poached in Custard

(*Serves 6 to 8*)

•

Meringue

> 6 *egg whites*
> 1 *cup confectioners' sugar*
> 3 *cups milk*

Whip the egg whites with an electric beater until they are stiff. Still beating, add the sugar; continue beating on high speed for 1 minute. Bring the milk to a boil in a large shallow pan. Take a large spoonful of the meringue mixture, sliding the full spoon along the side of the bowl to smooth the meringue and give it the shape of an egg. Drop in simmering, not boiling, milk. Cook for approximately 2 minutes on each side. *Do not over-*

cook or let the mixture expand too much or the "eggs" will shrink and be rubbery. Cook approximately 6 at a time. *Yield:* About 15 to 18.

Sauce

> 6 egg yolks
> ¾ cup sugar
> 1 teaspoon vanilla extract
> 1 tablespoon cornstarch
> 1½ cups milk

Mix the yolks, sugar, vanilla, and cornstarch in a bowl and whip with a whisk for 3 minutes, or until light and creamy. Pour in 1 cup of the milk, mix and pour into the hot milk used to poach the meringue. Cook on low heat, stirring constantly with a spatula until it starts to thicken, just before the boiling point. Strain right away through a fine sieve and add the remaining ½ cup of cold milk to avoid any further cooking. Allow the sauce to cool, stirring every so often to prevent a skin from forming on top. When cold, pour into a large deep serving platter or a shallow bowl and arrange the eggs on top of the sauce.

Caramel

> ½ cup sugar
> 3 tablespoons water

Mix the water and sugar in a saucepan and cook until the mixture thickens and turns into a nice brown color. Immediately pour directly on the eggs. Wait 10 minutes for the caramel to harden, then serve.

Gateau Saint-Honoré
Saint-Honore Cake

(*Serves 8*)

•

½ *recipe Pâte Brisée* (*see page 45*)

Line a baking sheet with waxed paper and set aside.

On a lightly floured board, roll the dough into a circle, approximately 12 inches in diameter. Roll up on the rolling pin, then center over the prepared baking sheet and unroll. Trim to have a nice circle. Refrigerate.

Pâte à Choux (Cream-Puff Dough)

> 1 *cup water*
> 6 *tablespoons* (¾ *stick*) *sweet butter*
> *dash salt*
> 1 *cup all-purpose flour*
> 5 *whole eggs*

Combine the water, butter, and salt in a heavy saucepan. Bring to a boil. Take off the heat and add the flour all at once. Mix in with a wooden spatula. Place back over low heat and cook 5 minutes, stirring constantly with the spatula until the dough leaves the sides of the pan and starts to dry around the edges. Take off the heat, transfer to a clean bowl and allow to cool for about 10 minutes, stirring once in a while to speed the cooling. Beat in 4 eggs, 1 at a time, beating hard after each addition. The finished paste should be smooth, shiny, and thick.

Spoon the dough into a pastry bag with a plain tube (with about a ½-inch opening) and pipe onto the circle of the pastry, making a ring all around the edge about ½ inch wide. Pipe the remaining dough onto the baking sheet to make miniature cream puffs about 1½ inches in diameter when uncooked. You should have about 10 puffs.

Beat the remaining egg. With a pastry brush, brush the top of each puff and the ring. Prick the pie dough with a fork. Let the egg wash dry on the dough in an airy place for about 10 minutes. Bake in a preheated 400° oven for 20 to 25 minutes. Using a wide spatula, carefully slide the circular base onto a cake rack. Lift the individual puffs to another rack. Cool to room temperature in an airy place.

Crème Saint-Honoré

> 2 cups milk
> 4 egg yolks
> ¾ cup sugar
> 1 teaspoon vanilla extract
> 1 envelope unflavored gelatin
> ¼ cup cornstarch
> 3 cups heavy cream

Bring the milk to a boil. Meanwhile, combine the yolks, sugar, vanilla, and gelatin in a heavy saucepan and beat with a rotary or electric beater for about 2 minutes. Then stir in the cornstarch until smooth. Stir in the hot milk. Place over moderate heat, bring to a boil and cook on low heat for about 5 minutes, stirring with a wooden spatula to avoid scorching. Take off the heat and pour into a bowl. Place plastic wrap directly on the surface and refrigerate until cold. Beat the cream until it will hold a shape, then fold into the basic cream. To fill the cream puffs, make an opening with a skewer in the bottom of each puff. Using a pastry bag and tube, fill each puff with the cream.

Caramel

> 1 cup sugar
> 1 tablespoon water

Combine the sugar and water in a heavy saucepan. Bring to a boil and continue boiling until the syrup has turned to a rich hazelnut color, approximately 10 minutes. Remove from the heat immediately and keep warm in a pan of hot water. Wait 3 to 4 minutes until the caramel thickens before glazing the puffs.

To glaze the cream puffs, dip the top of each puff into the caramel. Place each on the ring, using a dab of caramel to hold it in place. Fill the center of the *gâteau* with the remaining cream and place 1 puff in the center. If you have a little extra caramel, sprinkle it with a fork over the cream in the center of the cake. Keep cool until serving time in the refrigerator. Do not refrigerate for a long time because the puffs will lose their crispness; the caramel will "bleed."

Platée de Pommes au Caramel
Apple Tart with Caramel

(*Serves 6 to 8*)

•

Apple Filling

5 *medium-sized golden or red Delicious apples*
4 *tablespoons (½ stick) sweet butter*
grated rind of 1 lemon
1 *cup sugar*

Peel, halve, and core the apples, then slice into ¼-inch slices. Melt the butter in a large heavy skillet. Add the apple slices and sauté 5 minutes. Add the lemon rind. Set aside. Pour the sugar into a saucepan. Place over a low heat, stirring occasionally until the sugar melts and turns into a golden caramel. Pour at once into a 9-inch pie plate, tipping the plate back and forth so the bottom is completely coated. Arrange the apples in a pattern using the nicest slices on the bottom of the dish for the first layer. Keep in mind that the pie will be turned upside down and this layer will be the top of the dish.

Preparing the Tart

½ recipe Pâte Brisée (see page 45)

Roll the dough and place on top of the apples. With a sharp knife, cut off any surplus dough, keeping the dough even with the edge of the plate. Place the tart on a baking sheet in a pre-heated 375° oven and bake for 45 minutes. Cool to lukewarm. Place a serving platter turned upside down on top of the cake and invert the cake and the platter together. You now have a layer of crust on the bottom with the apples on top. If some of the apple slices stick to the bottom of the pan, arrange them back into the pattern with a knife. *If you let the cake cool off too much before inverting, the sugar will thicken and the slices will stick to the bottom. If you unmold the cake too early, it will be too runny.*

Glaçage (Glaze)

½ cup commercial apricot jam
1 tablespoon sugar
2 tablespoons water
2 tablespoons kirsch or cognac

Heat the apricot jam with the sugar and 2 tablespoons of water in a small saucepan. Bring to a boil, then strain. When cool, stir in the kirsch or cognac. Using a pastry brush, brush the apples with the glaze.

Pouding de Pommes et Brioche
Apple Brown Betty

(Serves 6 to 8)

•

Brioche Dough

> 1 *cup all-purpose flour*
> 3 *tablespoons sweet butter*
> 1 *envelope dry yeast*
> ¼ *cup lukewarm water*
> 1 *teaspoon sugar*
> ½ *teaspoon salt*
> 1 *small egg*

Mix the water and yeast together until the yeast is dissolved. Mix the yeast mixture, butter, sugar, salt, and egg until smooth. Add the flour and work for 2 or 3 minutes until smooth. Cover the dough with a towel and place in a warm place (like a 160° oven) for 1 hour to let the dough rise. Butter a cookie sheet and spread the dough on the sheet so that it is about ½ inch thick. Let the dough rise again in a warm place for about 20 minutes. Place in a 400° oven and cook for 15 to 20 minutes until well browned. You may let the dough rise for 10 minutes in the oven, then raise the heat to 400° and let the dough cook until browned (about 20 minutes). This may be done a few hours in advance because the dough is better when slightly stale.

Apple Mixture

> 4 to 5 *apples (red or golden Delicious, or*
> *McIntosh if you like it more tart) (about*
> 1¾ *pounds)*
> ¼ *cup sugar*

½ tablespoon ground cinnamon
2 ounces (½ cup) dark raisins
1 stick (¼ pound) melted sweet butter
¾ cup apple sauce

Peel, core, and slice the apples into about ¼-inch slices. Mix all the above ingredients carefully.

Slice the bread into ¼-inch slices and mix with the apple mixture. Do not overmix so that the slices of bread disappear completely. Place the mixture in a gratin dish and cook in a 400° oven for 40 to 45 minutes until nicely browned on top. Serve lukewarm.

Croûte aux Poires
Pear Pastry

(Serves 6 to 8)

•

You may substitute bananas, oranges, or peaches instead of the pears and follow the same directions.

1 9-inch Génoise (see page 56)
⅓ cup strong coffee
1 teaspoon vanilla extract
1 tablespoon confectioners' sugar

Slice the génoise in half horizontally with a long-bladed knife. You now have 2 disks of génoise, each about 1¼ inch thick. Use only 1 half. Set the cake, cut side up, on a serving platter. Mix the coffee, vanilla, and sugar together and sprinkle over the cake.

1 *cup heavy cream*
1 *tablespoon confectioners' sugar*

Whip the cream. Add the sugar and mix. Set aside.

¾ *cup apricot preserves*
1½ *tablespoons pear brandy or calvados*

Strain the preserves through a fine metal sieve and add the brandy to it. Heat to a slightly lukewarm temperature.

2 *large, well-ripened Anjou or Bartlett pears*

Not too long before serving time (no more than 1 hour because the cake will become too soggy if prepared ahead), spread the whipped cream on the cake. Peel, core, and halve the pears and slice into very thin slices (about ⅛-inch thick). Arrange the slices in concentric circles so that the whole surface of the cake is covered. Brush or spoon the lukewarm apricot sauce on top. Slice and serve.

Poires Bourdaloue
Pears in a Pastry Shell

(*Serves 6 to 8*)

•

Poaching the Pears

2 *cups water*
½ *cup sugar*
1 *vanilla bean*
grated rind and juice of 1 lemon
5 *medium-firm pears*

Combine water, sugar, vanilla bean, lemon rind, and juices in a large heavy saucepan. Bring to a boil and boil 3 minutes. Peel each pear, cut in half lengthwise, remove central core and seeds, and drop into the hot syrup. Place over low heat and simmer 15 minutes. Let cool in the syrup.

Feuilletage Shell

> 1 *cup all-purpose flour*
> ½ *cup* (1 *stick*) *sweet butter, cold, cut into pieces*
> ¼ *cup cold water*
> *pinch salt*
> 1 *tablespoon sugar*

Place all the ingredients in a bowl and work together with your hands (just enough to gather into a ball). On a lightly floured board, roll the dough into a large rectangle. In one movement, fold the dough over on itself into a piece 3 layers thick. Roll. Repeat folding over into thirds and rolling three more times for a total of four times. You may do the folding movements one after the other, however, if the dough seems too elastic, refrigerate for about 10 minutes between each folding. Roll out about ⅛ inch thick and fit into a 10-inch flan ring. Place a piece of waxed paper on the pastry and fill with dry beans or rice. *The beans or rice are used as a weight so that the dough keeps its shape during cooking.* After you finish using the rice or beans, set them aside for use another time. Bake in a preheated 400° oven for 30 minutes. Lift the paper and beans from the shell and continue to bake another 5 minutes.

Frangipane (Pastry Cream)

> ⅓ *cup sugar*
> 3 *tablespoons cornstarch*
> 2 *egg yolks*
> 1 *whole egg*

½ teaspoon vanilla extract
1 cup milk
⅓ cup sliced almonds
¾ cup heavy cream

Mix the sugar, cornstarch, yolks, whole egg, and vanilla together. Combine the milk and almonds in a saucepan and bring
to a boil. Stir in the egg mixture and bring to a boil. Boil 1
minute. Cover with plastic wrap directly on the surface of the
cream to keep a skin from forming and refrigerate until cold.
Whip the cream and fold into the frangipane.

Glaçage (Glaze)

Melt 1 cup of apricot or quince jam, then strain through a
fine sieve. Stir in 1 tablespoon of pear brandy, calvados, or kirsch.

Brush the bottom of the pastry shell with the glaze, then add
the frangipane. Drain the pear halves on a paper towel. You
may slice the pears or arrange the halves directly on the cream.
Brush with more of the glaze and serve immediately.

Note: It is best to do this last step not too long before serving,
as the dough will get soggy because of the cream.

Tarte aux Pommes Frangipane
Apple Tart with Almond Filling

(Serves 8)

•

Dough

1 recipe Pâte Brisée (see page 45)

Roll the dough out on a floured board and line a 10-inch pie
plate (see page 46).

Frangipane

> ¾ cup almonds
> ½ cup sugar
> 1 egg
> 1 tablespoon melted sweet butter

Grind the almonds in the electric blender to a powder. Then mix with the sugar, egg, and melted butter. Blend a few seconds to make a smooth paste. Spread over the top of the dough. Refrigerate.

Apples

> 4 to 5 red or golden Delicious apples, peeled
>   and cored
> 3 tablespoons sugar
> 2 tablespoons sweet butter

Cut peeled and cored apples in half and slice about ¼ inch thick. Arrange the slices, overlapping, in circles on top of the frangipane. Sprinkle with the 3 tablespoons of sugar and dot the top with the sweet butter, cut into small pieces. Bake in a preheated 400° oven for 1¼ hours, or until apples are tender and the pastry has browned. Let cool to room temperature.

Apricot Glaze

> 6 tablespoons apricot jam
> 2 tablespoons sugar
> ¼ cup water
> 1 tablespoon kirsch

Combine the apricot jam, sugar, and water in a small saucepan. Bring to a boil, then simmer slowly for 5 minutes. Strain through a fine sieve. Place a piece of plastic wrap directly on the surface of the mixture to prevent a skin from forming. When cool, stir in the kirsch.

Bring the glaze to a barely lukewarm temperature and brush the top of the tart with it.

Tarte aux Pommes de Ma Mère
Mother's Apple Tart

(Serves 6 to 8)

•

Dough

> 1¼ cups all-purpose flour
> 1 egg
> 3 tablespoons sweet butter
> 3 tablespoons vegetable shortening
> ¼ teaspoon salt
> 2 teaspoons baking powder
> 2 tablespoons boiling water

Place 1 cup of flour, the egg, butter, shortening, salt and baking powder in a mixing bowl and stir to have the ingredients just mixed together. Add the boiling water and mix just enough to combine everything into a ball. Use the remaining flour to roll the dough and line a 9-inch pie plate.

Note: The dough is very soft and can be used right away. If it breaks, patch it with small pieces of dough, pressing with your fingers.

Filling

> 2 to 3 apples, depending on size (red or golden
>   Delicious are fine)
> 3 tablespoons sugar
> ¼ stick (2 tablespoons) sweet butter

Peel, core, and slice the apples. Arrange the slices on top of the dough as artfully as you can. Sprinkle with the sugar and the butter broken into bits. Place in a preheated 400° oven for approximately 40 minutes. Eat lukewarm.

Tarte à la Rhubarbe
Rhubarb Pie

(*Serves 6*)

•

Try to buy small stalks of rhubarb of a nice red color. The rhubarb should be tender and sweet, and does not need to be peeled before cooking.

> 1 *pound rhubarb stalks, cleaned and cut into*
>   *2-inch sticks* (*3 cups*)
> ¼ *cup sugar*
> 3 *tablespoons all-purpose flour*
> ½ *seedless orange, sliced very thin* (*about ½*
>   *cup*), *unpeeled*
> 1 *tablespoon sweet butter*
> 2 *extra tablespoons sugar*

Line a pie plate or a 9-inch ring with Pâte Brisée, ⅛ inch thick (see page 45). Prick the bottom of the pie with a fork. Mix the ¼ cup sugar and flour together and place on the dough. Arrange the orange slices on top and the rhubarb last. Sprinkle with the butter and the 2 tablespoons of sugar. Place in a preheated 400° oven and cook for 1 hour. *While cooking, the rhubarb renders a lot of juices which will mix with the sugar-and-flour mixture and will give the filling its right consistency.*

½ cup apricot jam
¼ cup sugar
2 tablespoons water

Mix the above ingredients in a small pot and bring to a boil. Stir with a spoon until all ingredients are dissolved into a smooth mixture. After the pie has been removed from the oven, let cool for 15 or 20 minutes and brush the top (you may use a spoon to coat the pie) with the apricot mixture. Serve the pie slightly lukewarm or cool, but not ice-cold.

Galette au Citron
Open Lemon Tart

(*Serves 6*)

•

1 *recipe for Pâte Brisée* (*see page 45*)

Roll the dough into a ¼-inch-thick wheel, about 12 inches in diameter. Roll the edge of the wheel in on itself to make a border at least ½ inch high. You should have a shell about 11 inches in diameter. *It is easier to roll the dough on a floured board, then place it on a large cookie sheet. Then trim it to a round shape on the cookie sheet and roll the edges.*

2 lemons
4 egg yolks
¾ cup sugar
½ tablespoon cornstarch

Grate 1 lemon and press the juices. Mix the lemon juice, rind, egg yolks, sugar, and cornstarch in a bowl and work with a whisk for 3 to 4 minutes to give texture to the mixture. Pour the mixture on the dough, spreading it evenly. Peel the remaining lemon *à vif* (*i.e.*, the yellow and white skin should be completely removed to expose the flesh of the lemon). Cut the lemon into very thin slices, discarding the seeds. Arrange the slices on top of the filling in a circular pattern. Place in a 400° oven for 30 to 35 minutes. If the filling gets too brown during cooking, particularly during the last 10 minutes, place a piece of aluminum foil loosely on top, like a hat, so that it does not touch the filling.

> ¾ *cup heavy cream*
> 1 *tablespoon confectioners' sugar*

Whip the cream and add the sugar. Serve the *galette* with the cream on top as a decoration or served on the side.

Tarte à l'Orange
Open Orange Tart

(*Serves 6 to 8*)

•

Dough

> 1¼ *cups all-purpose flour*
> ⅛ *teaspoon salt*
> 2 *tablespoons sugar*
> 1 *stick sweet butter*
> 1 *egg yolk*
> 3 *tablespoons water*

Mix the yolk with the water until well blended. Set aside. Place the remaining ingredients into a large bowl and work with your hands until you have a yellow lumpy mixture. Add the yolk mixture and mix rapidly with your fingers until all the ingredients are well blended and assembled into a ball. Do not overmix.

Wrap the dough in a towel and refrigerate until ready to be used (it may be used right away).

Baking the Shell

Roll the dough on a lightly floured board to about ¼ inch thick. Place a 9- or 10-inch flan ring about 1 inch high on a cookie sheet. Roll the pastry on the rolling pin and unroll onto the flan ring. Ease the pastry down inside the ring, taking care not to break it. Press along the sides and bottom. With a knife, cut the dough off following the contour of the ring. You may make a decorative edge with a knife or a crimper. Line the dough with waxed paper and fill it up with raw rice or dried beans. This is used as a weight so that the dough keeps its shape during the cooking. Place in a 400° oven for 20 minutes. Remove the waxed paper and filler and store to be used some other time. Place the shell back in the oven (it is stiff enough by this time and it will not change shape) for 8 to 10 minutes, until the inside is slightly browned. Remove from the oven and let cool at room temperature.

Caramel

> ⅓ cup sugar
> 2 tablespoons water

Mix the sugar and water and cook over medium heat until it turns into a nice hazelnut color. Pour the caramel into the shell, trying to coat most of the bottom. Set aside.

Pastry Cream

> 3 egg yolks
> ¼ cup sugar
> ¼ teaspoon vanilla extract
> 1½ tablespoons cornstarch
> ¾ cup milk
> ¾ cup heavy cream

Bring the milk to a boil. Meanwhile, combine the yolks, sugar, and vanilla and work for 2 minutes with a whisk. Mix in the cornstarch. Combine with the milk and bring to a boil. Transfer to a clean bowl. Cover with plastic wrap and refrigerate until cold. When the cream is cold, mix it well with a whisk until smooth. Whip the heavy cream and fold in. Set aside.

Orange Garnish

> 4 *large oranges* (*seedless*)

With a sharp knife, peel the oranges so that the flesh is exposed and no white is left on. Cut the segments between the membranes to have little sections of pure orange flesh. Set aside.

Glaçage (Glaze)

> ¾ *cup apricot jam*
> 2 *tablespoons sugar*
> 2 *tablespoons water*

Combine all the ingredients, bring to a boil, and simmer 5 minutes. Strain through a fine sieve. Set aside.

The tart cannot be assembled more than 1½ hours before serving. Place the cream in the bottom of the shell. Arrange the orange segments in a pattern on top of the cream. Coat the top with the apricot glaze, which should be lukewarm, using a brush or a teaspoon.

Gâteau de Fromage aux Myrtilles
Cheesecake with Blueberries

(Serves 8 to 10)

•

2 tablespoons sweet butter
½ cup Graham cracker crumbs
4 8-ounce packages cream cheese, at room
    temperature
1¼ cups sugar
grated rind and juice of 1 lemon
½ teaspoon vanilla extract
4 large eggs

You need a round cake pan 8 inches in diameter and 3 to 4 inches deep, or a mold of the same capacity. Butter it well and add the crumbs. Shake the pan (best done over the sink), tipping it back and forth to coat the sides and bottom of the pan with the Graham cracker crumbs.

Place the cheese, sugar, lemon rind and juice, and vanilla extract in the bowl of an electric mixer (you can also mix it by hand using a strong whisk). Mix for 2 minutes on medium speed. Add 2 eggs and mix until incorporated. Add the remaining eggs and mix again until blended. Turn the mixer on high for 1 minute to thoroughly smooth the mixture. Pour mixture into the prepared cake pan. Place in a roasting pan or any implement which could be used as a double boiler. Add lukewarm water around the pan so that it reaches at least ⅔ the depth of the mold. Bake in a preheated 350° oven for 1 hour. (The water should not boil around the mold. If it does, remove some hot water with a ladle and replace with a few ice cubes.) At this point, turn off the oven and allow the cake to remain until lukewarm (about 1 hour). Remove the cake from the oven and allow to cool for at least 4 to 5 hours before unmolding. To unmold, place a round serving platter upside down on the top of the pan and invert. If the cake is hard to unmold, the butter around the mold might be set, especially if the cake has been refrigerated. Dip the pan in hot water a few seconds before inverting. If the cake has already been inverted, wrap the mold with a hot towel and wait approximately 1 minute before lifting the mold off.

> 1 12-ounce jar apricot jam
> ½ cup sugar
> ½ cup water
> 1 cup fresh blueberries, cleaned and washed
> 3 tablespoons kirsch

Combine the jam, water, and sugar in a saucepan. Bring to a boil and simmer for 5 minutes. Strain the sauce through a metal sieve, pushing with a metal spoon to extract as much jam as possible. Add the blueberries. *If the blueberries are frozen rather than fresh, do not add to the sauce as they would discolor it.* Cover the sauce with plastic wrap touching the surface of the mixture to prevent a "skin" from forming. When the sauce is cold, stir in the kirsch. *If you add the kirsch when the mixture is still hot, the alcohol will evaporate and most of the flavor will disappear.* If you are using frozen blueberries, add them to the sauce just before serving.

Serve each slice of cheesecake with 2 to 3 tablespoons of sauce.

Fromage Blanc à la Crème
Fresh White Cheese with Cream

(Serves 4)

•

This cheese is bought ready-made in all the little shops around Lyon or Bourg-en-Bresse. Often the housewife makes it herself with fresh unpasteurized milk and rennet (the gastric juices from the veal's or lamb's stomach used to curdle milk). A few drops of rennet are added to a quart of milk and left to stand in a lukewarm place for a couple of hours. When the milk has curdled, it is ready to be poured into small tins pierced with holes (called *faisselles*) and allowed to drain. At serving time, the cheese is turned upside down directly on the plate, covered with sweet cream and brought to the table. Most people sprinkle it with granulated sugar and mix it with fresh berries, such as raspberries or wild strawberries. In Bourg we mix it with garlic, chives, parsley—all chopped fine, sprinkle it with salt and pepper, and eat it as dessert.

It is not likely that you will find this fresh cheese ready-made in the local supermarket. This spurred me to work out a recipe, which turned out quite good, midway between a *fromage blanc* and a *fontainebleau*.

> 1 *cup cottage cheese*
> 2 *ounces* (¼ *package*) *cream cheese*
> ¾ *cup heavy cream*
> ½ *teaspoon salt*

Push the cottage cheese and the cream cheese through a fine metal sieve with a spoon or with your fingers. Work the cheese with the spoon until smooth. Add the salt. Whip the heavy cream separately until stiff and mix it with the mixture. *The texture of the cheese is too hard to fold the cream in; it has to be incorporated with the whip. Mix just enough to blend all ingredients. If you mix it too long it will turn into butter.* Pour the mixture into a square piece of cheesecloth and tie the 4 corners together. Hang it overnight in a cool place. You may push a spoon or a chopstick through the opening next to the knot and place across a deep pot so that the cheese has a chance to drain. Refrigerate. At serving time, turn the cheese upside down onto a serving platter.

> ½ *cup heavy cream*
> ½ *cup sour cream*
> 1 *small bunch chives, finely minced* (*or 2*
>   *scallions, finely minced*)
> 2 *cloves garlic, peeled, crushed, and chopped fine*
> ½ *cup parsley, chopped fine* (*about 3 to 4*
>   *tablespoons*)
> *salt*
> *freshly ground white pepper*

Mix the 2 creams together and pour over the cheese. Mix the chives, parsley, and garlic together and sprinkle over the cheese. Add some salt and sprinkle generously with pepper. Serve immediately.

Note: Even though the Bressan serve it as dessert, this is a delicious lunch or light supper dish.

Biscuits à la Cuillère
Ladyfingers
(*Yield: About 12 to 14*)

•

about 1 tablespoon butter
about 3 tablespoons flour
2 whole eggs, separated
1 extra egg white
½ teaspoon vanilla extract
⅓ cup confectioners' sugar
⅓ cup all-purpose flour
confectioners' sugar (extra)

Grease 2 baking sheets (about 12 by 18 inches) with the butter. Sprinkle the 3 tablespoons of flour on 1 sheet and shake the sheet to coat it evenly with the flour. Dump the excess flour onto the second sheet and repeat the operation. Bang each sheet upside down over the sink to get rid of any excess flour. Place the egg yolks, vanilla, and ⅓ cup sugar in a bowl and work it with a whisk for 2 to 3 minutes until the mixture is pale yellow. Add the ⅓ cup flour and stir with the whisk until it is smooth. Set aside. Beat the egg whites until they hold firm when the beater is held straight up. Add half of the whites to the first mixture and mix with a whisk. Add the remaining whites and fold in with a spatula. Do not overwork the mixture. *It is important that the whites be added to the mixture with the whisk very fast. The remaining whites will start to "grain" as soon as they are not whipped, so you cannot let them sit too long.* If the whites are grainy, the cakes will be porous and flat.

Scoop some of the batter into a pastry bag and squeeze out "fingers," approximately 4 inches long and 1½ inches wide, a good inch apart, on the prepared baking sheets. Continue until all the batter has been used. Sift confectioners' sugar over the fingers.

Bake on the middle and upper racks of a preheated 300° oven for 20 minutes. When properly baked the fingers should be a pale beige with a slight crust. Once they are taken from the oven, lift immediately from the baking sheets to racks to cool.

Diplomate au Kirsch
Diplomat Pudding with Kirsch

(Serves 8)

•

Ladyfingers

> *½ cup flour*
> *½ cup sugar*
> *3 eggs, separated*
> *1 teaspoon vanilla extract*
> *1 teaspoon sweet butter*
> *3 tablespoons confectioners' sugar*

Mix the ½ cup of sugar with the egg yolks and vanilla until the mixture becomes pale yellow (about 2 to 3 minutes). Mix in the flour. Whip the egg whites until they are fluffy and hold a peak and then fold them into the mixture. Butter a baking sheet and flour it, shaking off any excess flour by holding the sheet upside down over the sink. Scoop the mixture into a pastry bag with a plain tube that has approximately a ¾-inch opening. Make the ladyfingers about 4 inches long and 1 inch wide. The batter should yield about 20 fingers. Sprinkle with the confectioners' sugar and cook in a preheated 375° oven for 8 to 10 minutes.

¾ cup diced mixed candied fruit
1 cup good kirsch
8 egg yolks
1½ cups sugar
1 teaspoon vanilla extract
1 tablespoon cornstarch
4 cups milk
2 envelopes plain gelatin
¾ cup water
1½ cups heavy cream

Place the candied fruit and half of the kirsch in a bowl and let stand at least 2 hours or, if possible, overnight.

Line the bottom and sides of a 9- to 10-cup soufflé mold (or any other suitable mold) with the ladyfingers cut to fit the bottom and sides of the mold. (Be sure to place the top or curved side of the ladyfingers against the surface of the mold.) Place the egg yolks in a large mixing bowl and beat them with a whisk. Add the sugar and continue beating until they are light and lemon-colored. Beat in the vanilla and cornstarch. Meanwhile, boil 3½ cups of the milk and add it to the yolk mixture, beating constantly. When thoroughly blended, pour the mixture into a large saucepan. Stirring constantly with a wooden spatula, cook over low heat until the custard thickens slightly—just before the boiling point. *Do not let it boil or it will curdle. Immediately stir in the remaining cold milk and strain into a cold bowl. This will cool off the mixture and prevent curdling.* Remove 2 cups of the sauce and chill it in the refrigerator for later use. Combine the gelatin with ½ cup of water and cook, stirring until the gelatin is dissolved and transparent. Stir into the custard. Put the sauce in the refrigerator to cool it, but do not let it set. Stir often. Meanwhile, combine ¼ cup of kirsch with ¼ cup of water and brush the ladyfingers with it. Just before the custard sets, stir in the fruit-and-kirsch mixture. Whip the cream and fold it in. Pour the mixture into the prepared mold. Chill overnight, or at least 4 to 5 hours. To serve, unmold the Diplomate onto a round platter. Serve with the reserved sauce flavored with the remaining kirsch.

Beignets de Bananes
Banana Fritters

(*Serves 6*)

•

Batter

> 1¾ *cups all-purpose flour*
> 1 *tablespoon sugar*
> ½ *teaspoon salt*
> 1 *12-ounce can beer*
> 2 *eggs, separated*

Mix the flour, sugar, salt well, add the beer gradually until you have a smooth and shiny batter. Whip the egg whites and fold (see page 296) gently into the dough. Set the dough aside in the refrigerator for at least 30 minutes before using.

Sabayon

> 2 *egg yolks* (*reserved from above*)
> ¼ *cup sugar*
> ¼ *cup dry white vermouth*

Mix all ingredients in a small saucepan (do not use an aluminum pan because it will discolor the mixture) and using a whisk, beat the mixture on very low heat for 8 to 10 minutes. *Place an asbestos pad under the pan to distribute the heat evenly.* The mixture should never get so hot that you cannot hold your finger in it. Let the mixture cool (it will thicken as it cools). Then refrigerate.

5 bananas

Peel the bananas and cut into ¼-inch slices on a bias so you get longer slices. Heat some fresh vegetable oil in a skillet. You should use at least 1 inch of oil. The temperature should be from 360 to 375°.

Dip some slices of banana into the batter. Pick each slice out with your fingers so that it is completely coated with the batter, then drop into the hot oil. Cook 2½ to 3 minutes, turning the fritter so that it is browned evenly on all sides. Drain on a paper towel, sprinkle with sugar, stack on a plate and serve with the cold *sabayon*.

Beignets de Pommes (Apple Fritters)

Peel and core the apples so that they are left whole. Slice into ¼-inch rings. Follow the directions used for Banana Fritters. When cooked, place 1 teaspoon of jam (apricot, strawberry, apple, etc.) in the hollow center of each apple ring. Serve with or without the *sabayon*.

Crêpes Suzette
Thin Pancakes Flavored with Orange Liqueur

(Serves 6 to 8)

•

Batter

> 1½ *cups all-purpose flour*
> 3 *large eggs*
> 1 *tablespoon sugar*

¾ teaspoon salt
1½ cups milk
½ stick sweet butter, melted
½ cup cold water

Place the flour, eggs, salt, sugar, and approximately half of the milk in a mixing bowl. Stir with a whisk until the mixture is smooth and homogeneous, like a light bread dough. *If you add all the liquid at once you will have lumps; by doing this first step with half of the milk you eliminate any lumps.* Add the melted butter and mix well. Add the remaining milk and water and mix until smooth. It should have the consistency of a light syrup.

Use 1 or 2 crêpe pans or small cast-iron pans about 5 inches in diameter on the bottom. *You do not have to butter your pans because of the melted butter added to the batter.* Pour approximately 3 tablespoons of batter into each hot pan (use medium heat). As you are pouring the batter, move and tilt the pan back and forth so that the mixture spreads evenly in the bottom of the skillet. The entire bottom of the pan should be covered with the batter if you want a thin pancake. Do not worry if the first crêpe sticks, the pan has to "get in the mood." Cook the crêpe approximately 50 seconds on the first side. Then, flip it over (or turn over with a spatula) and cook about 30 seconds on the other side. You will notice that one side is more nicely and evenly browned than the other as you go along. When stacking the crêpes on a plate, place the best side down so that after the crêpes are folded the nicer side is on the outside. *Yield:* About 22 to 24 crêpes.

Sauce

2 sticks sweet butter, softened
*grated rind of 4 tangerines or 2 oranges (about
   2 teaspoons)*
juice of 2 tangerines or 1 orange
8 tablespoons sugar

With a rotary mixer or a whip, beat all ingredients together until you have a fluffy mixture.

Final Assembly at the Table

> 6 *tablespoons good cognac or brandy*
> 6 *tablespoons Grand Marnier or orange-flavored*
> *liqueur*

You need a gas or kerosene heater and a large skillet (copper, if possible). Heat about ⅕ of the butter mixture in the skillet. When sizzling hot, place 4 crêpes in the sauce. Dip the crêpes on both sides and fold each one into quarters to make small triangles as you go along. Add 1 tablespoon cognac and 1 tablespoon Grand Marnier and ignite. While it is flaming, turn the crêpes in the mixture and place on hot serving plates. You may serve 3 instead of 4 crêpes per person. Repeat the operation until you have used all the crêpes and all the sauce.

Note: If you have a very large crêpe pan and a powerful heater you may prepare 8 crêpes at a time.

Omelette Soufflée
Soufflé Omelet

(*Serves 6*)

•

> 1 *tablespoon butter*
> 6 *eggs, separated*
> *about 1 cup sugar*
> 8 to 10 *ladyfingers*
> ½ *cup Grand Marnier or cognac*
> *sifted confectioners' sugar*

Butter a large ovenproof platter, either silver or porcelain (approximately 12 by 15 inches). Sprinkle generously with granulated sugar. Turn it over and give it a good bang to get rid of any excess. Refrigerate. This not only makes a delicious crust but makes the omelet easier to serve.

Combine the yolks and remaining sugar in a bowl and beat with a rotary or electric beater until the mixture "makes ribbons" and is thick, creamy, and lemon-colored (about 3 to 5 minutes). Whip the whites with an electric beater or in an electric mixer until they hold firm, shiny peaks when the beater is held straight up. With a wire whisk, beat about ⅓ of the whites into the yolk mixture. With a rubber spatula, fold in the remainder.

Spread about ¼ of the mixture over the bottom of the platter. Arrange the ladyfingers on top and sprinkle with the liqueur. Pour the remainder of the mixture on top and smooth the surface with a metal spatula (you can set aside 3 to 4 tablespoons and decorate the top using a pastry tube). Sprinkle with confectioners' sugar.

Bake in a preheated 425° oven for 10 to 12 minutes. Serve immediately.

Soufflé Rothschild
Rothschild Soufflé

(Serves 6 to 8)

•

(See Soufflés, page 58.)

Crème Patissière (Base for the Soufflé)

1 *cup milk*
3 *eggs, separated* (*reserve the whites*)

½ cup sugar
½ teaspoon vanilla extract
2 tablespoons cornstarch

Bring the milk to a boil. Set aside. Combine the yolks, sugar, and vanilla in a bowl and beat with a wire whisk or electric beater until the mixture "makes ribbons" (see page 346) and turns pale yellow (about 3 to 4 minutes). Stir in the cornstarch until smooth. Add the hot milk slowly, whipping constantly. Pour the mixture back into the saucepan. Bring to a boil, beating constantly with the whisk. Cook for 3 to 4 minutes. Strain, if necessary (that is, if it is lumpy or has scorched at the bottom). Pour into a large bowl and place a piece of plastic wrap directly on the surface of the cream to prevent a skin from forming. Cool.

The Soufflé

½ cup diced mixed candied fruit
⅓ cup kirsch
½ tablespoon sweet butter, softened
1 tablespoon sugar
3 eggs, separated (reserve the yolks)
1 tablespoon confectioners' sugar

Mix the candied fruit and kirsch together in a bowl and set aside. Butter the inside of a 1½-quart soufflé mold, then coat with the granulated sugar. Refrigerate.

Combine the 3 egg whites with the 3 whites reserved from the *crème patissière* (above) in a large bowl. Beat with an electric beater or in an electric mixer until the whites hold firm, shiny peaks when the beater is held straight up. With a wire whisk, vigorously whip about ⅓ of the whites into the cooled *crème patissière*. With a rubber spatula, fold in the remainder of the beaten whites, then the fruit-and-kirsch mixture. Pour into the prepared soufflé mold, place on a tray, and bake in a preheated

375° oven for approximately 25 to 30 minutes. After 15 to 20 minutes, sprinkle the top with the confectioners' sugar. This gives a beautiful glaze to the top of the soufflé. When cooked, the soufflé should still be moist in the center.

Crème Anglaise (Sauce for the Soufflé)

⅓ cup sugar
3 egg yolks (see above)
½ teaspoon vanilla extract
½ teaspoon cornstarch
1 cup milk or half and half

Combine the sugar, egg yolks, and vanilla in a bowl and beat with an electric beater until the mixture "makes ribbons" and turns pale yellow. Stir in the cornstarch until smooth. Bring the milk to a boil and stir into the egg mixture. Pour back into the saucepan and cook, stirring constantly with a wooden spatula, until the cream coats the spoon (approximately 180° on a thermometer). Strain through a fine sieve. Cover with a piece of plastic wrap directly on the surface to prevent a skin from forming and refrigerate. Serve cold with the soufflé.

Note: If you have enough bad luck to curdle the crème, as soon as you realize it, transfer it as fast as you can to a cold vessel, add ¼ cup cold milk, mix and strain. If it is still very grainy it is hopeless, and you may as well discard the sauce and start all over again.

Soufflé Glacé Grand Marnier
Iced Soufflé Grand Marnier

(Serves 6 to 8)

•

1 cup sugar
⅓ cup water
1 tablespoon grated orange rind (about 1 large
    orange)
6 egg yolks
½ cup Grand Marnier
2½ cups heavy cream, whipped
6 to 8 Ladyfingers, or fingers of Génoise, or
    slices of Pound Cake (see pages 325, 56,
    and 295)
1 tablespoon cocoa powder

Combine the sugar, water, and orange rind in a saucepan.
Bring to a boil and boil 3 to 4 minutes.

Meanwhile, place the yolks in the bowl of an electric mixer.
Pour the syrup on the yolks, beating at high speed for 10 to 12
minutes. At this point the mixture should be thick, smooth, and
pale yellow. Add ¼ cup of the Grand Marnier and beat for
another 3 minutes on high speed.

With a rubber spatula, fold the whipped cream into the
mixture. Cover the bottom of a 1-quart soufflé mold with a thick
layer of the mixture (about 2 inches thick). Arrange the ladyfingers or génoise slices on top. Sprinkle with the remaining
Grand Marnier. Fill the mold right to the top with the mixture.
Refrigerate the remainder.

Take a double fold of waxed paper and make a collar around
the outside of the mold, 2 to 3 inches above the rim. Tie securely
with a string. Place the mold in the freezer for 1 hour, or until

it is firm. When firm, add the remainder of the mixture, which should bring the soufflé to about 1½ to 2 inches above the rim of the mold. Return to the freezer until frozen. Just before serving, sprinkle the top with the cocoa. Remove the collar and serve immediately. The cocoa is added to give the illusion of a brown, baked soufflé. The collar is added to imitate the rising of a hot soufflé.

Roulade au Chocolat
Chocolate Roll

(*Serves 8*)

•

6 *squares semisweet chocolate*
½ *cup sugar*
¼ *cup water*
6 *eggs, separated*
1 *tablespoon very strong coffee, or 1 teaspoon*
   instant coffee
1½ *cups heavy cream*
2 *tablespoons confectioners' sugar*
½ *teaspoon vanilla extract*
2 *teaspoons kirsch*
1 *tablespoon bitter cocoa powder*

Place the chocolate in a double boiler or in a 200° oven and melt. Mix the granulated sugar and water in a saucepan. Bring to a boil and cook for 2 minutes over medium heat. Meanwhile, place the egg yolks in a bowl. Slowly pour the hot sugar syrup over the yolks, mixing vigorously with a whisk. Continue whipping the mixture for about 5 minutes to have it fluffy and smooth and pale yellow in color. Add the melted chocolate and the coffee. Mix. Whip the egg whites until they hold firm peaks. Add about ⅓ of the whites to the chocolate mixture and mix vigorously with the whisk. Add the remaining whites and fold in with a spatula—mix just enough to combine the ingredients. (See page 296). Do not overwork. Cut a piece of waxed paper large enough to line a 12- by 16-inch cake-roll pan (you may have to use 2 pieces of waxed paper running the length of the pan, be sure they overlap a bit, otherwise the mixture will stick to the pan). Butter the paper and coat with flour, shaking off any excess. Spread the mixture into the prepared pan. The mixture will be about ½ inch thick. *Again, avoid stirring and mixing the mixture too much.* Place in a preheated 375° oven for 15 minutes. Initially cool at room temperature; then cover with plastic wrap and allow to cool for at least 2 more hours. Start whipping the cream; when half-whipped, add the confectioners' sugar, vanilla, and kirsch. Continue beating until the cream is firm. Now begin rolling the cake. This is a delicate operation. You have just cooked a soufflé mixture which rose in the oven and collapsed to about ¾ to 1 inch thick. It is important that the pan be lined because the paper aids in removing the cake and in rolling. The plastic wrap keeps the cake moist, making it possible to be rolled. Remove the plastic wrap, slide a knife all around the sides to loosen the cake. Spread the whipped cream on the cake. Start rolling the cake with the paper still on, peeling the paper off, then rolling a little. Avoid pressing down on the cake as you roll so that the whipped cream is not squeezed out. Continue rolling and removing the paper alternately. Try to have the end of the cake underneath so that the cake looks smooth on top. Use 2 large spatulas to slide the cake to a serving platter. Place the cocoa powder into a sieve and shake it over the cake to coat the top. Refrigerate.

There are two delicate operations, folding the egg whites into the chocolate mixture and rolling the cake. If the cake is brittle and cannot be rolled you probably did not incorporate the egg whites properly in the mixture. To salvage the cake, cut into 3 lengthwise strips, cutting through the paper. Place the first strip upside down on a serving tray, remove the paper and spread with cream; place the second strip upside down on top of the first, remove the paper, spread with cream, and repeat the operation with the last strip. Coat all around with cream and sprinkle the top with cocoa.

Truffettes du Dauphiné
Small Chocolate Truffles

(Yield: 2 Dozen)

•

Chocolate is often a tricky and delicate product to utilize. It can scorch, curdle, or change color easily and go from the brightest to the very dull depending on the amount of cooking heat. So temperatures are very important when cooking with chocolate. If you are not too familiar with chocolate, remember that it contains cocoa butter and that fat is not easily incorporated with liquid. Sweet chocolate, which has already a percentage of moisture added to it, will absorb liquid more readily than the bitter chocolate. Therefore, sweet or semisweet chocolate is easier to handle than the bitter kind. *If the chocolate curdles or tightens too much after addition of a liquid, add more liquid and keep beating it with a spatula and it will become smooth again.* Only melted fat, butter or shortening, and sugar syrup are added to bitter chocolate.

This is a simpler version of the more elaborate, classic recipe for chocolate truffles.

6 ounces semisweet chocolate (you need a dark
coating chocolate of the best quality)

DESSERTS • 339

2 *egg yolks* (*medium-sized eggs*)
2 *tablespoons milk*
1 *teaspoon coffee or orange liqueur* (*optional*)
⅓ *stick sweet butter*

Melt the chocolate in a double boiler (a skillet with some water can be used as a double boiler), or in a lukewarm oven until the chocolate is on the warm side. Add the egg yolks and stir with a whisk for a few seconds. It may curdle. Add the milk and the alcohol and place back on heat or hot water for a few seconds, stirring with the whisk. The mixture should be smooth. Remove from heat and add the butter bit by bit, whisking after each addition. Beat with the whisk for 2 to 3 minutes to let the mixture absorb some air and become fluffier. Cover with plastic wrap and refrigerate for 4 to 5 hours. With a spoon, divide the mixture into little balls the size of cherry tomatoes. Roll in the palm of your hand to make them smooth. Roll in bitter cocoa or chocolate shavings or dip them in melted chocolate by piercing each ball with a skewer and lowering it into the liquid chocolate. The balls rolled in the chocolate shavings can also be sprinkled with confectioners' sugar.

Note: The chocolate truffles are served to guests after dinner in France, especially during the Christmas season.

Dentelles Lily
Lily's Lace Cookies

(*Yield: 45 to 50 Cookies*)

•

One of the best and easiest cookies to make is this recipe of a very dear friend of mine.

1 *stick sweet butter, melted*
½ *cup sugar*
1 *cup ground almonds, or a mixture of almonds*
    and other nuts
2 *tablespoons flour*
2 *tablespoons milk*

Mix the sugar and butter together. Stir in the almond powder. When smooth, mix in the flour and then the milk. Butter and flour several cookie sheets. Place ½ teaspoon of the mixture for each cookie on the sheets, leaving enough space for the cookies to spread during the cooking. Place in a preheated 350° oven for 8 to 10 minutes. Remove the sheets from the oven and allow the cookies to rest 1 minute. With a spatula, transfer cookies to a wire rack and allow to cool and harden.

Langues de Chat
Cats' Tongues

(*Yield: About 45 Cookies*)

•

¾ *stick sweet butter*
½ *cup sugar*
dash of vanilla extract
2 *egg whites*
½ *cup all-purpose flour*

Grease and flour 3 or 4 baking sheets and set aside.

Work the butter with a whisk until soft and fluffy. Then gradually work in the sugar and vanilla until you have a creamy, homogeneous mixture. Add the egg whites, beating them in thoroughly. Fold in the flour with a wooden spatula.

Fit a pastry bag with a plain, small *douille* or tube, then fill about ⅔ full with the batter. Press the batter out on the prepared pans in strips about as thick as a cigarette and 3 inches long, leaving 1 inch between strips to allow for spreading. Before placing in the oven, give the sheet a good bang on your worktable to flatten the dough.

Bake in a preheated 400° oven for 12 minutes, or until light brown. Remove from cookie sheets onto cake racks at once, but allow to cool for at least 45 minutes before serving.

Cats' Tongues keep well if stored in a tightly covered tin in a cool place.

Note: For Lemon Cats' Tongues, in place of the vanilla add the grated rind and juice of half a lemon. Follow the same directions for preparation and baking.

Tuiles à l'Orange
Orange Cookies

(*Yield: About 20 Cookies*)

•

½ cup sugar
dash of vanilla extract
2 egg whites
⅓ cup all-purpose flour
4 tablespoons butter, melted
½ cup slivered, blanched almonds
grated rind of ½ orange

Butter and flour a baking sheet and set aside.

Combine the sugar, vanilla, and egg whites in a bowl and beat with a whisk for 1 minute, or until the mixture is foamy. Add all the remaining ingredients, mixing them in well.

Drop the batter from a coffee spoon onto the prepared pan, leaving enough space between mounds to allow for spreading. Bake in a preheated 400° oven for 10 to 12 minutes. While still hot, remove the cookies from the baking sheet and place over a rolling pin so each takes the shape of a curved roof tile. The *tuiles* should be allowed to dry on the rolling pin long enough to maintain the shape when cold.

Petits Pots de Crème Vanille
Rich Vanilla Custard

(*Serves 6 to 8*)

•

1 *cup sugar*
10 *egg yolks*
¼ *teaspoon arrowroot*
1½ *tablespoons vanilla extract*
¾ *quart milk* (3 *cups*)
1 *cup heavy cream*

Combine the sugar, yolks, arrowroot, and vanilla in a large bowl and whip together with a wire whip for about 5 minutes, or until the mixture becomes pale yellow and "makes ribbons." Bring the milk to a boil, then gradually add to the yolk mixture in a thin stream, whipping constantly. Add the cream. Strain through a fine sieve or several layers of cheesecloth. Allow to stand for 2 to 3 minutes, then remove any foam that rises to the top.

Pour into 6 or 8 individual molds, ramekins, or *petits pots*. Set them in a large baking pan, add enough hot water to reach to about half the depth of the molds, and bake in a preheated 400° oven for 30 minutes. Do not allow the water in the pan to boil or the custard will become grainy. Should it boil, add enough cold water to stop the boiling.

Pots de crème are served right in their little pots and never unmolded. They should be ice-cold. Serve with dry petits fours.

Crème Caramel au Rhum
Caramel Custard with Rum

(*Serves 6*)

•

Sauce

1 *cup sugar*
⅓ *cup water*
2 *tablespoons good rum* (*either white or dark*)

Mix the sugar and water in a heavy saucepan and cook on high heat until it turns into caramel (takes about 6 to 8 minutes). As soon as the sugar caramelizes, remove from the heat and pour about ⅓ of the mixture into a soufflé mold (porcelain is the best, about 1 to 1½ quarts). If you use a metal mold the transfer of heat is faster and you have more of a chance of getting a custard with little holes around the edges. Move the mold around so that the mixture runs and covers the bottom (only the bottom) of the mold with a layer about ¼ inch thick. Pour ¾ cup of cold water in the remaining caramel. Be careful to pour the water slowly because it splashes and you may burn yourself. Place the saucepan back on the heat, bring to a boil and boil for ½ minute. The mixture should be liquid without any solidified sugar sticking to the bottom of the pan. Pour in a bowl and cool in the refrigerator. When cold, add the rum. *If you add the rum when the mixture is hot, the alcohol will evaporate and most of its flavor will be gone.* When cold, the sauce should have the consistency of a heavy maple syrup. If too thick, add a little water.

Custard

> 2 cups milk
> 5 tablespoons sugar
> 4 whole eggs, 1 extra egg yolk
> 1 cup heavy cream
> 1 teaspoon almond extract
> 2 tablespoons rum

Bring the milk and sugar to a boil. Mix the eggs, extra egg yolk, cream, almond, and rum in a bowl with a whisk until everything is well blended. Pour the hot milk into the egg mixture, stirring to blend everything. *Do not over-mix or whip the mixture or a thick layer of foam will form on the surface.* Strain the mixture into the caramel-lined mold, pouring through the sieve slowly to avoid making more bubbles. Place the mold in a pan of lukewarm water. An iron skillet will do as a *bain-marie*. The water should come up to ⅔ of the mold, and it should never boil during the cooking. If it boils, add a little cold water to stop the boiling. Place in a 330° oven for 1 hour. A knife inserted in the center of the custard should come out without any liquid mixture adhering to it. Let cool at least 4 hours before serving. At serving time, run a sharp knife around the sides of the mold, place a serving platter upside down on top of the mold and invert. The custard should slide out easily. Some extra liquid will come out of the mold, like a light caramel. You may add it to the sauce. Serve with the sauce on the side.

Note: If there are some little holes on the sides of the custard, it cooked slightly too fast and the water boiled. If there are holes inside the custard as well, it cooked much too fast and too long.

Bombe aux Fraises
Cold Strawberry Cream

(Serves 6 to 8)

•

*3 pint baskets of strawberries, hulled and
cleaned (about 6 large cups)*

Syrup

*¾ cup sugar
2 tablespoons kirsch*

Place 3 cups of strawberries with the sugar in an electric blender and puree. Place on the stove and bring to a boil. Simmer for 3 minutes, then strain through a fine metal sieve. Cool. When cool, mix in the kirsch and set aside.

Sauce

*½ cup sugar
½ cup water
5 egg yolks
4 tablespoons kirsch*

Place the remaining strawberries, sugar, and water in a saucepan. Bring to a boil and cook on medium heat for 5 minutes. Let cool, then strain the juices. Reserve the strawberries. Place the juices with the egg yolks in a heavy saucepan (not aluminum, or it will discolor). Place on very low heat and beat with a wire whisk for 7 to 8 minutes to have a *sabayon* the consistency of a light mayonnaise. *It should never be so hot that you cannot hold your finger in the mixture. If it gets too hot during cooking, remove from the heat and continue beating until the tempera-*

ture lowers. When cooked, place the saucepan in cold water and continue beating for a few minutes until the mixture is cold. Add the kirsch and the reserved strawberries.

Assembly

> 2 *cups heavy cream*

Whip the cream—not too firm—and fold into the strawberry-egg mixture. Place in a 2-quart mold (any one that suits your fancy) and freeze for at least 5 hours. Run the mold under lukewarm water for a few seconds and unmold onto a tray. Pour a few tablespoons of the strawberry sauce on top and around and serve with the remaining sauce on the side. The *bombe* should not be too cold so that it can be served easily with a spoon.

Crème au Chocolat
Chocolate Cream

(*Serves* 8)

•

> 2 *cups milk*
> 6 *squares* (6 *ounces*) *semisweet chocolate*
> 4 *egg yolks*
> ¾ *cup sugar*
> ¼ *teaspoon grated orange rind*
> ½ *package gelatin* (1 *teaspoon*)
> 3 *tablespoons cornstarch*

Bring the milk to a boil, add the chocolate and set aside. Mix the yolks, sugar, orange, and gelatin in a bowl, using a whisk until it forms a "ribbon." *This means that when you lift the whisk full of mixture, the mixture falls back on itself in the same manner as a silky ribbon would. The ribbon of mixture from the end of the whisk to the bowl should be continuous and smooth.* This will take a couple of minutes only. Add the starch and mix well. Stir the milk-and-chocolate mixture and combine with the egg mixture. Bring to a boil, stirring constantly with the whisk to avoid scorching. Allow to boil for a few seconds. Remove from the heat and cool, then cover with plastic wrap to prevent a skin from forming on top.

> 4 *squares (4 ounces) semisweet chocolate*
> 2 *cups heavy cream*

Place the chocolate in a bowl and melt in a double boiler or place in a lukewarm oven (about 180°) to melt. *Whip the cream until it holds firm but is not too stiff or it will have the taste of butter instead of sweet cream.* Place about ⅓ of the cream in the first mixture and mix with a whisk. Fold in the remaining cream (page 296). Pour the mixture into a serving bowl. Pour the hot chocolate on top, letting it fall like a string so that the whole top is marbled with a lacy chocolate design. Refrigerate. Serve with Langues de Chat cookies (see page 340).

Pouding au Caramel
Caramel Pudding

(Serves 8)

•

> ½ *cup sugar*
> ¼ *cup water*

Combine the water and sugar in a saucepan and cook over medium to high heat until it turns into a light caramel color (about 6 minutes). Immediately pour the caramel into a 1½-

to 2-quart soufflé mold. Tip the mold back and forth so that the caramel coats the bottom and the sides of the mold. *You must do this as quickly as possible because the caramel will harden fast.*

> 1½ cups milk
> 4 egg yolks
> ⅓ cup sugar
> 1 teaspoon vanilla extract
> 1 teaspoon lemon rind
> 2 tablespoons cornstarch

Combine the yolks and sugar and work together for a few minutes until the mixture forms a "ribbon" (see page 346). Add the vanilla, lemon rind, and starch and mix until combined. Bring the milk to a boil. Pour half of the milk into the mixture, stirring with a whisk until smooth. Pour back into the pot with the remaining milk and bring to a boil, stirring constantly to avoid scorching. Bring to a good rolling boil. Set aside.

> 6 egg whites

Whip the egg whites until stiff. Add ⅓ of the whites to the cream mixture and stir until smooth with the whisk. Fold (see page 296) in the remaining whites. Work fast to prevent the whites from becoming grainy. Pour the mixture into the caramel-lined mold. Place in a double boiler, a regular ovenproof casserole is fine, and cook in a 350° oven for 1 hour. The soufflé will rise and hold its peak for a while. Finally it will collapse. Remove from the double boiler and cool in the refrigerator or in a cool place. At serving time, run a sharp knife around the sides of the mold and invert on a serving platter. *If the pudding does not come out easily, the caramel must have hardened and you will have to heat the mold slightly on top of the stove to help the unmolding.* The pudding may be served with whipped cream, or glazed with apricot sauce and surrounded by sliced pears or peaches, or served (our version) with *sabayon*. *Do not serve it too cold.*

Sabayon

> ½ *cup sugar*
> 6 *egg yolks*
> ½ *cup dry sherry*
> ½ *cup dry white wine*

Place all the ingredients in a heavy saucepan (not aluminum). Cook, whipping with a whip, in a double boiler or on a very, very low fire for 8 to 10 minutes. *The sauce should never get so hot that you cannot stick your finger in it. Be careful not to scramble the eggs, especially around the bottom edge of the saucepan. Do not whip before the mixture is lukewarm.* The mixture will whip to the consistency of a light whipped cream. Serve generous spoonfuls with the pudding.

Note: The *sabayon* is best served lukewarm, but can also be served cold.

Pouding Brésilien
Bread and Butter Pudding

(*Serves 6 to 8*)

•

> ½ *cup mixed candied fruit*
> ¼ *cup good kirsch*
> ½ *cup seedless dark raisins*
> 10 *thin (about ¼ inch thick) slices French bread*
> 3 *tablespoons soft sweet butter*

1 *quart milk*
1 *cup heavy cream*
5 *eggs*
4 *extra egg yolks*
1 *cup sugar*
1 *teaspoon vanilla extract*
2 *tablespoons confectioners' sugar*

Preheat the oven to 375°. Combine the candied fruit and kirsch and set aside. Cover the raisins with boiling water, let stand 5 minutes, then drain and set aside. Generously butter 1 side of each slice of French bread and set aside.

Bring the milk to a boil. Mix the eggs, extra egg yolks, sugar, and vanilla together with a whip until well combined. Add the cold cream to the milk and mix. Combine the egg mixture with the milk and cream until well homogenized. Strain through a fine sieve. Butter a 2-quart baking dish. Put the candied fruit-and-kirsch mixture in the bottom of the dish. Place the raisins and the bread, buttered side up, on top of the fruit.

Place the baking dish in a large pan and pour boiling water around it. Bake 35 to 40 minutes, or until set. Sprinkle with confectioners' sugar and glaze under the broiler for approximately 1 minute, or until golden. Cool off to room temperature. The pudding may be served with a Sabayon (see page 328).

Pêches Ninon
Ninon Peaches

(Serves 8)

•

2 *cups milk*
1 *teaspoon grated lemon rind*
1½ *ounces farina or cream of rice*
5 *egg yolks, lightly beaten*
4 *ounces sugar* (½ *cup*)
1 *teaspoon vanilla extract*
1½ *packages gelatin*
1½ *cups heavy cream*
2 *tablespoons sifted confectioners' sugar*

Bring the milk and lemon rind to a boil. Stir in the farina and continue cooking for 5 minutes, stirring constantly. Remove from the heat. Beat the egg yolks and sugar until they form a "ribbon" (see page 346), add the vanilla and gelatin, mix well and add to the farina mixture. Bring this mixture to a boil quickly over medium heat, stirring constantly with a whisk. As soon as it starts boiling, remove from the heat, transfer to a clean bowl, and cover tightly with plastic wrap (the plastic wrap touching the surface so a skin doesn't form on the mixture). When the farina is cool (if it gets too cold, it will set), whip the cream and confectioners' sugar together until the mixture forms soft peaks. Fold (see page 296) the whipped cream into the chilled farina mixture, then pour into a very lightly oiled 6-cup savarin mold, charlotte mold, or any other mold which will serve the purpose. (To oil the mold, use a paper towel and a small amount of vegetable oil.) Refrigerate for at least 4 hours, preferably overnight.

4 *cups sugar*
2 *quarts water*
1 *stick of vanilla*
rind of 2 lemons
8 *peaches*

Bring the water, sugar, vanilla bean, and lemon rind to a boil, then let boil gently for 10 minutes. Let the syrup cool for 10 to 15 minutes. Set the peaches, unpeeled, in the syrup and bring to a simmer; simmer for 2 to 3 minutes. Remove from the heat and let the peaches cool in the syrup until ready to serve. Just before serving, peel them (they will slide out of their skins easily) and set them around the farina ring. *Sometimes the peaches are blanched to remove the skin before poaching in the syrup. By cooking the peaches with the skin on, the color of the skin "decals" on the flesh and makes the peaches more attractive.*

Apricot Sauce

12 *ounces apricot jam*
⅓ *cup sugar*
¼ *cup water*
3 *tablespoons kirsch*

Bring the jam, water, and sugar to a boil over medium heat, then simmer for 5 minutes. Strain through a fine sieve. Let the mixture cool and add the kirsch.

1½ *cups heavy cream*
4 *tablespoons confectioners' sugar*

Whip the cream halfway. Add the confectioners' sugar, then finish whipping the cream.

To unmold the farina ring, run a sharp knife around the sides, cover the ring with a serving plate, then invert. If the unmolding is difficult, you can place a hot wet towel around the mold for 15 to 20 seconds to help the unmolding. Dry the peeled peaches and arrange around the "pudding" mixture. Pour the apricot sauce on the peaches and around the farina ring. Using a pastry tube, decorate the dish with the whipped cream, or serve separately.

Charlotte de Pommes Sauce Abricot
Apple Charlotte with Apricot Sauce

(*Serves 6*)

•

6 red or golden Delicious apples, peeled, seeded,
    and cut into eighths
3 tablespoons sweet butter
½ cup sugar
1 tablespoon grated orange rind
1 tablespoon grated lemon rind
3 tablespoons apricot preserves
½ cup melted sweet butter
2 slices white bread, trimmed, each cut into
    4 triangles
5 slices white bread, trimmed and cut into
    halves

Melt the 3 tablespoons of butter in a saucepan and add the apples. Cook 4 to 5 minutes, stirring constantly, and add the sugar, orange, and lemon rind. Cook 15 to 20 minutes, stirring until all the juices have evaporated and the apples are soft. Mix in the apricot jam. Brush a charlotte mold (about 1½-quart size) with the melted butter. Arrange the triangles of bread on the bottom of the mold, so that the points of the triangles meet in the middle and the bread covers the bottom of the mold entirely. Arrange the half slices of bread around the sides so that they overlap. Fill the center with the apple mixture and cover with waxed paper and cook in a preheated 400° oven for approximately 50 minutes. If the apple mixture shrinks during cooking, the slices of bread will be higher than the filling. If so, fold the excess bread over the apples. Unmold on a serving platter and brush with Apricot Sauce (see page 352). Serve lukewarm with apricot sauce perfumed with kirsch.

Mousse au Chocolat
Chocolate Mousse

(*Serves 6 to 8*)

•

8 *squares* (*1-ounce size*) *semisweet chocolate*
½ *cup sugar*
¼ *cup water*
2 *eggs, separated*
2 *extra egg yolks*
⅓ *cup coffee concentrate*
2 *tablespoons Grand Marnier*
6 *tablespoons* (¾ *stick*) *sweet butter, softened*
2 *cups heavy cream, whipped*

Melt the chocolate over hot, but not boiling, water or place in a very low oven (180°).

Mix the sugar with ¼ cup of water in a saucepan and bring to a boil. Boil 3 to 4 minutes. Meanwhile, place the 4 egg yolks in the bowl of an electric mixer. Gradually add the sugar syrup, beating constantly. Continue beating for 5 to 6 minutes at high speed, or until the mixture is thick and creamy. Add the coffee concentrate, Grand Marnier, and softened butter and beat thoroughly. Stir in the melted chocolate.

Beat the egg whites with a rotary or electric beater until stiff and shiny. As soon as they are ready, add to the chocolate mixture and beat in with a wire whisk. Finally, fold in the whipped cream. Pour into a large serving bowl and refrigerate until serving time.

You can, if you like, garnish the top with cocoa, whipped cream, or chocolate curls. You may also omit the egg whites and add 1 more cup of heavy cream to the recipe.

Mousse aux Fraises
Strawberry Mousse

(*Serves* 8)

•

Mousse

2 *baskets strawberries*
¾ *cup sugar*
6 *egg yolks*
¾ *ounce plain gelatin* (3 *envelopes*)
½ *cup hot water*
red food coloring
1 *quart heavy cream*
2 *tablespoons strawberry or raspberry kirsch*

Mix the sugar and yolks with a wire whisk. Work in a double boiler with hot, but not boiling, water for approximately 8 minutes, or until the mixture becomes very pale in color and thickens. Place the pot in cold water and stir until the mixture further thickens (until it's like a mayonnaise). Melt the gelatin with the ½ cup of hot water and add to the mixture.

Blend ½ basket of strawberries in a blender and add to the

mixture. Slice the rest of the basket of strawberries and add to the mixture, along with about 10 drops of red food coloring to give a nice pink color. Add the alcohol.

Whip the cream until almost hard and fold ¾ of it into the mixture. Set the rest aside. Line a mold with waxed paper in the bottom and around the sides. Pour in the mousse mixture. Cover with plastic wrap and place in the refrigerator for at least 5 to 6 hours.

Sauce

> 3 *tablespoons good cognac*
> ½ *cup sugar*

Divide the second basket of strawberries into 2 parts. Clean the nicest strawberries and pat them dry with a paper towel. Set aside. Place the remaining strawberries in a blender with the sugar and cognac and puree until smooth. Refrigerate.

Unmold the mousse and remove the waxed paper. Pour some of the sauce around the mousse and garnish with the whole strawberries and reserved whipped cream. Serve with the remaining sauce on the side.

Fraises aux Framboises
Strawberries with Raspberry Sauce

(*Serves 6*)

•

This very simple recipe can finish up a light meal as well as an elaborate one. The simplicity of this dessert is equal to its superbness. Serve it in a plain crystal bowl. Thin slices of Génoise (page 56) or Pound Cake (page 295) go well with it.

2 *small baskets fresh strawberries* (2 *pints*)
1 *small basket fresh raspberries* (1 *pint*)
½ to ¾ *cup sugar, depending on the sweetness
    of the fruit*
⅓ *cup good quality kirsch*

Trim the strawberries and the raspberries and wash in cold water. Drain on paper towels. If you have any imperfect strawberries, trim and place the remaining parts along with the raspberries in the blender. Add the sugar and kirsch and blend for 30 to 50 seconds. Pour this sauce over the fresh strawberries and cover with plastic wrap and place in the refrigerator. Allow the sauce to impregnate the strawberries for at least 5 to 6 hours. Toss the berries from time to time. Serve cold.

Salade de Fruits au Kirsch
Fruit Salad with Kirsch

(*Serves 6 to 8*)

•

Maceration

juice of ½ lemon
¼ *cup sugar*
3 *tablespoons apricot jam*
3 *tablespoons kirsch*

Fruits

1 *cup fresh cherries or strawberries*
1 *small bunch seedless white grapes*
1 *small bunch red grapes*
1 *banana*

2 *red or golden Delicious apples*
2 *pears*
3 *navel oranges*

Combine the lemon juice, sugar, apricot jam, and kirsch in a bowl large enough to accommodate the fruit.

Wash and pit the cherries or wash and hull the strawberries. Add to the bowl. Wash the grapes, strip off the stems, and add to bowl. Peel the banana, peel and core the apples and pears, then slice right into the bowl. Using a sharp knife, peel the oranges right down to the flesh. Loosen the sections by cutting down as close to the membrane as possible on both sides of each section. Drop the sections into the bowl as you cut them and remove the seeds, if any. Squeeze the membrane to extract any juices.

Once all the fruit has been added to the maceration, mix very carefully, then refrigerate for 3 to 4 hours before serving. Serve cold with a good, rich Pound Cake (see page 295).

Compote de Pommes au Calvados
Apple Compote with Calvados

(*Serves 6*)

•

7 or 8 *large apples, red or golden Delicious,*
    peeled, quartered, and seeded (about 3
    pounds)
½ *cup sugar*
½ *cup water*
juice and grated rind of 1 lemon
2 *tablespoons sweet butter*
2 *tablespoons calvados (apple brandy)*

Place all ingredients (except the brandy) in a heavy casserole with a cover. Bring to a boil and simmer on low heat, covered, for 30 minutes. Uncover the pot and push the apple pieces down into the juices. Continue cooking uncovered on very low heat for 30 more minutes. *By this time, practically all the liquid should have evaporated. Keep pushing the apples down in the juices with a spoon.* Stir the mixture with a spoon to break the pieces into a very coarse mixture. Cover with plastic wrap and refrigerate. When cold, add the calvados.

> 1 *cup heavy cream*
> 1 *tablespoon confectioners' sugar*
> 2 *tablespoons calvados*

Whip the cream and add the sugar and calvados to it. Place the cold apples in an attractive glass bowl. Put the cream in a pastry bag with a tube and decorate the top of the compote. Serve with very thin slices of Pound Cake (see page 295).

Gâteau de Riz Sauce Groseille
Rice Pudding with Red Currant Sauce

(*Serves 8*)

•

> ½ *cup mixed candied fruits*
> 4 *tablespoons kirsch*
> 1 *quart milk*
> ⅔ *cup long-grain rice* (*not par-boiled*)
> 4 *egg yolks*
> ¾ *cup sugar*
> 1 *teaspoon vanilla extract*
> *grated rind of* ½ *lemon*

grated rind of ½ orange
2 envelopes unflavored gelatin
1½ cups heavy cream
vegetable oil

Combine the fruits and the kirsch in a bowl. Cover and macerate overnight.

Bring the milk to a boil in a heavy ovenproof casserole or saucepan. Stir in the rice, cover tightly and place in a preheated 400° oven. After 30 minutes, give the mixture a stir. Cook for another 30 minutes for a total of 1 hour.

In a large bowl, combine the egg yolks, sugar, vanilla, lemon and orange rinds, and gelatin. Stir rapidly and thoroughly into the rice, cover and return to the oven. Cook another 5 minutes.

Pour the rice mixture into a bowl, cover with a piece of plastic wrap and cool in the refrigerator. Whip the cream until it holds a shape, then fold (see page 296) into the rice mixture. Brush a 2-quart mold (it may be a ring mold, a charlotte, or a plain round mold) lightly with vegetable oil. Add the rice mixture. Cover with plastic wrap and refrigerate overnight to set.

At serving time, unmold by running a sharp knife around the sides of the mold and inverting on a serving platter. If the *gâteau* does not slide out easily, place a hot wet towel around the mold for a few seconds to help the unmolding.

Sauce Groseille

1 10- to 12-ounce jar good red currant jelly
2 tablespoons sugar
¼ cup water
¼ cup kirsch or cognac

Combine the jelly, water, and sugar in a saucepan. Bring to a boil, then simmer for 5 to 6 minutes. Strain. Refrigerate. When cold, stir in the liqueur.

Pour some of the sauce around the unmolded *gâteau* and

serve the rest separately. The *gâteau* may also be decorated with whipped cream and candied violets, or with little strips of melted chocolate imitating flowers and tinted apricot jam for the petals of the flowers.

Bananes Flambées au Rhum
Bananas Flambeed with Rum

(*Serves 6*)

•

6 *large, well-ripened bananas*
1 *stick sweet butter* (*4 ounces*)
⅓ *cup sugar*
juice of 1 lime
¼ *cup water*
⅓ *cup good white or dark rum*

Although this dish is usually made in the dining room, a couple of steps can be done in advance. Place the bananas in a 400° oven on a cookie sheet and cook for 15 minutes. *The skins should be black and the bananas soft to the touch.* Cut the ends off and make an incision down the entire length of each banana. Set aside. This step can be done 45 minutes to an hour before serving time.

Place the butter, sugar, lime juice, and ¼ cup water in a large copper skillet (a skillet that can be used in the dining room). Cook on medium heat, stirring constantly with a wooden spatula. In about 4 to 5 minutes the mixture should turn to a light caramel color. Remove immediately from the heat. *It will continue to cook and darken off the heat, so be careful not to let the mixture take on too much color before you remove it from the heat.* This step also may be done ahead of time.

At serving time, place the pan with the butter mixture over a heater or flame in the dining room. Add 1 tablespoon of water and mix with a spoon to dilute the basic sauce, which has thickened. Open the bananas and "unwrap" into the skillet. Cook 2 to 3 minutes, basting the bananas with the sauce. When very hot, add the rum. Ignite and keep basting until the flames die out. Turn off the heat and serve immediately.

Poires au Vin Rouge
Pears Braised in Red Wine

(Serves 6)

•

Pears cooked in red wine are served in all the different wine-growing regions of France. The dish is most successful, in my opinion, when made with a strong, robust wine that sustains hours of cooking and still retains some of its original flavor. An earthy Beaujolais is excellent. The best pears are the hard species, such as the Bosc (which is the brown, long tapered-neck variety); the Anjou (speckled with red and green); and the Comice (usually large and pot-bellied with green marking). The Bartlett will fall apart too easily for this recipe and it should be avoided or the cooking time should be adjusted accordingly.

> 6 *large pears*
> ½ *cup sugar*
> 1 *quart good dry red wine*
> *the skin (yellow part only) of 1 lemon*

Peel the pears, trying not to sever the stem (the reason is esthetic). You need a kettle in which the pears can stand up, tightly pressed against each other. Add the sugar, the wine, and the lemon peel. The liquid should just cover the pears. (The pears are poached standing up so that they retain their shape.) Bring to a boil and place in a 350° oven for 3½ hours. *Be sure to place the kettle on a metal tray to have a uniform transfer of heat. Cover the pears so that they do not dry, but leave a little space open for the steam to escape and for the liquid to reduce.* Let the pears cool off slowly in their juices. When done, they should be a nice mahogany color. At serving time, place them standing up on a large platter. You will have approximately 1 to 1½ cups of liquid left. You may add 2 to 3 tablespoons of liqueur (such as cognac or kirsch) to the liquid if you wish. Pour over the pears. Excellent with a rice pudding or fresh slices of brioche.

Poires Braisées au Caramel
Braised Pears in Caramel Sauce

(*Serves 6*)

•

6 *medium-sized pears, not too ripe* (*Anjou,
    Bosc, or Comice*)
3 to 4 *tablespoons sugar*
⅓ *stick sweet butter*
1½ *cups heavy cream*
1 *tablespoon confectioners' sugar*
¼ *teaspoon vanilla extract*

Peel and split the pears lengthwise. Remove the seeds and core. Place the pear halves, flat side down, in a gratin dish. You need a large dish in order not to have the pieces overlap. Sprinkle the sugar on top, add the butter broken into bits, and place in a 425° oven for 35 minutes. By this time the sugar should have caramelized and the pears should be tender when pierced with the point of a knife. If the pears are still hard, cook another 5 or 10 minutes. Add 1 cup of the cream and place back in the oven. Cook for approximately 10 to 15 minutes, basting every 5 minutes. The sauce should have reduced, be thick, and of a nice ivory color. The caramel cooking with the cream will form a rich and delicious sauce. *If it reduces too much and you see that the sauce is breaking down, add 3 or 4 tablespoons of water.*

Whip the remaining ½ cup of heavy cream and mix in the confectioners' sugar and the vanilla. Serve the pears lukewarm. Turn each half flat side up and spoon some sauce into the hollow cavity. Bring to the table and at the last moment add 1 tablespoon of cold whipped cream on top of each pear. Eat immediately, otherwise the whipped cream will melt.

Index

3|7